Leisure Education III

More Goal-Oriented Activities

Norma J. Stumbo, Ph.D., CTRS

Illinois State University

Venture Publishing, Inc.

State College, Pennsylvania

Production Manager: Richard Yocum
Design, Layout, and Graphics: Diane K. Bierly
Manuscript Editing: Diane K. Bierly
Additional Editing: Matthew S. Weaver

Library of Congress Catalogue Card Number 97-61628
ISBN 0-910251-91-6

Contents

Preface ix

Acknowledgments xi

Chapter One 1
    A Proposed Intervention Model for Therapeutic Recreation Services

Chapter Two 15
    Issues and Concerns in Therapeutic Recreation Assessment

Chapter Three 31
    An Examination of the Logical Assumptions Underlying the Use of Activity Interest
    Inventories in Therapeutic Recreation Assessment

Leisure Awareness Activities 43
    Leisure Jeopardy (Lisa Scherer and David Griggs) 45
    Spin and Write (Julie Keil) 47
    By Any Stretch of the Imagination (Norma J. Stumbo) 49
    Leisure Awareness Box (Theresa M. Connolly) 51
    Top 10 Countdown (Patti Tanner Florez) 53
    Where Is My Playground? (Theresa M. Connolly) 57
    The Wall of Leisure (Shelley A. Vaughan) 59
    Magic Leisure Box 61
    Up and Down 63
    Leisure Scattergories (Jennifer Harz-Morgan) 67
    Mime or Go Fish 71
    Story Time Tag (Norma J. Stumbo) 73
    Leisure Hangman (Bonnie Beasley) 77
    Leisure Memory (Jennifer Matkowich) 79

Leisure Perceptions and Well-Being (Marcia Jean Carter) 81
Leisure Outburst (Stacey Zimmerman) 85
Recipe for the Perfect Leisure Day (Norma J. Stumbo) 89
Leisure Activity Bull's-Eye (Beth Turner) 93
Mini-Vacation (Linda Traylor) 97
Leisure Around the World (Bonnie Beasley) 99
Time Capsule Keepsake (Judy K. Hoogewerf) 103
Share Something Wonderful (Susan Leifer Mathieu) 107
My Personal Newsletter (Becky Klein) 109
Spiral About Me (Julie Keil) 111
Myself in Leisure (Julie Keil) 115
What If . . . (Julie Keil) 117
Positive Messages Box (Theresa M. Connolly) 121
Personal Leisure Values (Julie Keil) 123
My Top Four Choices (Julie Keil) 127
Barriers Busters (Jennifer Harz-Morgan) 131
Excuses, Excuses (Angela Rice and Janine Roe) 135
Luck of the Draw (Jennifer Laughrun) 139
Diamond in the Rough (Becky Klein) 143
Leisure Benefits Box (Theresa M. Connolly) 147
How Does My Family Play? (Theresa M. Connolly) 149
I'll Be There (Tim Leer) 153
Leaves of Change (Shelley A. Vaughan) 155
Calendar Day (Nikki Colba Harder) 159
Stress Buster Ball (Shelley A. Vaughan) 161
Family Leisure Go Fish (Nikki Colba Harder) 163

Social Skills Activities **165**
How I Feel (Norma J. Stumbo) 167
The Look of Emotions (Theresa M. Connolly) 171
How Do You Feel? (Norma J. Stumbo) 175
Emotional Expressions (Nikki Colba Harder) 179
A Little Character (Deland DeCoteau) 181
Emotions Charades (Norma J. Stumbo) 183
Anger Envelopes 185
Drawing Together (Norma J. Stumbo) 187
Positive and Negative Statements (Norma J. Stumbo) 191
How Do I (Should I) Respond? (Nikki Colba Harder) 195
Listening and Interrupting Skills (Norma J. Stumbo) 199
What Are You Saying? (Deland DeCoteau) 203
I Hear You (Norma J. Stumbo) 205
Self-Disclosing Cards (Cathy Pacetta and Julie Beck) 207
One Step Ahead (Deland DeCoteau) 209
M.Y.O. Business Cards (Deland DeCoteau) 213
What Did You Say? (Amy Payne-Johnson) 215
I'm Listening (Norma J. Stumbo) 217
Welcoming Newcomers (Norma J. Stumbo) 219
Friendship Pizza (Becky Klein) 223

Friendship Mobile (Norma J. Stumbo) 225
Role Models (Penny J. Hogberg) 227
Conflicts Between Friends (Norma J. Stumbo) 231
Handling Conflicts (Norma J. Stumbo) 233
1 + 1 + 1 = 3 (Norma J. Stumbo) 235
Comfort Level (Penny J. Hogberg) 239
My Group Comfort Level (Norma J. Stumbo) 243
The ABC'S of Compliment (Nikki Colba Harder) 247
Compliment Web 249
Express Ways (Deland DeCoteau) 251
Dear Abby, Dear Abby I (Norma J. Stumbo) 253
Dear Abby, Dear Abby II (Norma J. Stumbo) 255
What's a Good Option? (Norma J. Stumbo) 259
Beads in a Bottle (Norma J. Stumbo) 263
Holiday Wall Mural (Nikki Colba Harder) 265
First Impressions Bouquet (Lisa Scherer and David Griggs) 267
Body Image Awareness (Jennifer Matkowich) 269
Healthy Selves (Norma J. Stumbo) 271
Cage Ball Dare (Stacy McNerney, Stacy Zawaski and Sherby Philpot) 275
Short Story Writing (Barb Sauer and Kristen Geissler) 277
Social Skills Game (Norma J. Stumbo) 279

Decision-Making Activities **283**
Problem-Solving Skill Building (Norma J. Stumbo) 285
Three Weeks (Julie Keil) 289
An Adventure in Leisure (Angela Rice) 293
The Decision Tree (Nikki Colba Harder) 297
Problem-Solving Journal (Theresa M. Connolly) 301
So Much Leisure, So Little Time (Theresa M. Connolly) 305
Things to Do List (Samantha Rudolph and Norma J. Stumbo) 309
House on Fire (Linda Maurer) 313
Leisure Choices (Marcia Jean Carter) 315
Planning a Luncheon (Shelley A. Vaughan and Patricia Grimm) 319

Leisure Resources Activities **321**
Back to Back 323
Personal Leisure Directory (Nikki Colba Harder) 327
Leisure Circle (Becky Klein) 329
Leisure Phone Book (Jeff Thompson) 333
Find a Resource (Becky Klein) 337
I Walk the Line 339
Leisure Resources Box (Theresa M. Connolly) 341
Leisure Resource Tick-Tack-Toe (Julie Keil) 343
The Resource Exchange (Julie Keil) 345
Leisure Resources Game (Norma J. Stumbo) 347
Leisure Resource Influences (Marcia Jean Carter) 353
Scavenger Hunt Community Outing (Shelley A. Vaughan) 357
What's Out There? (Tim Leer) 359

Leisure Treasure Hunt (Amy Payne-Johnson) 361
Leisure Resources Bingo (Melissa Capenigro) 365
In the Bag (Norma J. Stumbo) 369
Community Reintegration Trips (Cathy Pacetta and Julie Beck) 373

Preface

Leisure Education III was developed in response to the very positive reception that was received from professionals for *Leisure Education I* and *Leisure Education II*. We appreciate the kind words, letters of encouragement and many requests we get for these volumes. Since it has been 12 years since the first volume and five years since the second volume was published, it was time to introduce new ideas to keep those creative juices flowing. We hope to continue to provide new and innovative activities that meet the needs of participants and specialists alike.

Feedback from practicing professionals has helped guide the development of this new manual. A few changes have been made in an attempt to keep abreast of the demands of practice and to make service delivery as easy as possible, yet meet the needs of participants. One of the most noticeable changes is that there are no leisure activity skills activities in this manual, as there are many activity books now available on the market. In their place a new section on Decision-Making Skills activities, a primary area of need for many of our participants, has been added. For similar reasons the number of Social Skills activities—again, a primary deficit for many participant groups—has nearly doubled. We hope these changes help specialists respond to these growing areas of concern for many types of clients.

Another difference is the beginning chapters. In *Leisure Education III*, the focus is on some basic conceptual foundations for service provision. One chapter highlights a conceptual framework that shows how the different elements of service provision, such as protocols, activity analysis, and quality improvement, are related. Another provides an examination of assessment issues and concerns that need to be addressed to meet increasing accountability demands. The third chapter reviews some problems and concerns with the use of activity interest inventories as a primary source of client assessment information. The combination of these three beginning chapters provides therapeutic recreation professionals with some food for thought about improving their service delivery to clients.

It is our hope that the entire manual assists professionals in improving practice in a time of increasing work demands and stresses. Please let us know if this hope has been realized.

NJS

Acknowledgments

Many individuals have touched this work and made it a better product. Four individuals helped tremendously in initial editing and inputting of submitted activities, and creating many of their own: Julie Keil, Nikki Colba Harder, Becky Klein and Theresa Connolly. Hopefully they learned as much as they gave. Terri was especially helpful in the final editing stages and her unflagging eye for detail was invaluable.

As with the *Leisure Education II* manual, an attempt was made to get as many professionals involved in submitting activities as possible, so that users would be assured of high quality and relevant activities. We were pleased that so many individuals responded, and their contributions clearly enhanced the utility and applicability of this manual. Also included are many Illinois State University student contributions, as they are very creative and innovative. The contributors are listed alphabetically here. A few activities with no author's name listed have been included—these appear to be "public domain" activities to which no one has claimed authorship. We included them because we thought they were worthwhile and unique. Thanks so much to all!

Bonnie Beasley, CTRS, Orchard Place Child Guidance Center, Des Moines, Iowa

Julie Beck, Elgin Mental Health Center, Elgin, Illinois

Melissa Capenigro, Illinois State University, Normal, Illinois

Marcia Jean Carter, CTRS, Ashland University, Ashland, Ohio

Nikki Colba Harder, CTRS, Illinois State University, Normal, Illinois

Theresa M. Connolly, CTRS, Illinois State University, Normal, Illinois

Deland DeCoteau, West Central Human Service Center, Bismarck, North Dakota

Kristen Geissler, CTRS, Anoka-Metro Regional Treatment Center, Anoka, Minnesota

David Griggs, CTRS, Choate Mental Health and Developmental Center, Anna, Illinois

Patricia Grimm, OTR/L, St. John's Hospital, Springfield, Illinois

Jennifer Harz-Morgan, CTRS, Elmhurst Memorial Hospital, Elmhurst, Illinois

Penny J. Hogberg, CTRS, Anoka-Metro Regional Treatment Center, Anoka, Minnesota

Judy K. Hoogewerf, CTRS, Neighborhood Resources, Colorado Springs, Colorado

Julie Keil, CTRS, Illinois State University, Normal, Illinois

Becky Klein, Illinois State University, Normal, Illinois

Jennifer Laughrun, University of North Carolina at Chapel Hill, Chapel Hill, North Carolina

Tim Leer, West Central Human Service Center, Bismarck, North Dakota

Susan Leifer Mathieu, CTRS, California State University–Dominguez Hills, Carson, California

Linda Maurer, CTRS, Veterans Administration Medical Center, Chillicothe, Ohio

Jennifer Matkowich, Illinois State University, Normal, Illinois

Stacy McNerney, CTRS, Glen Oaks Medical Center, Glendale Heights, Illinois

Cathy Pacetta, Elgin Mental Health Center, Elgin, Illinois

Amy Payne-Johnson, CTRS, Orchard Place Child Guidance Center, Des Moines, Iowa

Sherby Philpot, Glen Oaks Medical Center, Glendale Heights, Illinois

Angela Rice, CTRS, Four County Mental Health, St. Charles, Missouri

Janine Roe, CTRS, Barnes Extended Care, Clayton, Missouri

Samantha Rudolph, Illinois State University, Normal, Illinois

Barbara Sauer, CTRS, Anoka-Metro Regional Treatment Center, Anoka, Minnesota

Lisa Scherer, CTRS, Choate Mental Health and Developmental Center, Anna, Illinois

Norma J. Stumbo, CTRS, Illinois State University, Normal, Illinois

Patti Tanner Florez, CTRS, Chestnut Health Systems, Bloomington, Illinois

Jeff Thompson, Heart of Illinois Special Recreation Association, Peoria, Illinois

Linda Traylor, CTRS, VA Healthcare System, Fort Howard Division, Fort Howard, Maryland

Beth Turner, Illinois State University, Normal, Illinois

Shelley A. Vaughan, CTRS, St. John's Hospital, Springfield, Illinois

Stacy Zawaski, Glen Oaks Medical Center, Glendale Heights, Illinois

Stacey Zimmerman, CTRS, Mission Nursing Home, Plymouth, Minnesota

Chapter One

A Proposed Intervention Model for Therapeutic Recreation Services

In a discussion of a personal, historical perspective of the field, Navar (1991) provided a longitudinal look at how the evolving profession of therapeutic recreation has defined accountability. Through the years, there has been a growing sophistication in the way therapeutic recreation specialists have defined and provided appropriate, quality services. Most recently, quality has been equated with the "degree of adherence to standards," according to Navar (1991, p. 5), while appropriateness has been defined as "providing the right patient with the right service [at] the right time in the right setting at the right intensity and for the right duration" (Navar, 1991, p. 5). In this way, quality and appropriateness have been linked with service accountability (Russoniello, 1991). "Healthcare professionals should appreciate that the cornerstone of accountability is evolution. Systems should develop over time to become more sophisticated approaches for monitoring and evaluating the quality and appropriateness of care" (Scalenghe, 1991, p. 30). These accountability systems, often proposed by external regulators, have moved the profession (and others) from beyond a more simplified approach of

examining "structure" and "process" indicators to measuring "client outcomes" (Scalenghe, 1991, p. 33). The implication for therapeutic recreation is that the accountability focus shifts from designing and implementing quality intervention programs to also monitoring their cohesiveness and their success at producing client outcomes. While therapeutic recreation professionals continue to do a commendable job of designing and implementing quality programs, the task of developing and using "monitoring systems" (Riley, 1991a) to measure their cohesiveness and effectiveness has received less attention. One reason may be that the therapeutic recreation literature has not had adequate models to assist in conceptualizing and completing these systems.

One intent of this chapter is to introduce a conceptual model of accountability within therapeutic recreation service delivery. The Therapeutic Recreation Intervention Model (TRIM) highlights the various accountability and documentation procedures used by the therapeutic recreation specialist to monitor and make decisions about the delivery of services for producing client outcomes. The model

---

Chapter One is adapted from Stumbo, N. J. (1996). A proposed accountability model for therapeutic recreation services. *Therapeutic Recreation Journal, 30*(4), 246–259.

synthesizes several concepts that are found usually singularly elsewhere in the literature (e.g., program planning, client assessment, or quality improvement) into a comprehensive system of accountable provision of intervention services. In this way, the contribution of this model to the literature is its ability to depict interrelationships between various decision or documentation points used by the specialist to provide and monitor appropriate, quality services. These logical linkages are crucial to providing clients with goal-oriented, outcome-based interventions. The need and logic behind outcome-oriented intervention will be discussed as the foundation for and prior to the introduction of TRIM.

Importance of Client Outcome-Oriented Intervention

"Outcomes are the observed changes in a client's status as a result of our interventions and interactions. . . . Outcomes can be attributed to the process of providing care, and this should enable us to determine if we are doing for our clients that which we purport to do" (Shank and Kinney, 1991, p. 76). "Determining what is effective therapeutic recreation intervention depends upon examining the relationships between various program/treatment protocols for a specific illness/diagnostic category and the associated outcomes of those treatments" (Riley, 1991a, p. 54). These statements emphasize that there must be a direct connection or match between the services provided and the expected client outcomes (Dunn, Sneegas and Carruthers, 1991; Navar, 1991; Shank and Kinney, 1991). In other words, the "right services" must be delivered to produce the "right outcomes" (Navar, 1991, p. 5).

According to Connolly (1984):

. . . the bottom line of designing a program is to put together a strategy, intervention, or approach that will aid those who participate in the program to ac-complish behavioral change in the form of improved functional abilities and/or acquisition of new knowledge and skills. One measure of the effectiveness of a program, therefore, is documenting the outcomes clients attain as a consequence of participating in the program. (p. 159)

Riley (1991a) draws attention to the concepts of "measurable change" and "relationship" (p. 59). "The causal relationship between the process of care (intervention) and the outcomes of care (change in patient behavior) is critical" (Riley, 1991a, p. 59). These authors, among others, advocate that there must be a direct and proven link between the goals of the program, the type of program being delivered, and the client outcomes expected from participation in the program. It is this link that is central to the concept of intervention and accountability for services.

Outcome-Oriented Versus Non-Outcome-Oriented Programming

Dunn (1991) referred to non-outcome-oriented programs as *Type I* programs, while Stumbo (1992) labeled them *cafeteria-style*. Dunn (1991) expanded on this concept: "all the clients on the unit attend whatever has been planned for the day. There is no provision which matches his or her unique treatment goals. All clients are essentially seen as having the same treatment needs and thus receive the same services" (p. 3). Client assessment to collect essential baseline information, in this case, is minimal or nonexistent, resulting in a lack of or misdirected individualized treatment goals and action plans. The lack of client goals and directed involvement translates into programming (typically large group) that does not produce behavioral change nor measurable, useful client outcomes.

Intervention or outcome-oriented programs, labeled as *Type II* by Dunn (1991, p. 3), are designed to produce measurable, relevant and meaningful client outcomes. The process begins with an assessment procedure that produces valid and reliable results. This information is interpreted into individualized goals and objectives (cf., Dunn, Sneegas and Carruthers, 1991) forming the basis for meaningful placement into appropriate programs that address the specific needs of the client. Client goals are worked on during these programs, and measurable client outcomes are likely to be produced. Programs that focus on individual client outcomes often are provided to small groups or on a one-to-one basis.

Intervention or outcome-based programs are very different in intent, content, and delivery from nonintervention programs. In order for therapeutic recreation programs to be considered intervention, they must possess the following characteristics:

a. be systematically designed prior to their implementation;
b. be a part of a larger system of programming;
c. be individualized, based on client needs;
d. have relevance to the clients;
e. have importance to the clients;
f. have timeliness to the clients; and
g. be able to produce desired results.

These seven factors will be discussed in three parts: (a) systematic program design, (b) client placement based on need, and (c) producing client outcomes.

Systematic Program Design

According to Peterson and Gunn (1984), a systems approach for designing therapeutic recreation programs implies that the designer must specify the intended outcomes as well as the process to accomplish the outcomes *prior* to the implementation of the program. That is, systems design assumes that there is a well-defined, goal-oriented *purpose* to the activity or program being provided. Enabling objectives, terminal performance or behavioral objectives, and performance measures help define where

the program is going and how it is going to get there. There is a well-defined plan for getting the participant from point A to point B, through his or her participation in a program that has been specifically designed for that purpose (Peterson and Gunn, 1984). These linkages are one of the major factors that help systems-designed programs produce client change.

A program that is designed and implemented to be an *intervention program* has as its outcome, some degree of client behavioral change (that is, behavioral change is the purpose of the program) (Riley, 1987a, 1991a; Shank and Kinney, 1991). This may mean an increase in knowledge, an increase in skill, a decrease in some behavior, an increase in functional ability, and so forth. To be accountable in being able to produce change, a program has to be well-designed and implemented according to a plan that addresses that specific participant change. On the other hand, programs that are not accountable often lack forethought into the content and process of delivery, or the intended outcomes.

In addition, designing and providing intervention programs assumes that each program is part of larger whole—a comprehensive set of programs that are designed to meet the diversity of needs of clients entering the program. This applies to the comprehensive series of therapeutic recreation programs as well as implying that departmental programs also need to align with the overall agency's system of services. Each program part should complement other programs within the department and agency.

Client Placement Based on Needs

A comprehensive set of programs designed and available to meet the range of incoming client needs is required so that each client may be placed into programs based on individual need (Peterson and Gunn, 1984). This depends on an assessment procedure that produces valid and reliable results. Other literature (Dunn, 1983, 1984, 1987, 1989, 1991; Stumbo, 1991, 1992, 1993/94, 1994/95, 1996) discusses the need for validity and reliability in any measurement procedure, specifically client assessment.

A major requirement to establish validity and reliability is the alignment between the content of the programs offered and the content of the assessment. The importance of this match cannot be overstated. When the match exists, the potential for the clients to receive the right services is maximized; when the match does not exist, the potential for clients receiving the wrong or unnecessary services is maximized. The alignment was highlighted by Navar (1991) in explaining the term *appropriateness* (as quoted in the first paragraph of this chapter). The right client cannot be placed into the right program unless the assessment contains the right information (valid) and is refined to the point that placement is accurate (reliable).

Figure 1.1 helps to explain the relationship between program placement and client needs. Quadrants I and IV indicate correct decisions—the match between the client needs (from assessment results) and their placement into programs is correct. Clients who need programs receive services, while clients with no need do not. In Quadrant II the assessment results indicate needed program involvement that is not realized—an incorrect decision. The end result is that clients involved with erroneous Quadrant II decisions do not receive the necessary services. Quadrant III also indicates faulty matches or decisions. In these cases, clients receive services that do not match their needs. Programs provided in Quadrant III are likely to be misdirected in that clients without need are involved in programs without clearly defined outcomes. Whether this is due to agency mandates, high staff to client ratios, client diversity or other reasons, the specialist often resorts to Type I (Dunn, 1991) programming, often with the intent of keeping clients busy. Producing meaningful and reliable client outcomes is less likely in situations where clients with widely varying characteristics and needs are placed into one program.

Clearly, Quadrant I contains the "right" programs in which the "right" clients are placed. As such, it has the greatest likelihood to be outcome-based intervention; that is to produce measurable, predetermined client outcomes. It requires the mix of an appropriate assessment procedure that is able to produce valid and reliable assessment results and appropriate programs that are designed based on common client needs. This match is essential for correct client placement decisions.

Producing Client Outcomes

The ability to produce client outcomes is contingent on well-designed and systematic programs in which clients are placed based on the needs shown from assessment results. The relationship or causal link (Riley, 1987a, 1991a) is a strong one. It assumed that client outcomes have relevance and importance and are attainable.

Relevance can be determined by judging which outcomes are most crucial to the client's future status. For some that translates into future independence post-discharge, for others it might mean living with dignity in their remaining years, and for still others it may mean being better able to cope with their current disability or illness. What knowledges, abilities, and skills are needed most frequently or are most likely to be used by the client in his or her home or other future environment? How generalizable or transferable are the skills being taught to settings to which the client will go or return? How relevant is the content of the program(s) to the future lifestyle of the client?

Importance is related to relevance in that the specialist is probably limited in the amount of time that can be spent with any given client. Therefore, client contact time must be spent in the most efficient and effective way possible. How can time be best spent with the client? What is the most productive use of the client's time? How can the client's treatment time be maximized to the fullest extent possible? What are the most important knowledges, abilities or skills for the client's independent leisure lifestyle?

The *attainment* of outcomes often depends on the logistics of the therapeutic recreation program. How often is the client expected to participate in the program? What is the

Figure 1.1. Relationship Between Client Placement Into Programs and Client Needs.

	Client Placed Into Program	**Client Not Placed Into Program**
Client Needs Program	**I. Correct Decision** Client receives necessary services—likely to be intervention	**II. Incorrect Decision** Client does not receive necessary services—no or unnecessary program involvement
Client Does Not Need Program	**III. Incorrect Decision** Client receives unnecessary services—not likely to be intervention	**IV. Correct Decision** Client does not receive services—program involvement not necessary

frequency, duration and intensity of client participation? When are outcomes to be measured? How are the individual characteristics (variations) of the clients accommodated within the programs? How will the outcome data be collected? How reliable is this process?

A great deal of effort on the part of the specialist should be spent considering what client behaviors, skills or attitudes can be changed, given the goals and design of the program. For example, if clients' average length of stay is seven days, it would seem difficult to change attitudes that took a lifetime to develop. Instead the specialist might choose to help the client increase his or her knowledge of community leisure resources, an outcome that typically can be expected within seven days of intervention. The outcome has relevance, importance and is attainable. Smaller, more measurable client outcomes may be preferable to larger, less measurable outcomes.

Several authors have provided guidelines for selecting and developing client outcome statements (Anderson, Ball, Murphy and Associates, 1975, as cited in Dunn, Sneegas and Carruthers, 1991; Shank and Kinney, 1991). These authors suggest that the specialist create and implement client outcome statements that consider:

a. the efficiency and effectiveness of demonstrating client change;

b. a reasonable expectation or relationship between the services provided and the expected outcome;

c. the connection between occurrence of the outcome and the timing of data collection;

d. the relevance to the client and society;

e. the goals and intent of the program;

f. an appropriate level of specification, but not reduced to trivial detail;

g. individual client variation within any given program;

h. both long-term and short-term goals and objectives;

i. the social and home environment to which the client will return; and

j. behaviors that are generalizable and transferable to a variety of settings and situations.

Client outcomes are vital to survival in today's healthcare arena. The ability to produce client outcomes is largely a factor of providing well-designed, systematic programs that are part of a comprehensive whole. It is important for specialists to be able to visualize and understand how individual components fit into the comprehensive whole. One of the major intentions of the Therapeutic Recreation Intervention Model is to provide this comprehensive perspective to design, implement and justify programs.

Components of the Therapeutic Recreation Intervention Model

The Therapeutic Recreation Intervention Model (TRIM) was created to help specialists visualize the interactive nature of documentation and decision points involved in the delivery, implementation and evaluation of accountable programs. Expanding on the models and concepts documented by Peterson and Gunn (1984) and Carter, Van Andel and Robb (1995), the TRIM attempts to depict the relationship between program input factors (such as activity analysis and assessment) and output factors (such as program outcomes and client outcomes).

The Therapeutic Recreation Intervention Model is presented in Figure 1.2. Each component of the model will be discussed separately, beginning with Comprehensive Program Design. The reader should note that, in practice, these elements are highly interactive. Interactive arrows virtually could be drawn between all components of the TRIM Model; those with the strongest relationships are provided.

Comprehensive Program Design

Program design involves establishing the direction of the therapeutic recreation department, unit or agency (Peterson and Gunn, 1984). This process entails gathering data about those factors (such as the community, agency and/or department, clients and profession) that impact the program and its clients, and prioritizing and selecting those programs that best meet client needs. Implementation and evaluation plans are created to ensure that the right programs will be delivered and reviewed systematically. Details about carrying out this process are provided through the Peterson and Gunn (1984) and Carter, Van Andel and Robb (1995) therapeutic recreation program planning models. The direction taken by the therapeutic recreation department at this point is crucial to the success of its remaining operations.

Activity Analysis, Selection and Modification

To make sure that the participation requirements of each planned activity are understood fully, an activity analysis is conducted. This helps planners understand, for example, that softball, volleyball and bingo are not primarily social activities; that there is little in the rules of these activities that teaches and/or requires social interaction, and therefore, social interaction skills. An activity analysis helps the programmer select specific activities that are more likely to be delivered as intervention, simply because the planner has had to look at the activity's requirements systematically through this process (Peterson and Gunn, 1984). "Through the processes of activity and task analyses, the [Therapeutic Recreation Specialist] selects and sequences potential content so the desired client changes will result from participation" (Carter, Van Andel and Robb, 1995, p. 127). The professional should "understand the activity and its potential contributions to behavioral outcomes" (Peterson and Gunn, 1984, p. 180). An activity analysis helps the programmer determine if any modifications need to be made to the selected activity in order that clients will benefit most fully. Thorough activity analysis is a critical link to program planning because it helps ensure that the specialist is providing programs that meet client needs and abilities. Activity analysis is an additional accountability factor that helps the specialist know that the "right service" or intervention is being delivered.

Peterson and Gunn (1984) have developed a system for completing an activity analysis and determining what modifications might be needed. This system complements the efforts taken by the specialist within comprehensive program design, protocol development, and assessment.

Protocols

Protocols are meant to aid in the "standardization of interventions" (Knight and Johnson, 1991, p. 137). Protocols are "a group of

Figure 1.2. The Therapeutic Recreation Intervention Model.

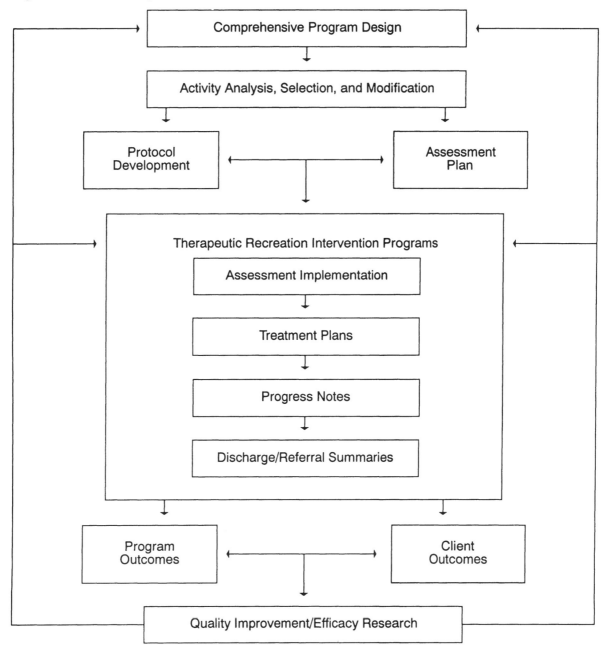

strategies or actions initiated in response to a problem, an issue, or a symptom of a client. They are not programs or program descriptions . . . but are approaches or techniques that will lead to expected treatment outcomes" (Knight and Johnson, 1991, p. 137). Protocols are meant to provide a blueprint of treatment for a specific diagnosis or client problem, and when

validated through professional use and consensus, allow for program benchmarks to be set. They are useful methods of increasing the standardization of intervention programs within various service delivery agencies and departments across the country, primarily because they help define the input, process and projected outcomes of well-designed intervention procedures. Connolly and Keogh-Hoss (1991) and Knight and Johnson (1991) asserted that protocols are a link between standards of practice and both efficacy research and quality improvement activities.

Kelland (1995) provided examples of 25 protocols, such as fitness, community living, and leisure education. The seven-part format used was adapted from Ferguson (1992) and includes categories of (a) general program purpose, (b) program description, (c) deficits the program might address, (d) facilitation techniques, (e) staff responsibilities and requirements, (f) expected program outcomes, and (g) appendices (samples). Connolly and Keogh-Hoss (1991) and Knight and Johnson (1991) also provided several examples of completed protocols.

Assessment Plan

Client assessment is the process used to place clients into therapeutic recreation programs based on their individual needs, strengths and limitations. Without a valid and reliable assessment, a program has little chance of being intervention and a client has little chance of attaining outcomes. That is, when clients are not assessed individually for their strengths, weaknesses and program needs, and all participants are encouraged or invited to come to all programs, this is a major signal of Type I (Dunn, 1991) programming.

In this phase of the model, a plan for developing or selecting, and implementing an assessment procedure is formed. Decisions about assessment content and implementation procedures are made.

Figure 1.1, introduced earlier in this chapter (page 5), helps explain the necessary relationship between assessment results and program placement, and points to key factors in assessment selection or development. At least four major concepts are important to understanding this relationship:

a. the content of the assessment must reflect the content of the programs that have been selected for delivery to clients;

b. the match between the assessment content and the program content implies that the assessment must be valid for its intended use, primarily for placing clients into the most appropriate programs to address their needs;

c. the assessment process must be able to deliver reliable results, indicating that specialists need to have standardized procedures and tools; and

d. client assessments play an important role in determining the baseline of client needs, abilities and limitations, and this baseline is crucial to proving outcomes during or after the process of intervention.

Client assessment, conducted in a systematic and meaningful manner, is a major foundation for providing outcome-based programs as it helps determine what types of behavioral change(s) are needed by the participant. Several pieces of literature have discussed the need for quality assessment procedures and tools, and their relationship to intervention programming (cf., Dunn, 1983, 1984, 1987, 1989, 1991; Stumbo, 1991, 1992, 1993/94, 1994/95, 1997).

Intervention Programs

Therapeutic recreation intervention programs are provided to clients based on need. It is common practice to group participants in programs based on their disability and/or illness characteristics that imply similar needs. For example, individuals with traumatic brain injury may demonstrate similar needs to develop impulse control. Planning for intervention programs relies heavily on the programmer's knowledge of the disability and/or illness characteristics of the participant group.

Shank and Kinney (1987) imply that the intervention process is one that requires careful and directed planning. "The clinical or therapeutic use of activity implies a careful selection and manipulation of the activities in a prescriptive sense" (Shank and Kinney, 1987, p. 70). This means that intervention programs must have the specific intention of modifying client behavior and be presented in a manner most likely to systematically produce these changes.

The likelihood of program success is improved by the forethought given during planning. As mentioned previously, well-designed and systematic programs that include processes such as protocol development and activity analysis are much more likely to be planned as intervention and produce client behavioral changes.

The baseline for intervention is documented in a client assessment. Problems, strengths, limitations and the like are documented in order to determine the client's needs for services. As services are delivered, additional client documentation includes the client's individualized treatment or program plan, a periodic progress note(s), and a discharge and/or referral summary of services. The treatment plan outlines the goals and specific plan of action to be taken with a client (sometimes co-planned by the client). Progress notes are used to monitor progression toward or regression from the goals established in the treatment plan and to modify, if necessary, the original plan of action. Discharge and referral summaries are a compilation of the services received by the client, his or her reaction to the plan of action, as well as any future recommendations for leisure service involvement.

The focus of these action plans and summaries is on the expected or planned behavioral change (outcomes) within the client as a result of receiving appropriate and quality services. These pieces of documentation flow from the efforts taken within the program design, activity analysis phases, protocol development, and assessment. As a result of quality documentation, the specialist is better able to prove client outcomes and program effectiveness.

Navar (1984) outlined guidelines for producing quality client documentation and provided several examples of these forms within her chapter on Documentation in the Peterson and Gunn text (1984). These guidelines and examples can help the specialist improve the quality of his or her written documentation, and ensure alignment with other professional accountability activities.

Program Evaluation and Program Outcomes

In specific program evaluation, the specialist must gather and analyze selected data in a systematic and logical manner, for the purpose of determining the quality, effectiveness and/or outcomes of a program. It makes sense that the plan for program evaluation closely follows the plan for program implementation (Peterson and Gunn, 1984). For example, program factors such as facilities, equipment, staff, budget, advertisement and promotion, and the like can be evaluated as a function separately from individual client outcomes. Although they are undoubtedly interrelated, program documentation and evaluation focuses on program outcomes and client documentation and evaluation focuses on client outcomes.

Program evaluation questions might include the following: Were there adequate staff to implement the program and supervise clients? Was the facility adequate for the purpose of the program—enough space? accessible? Was the equipment functioning properly? How effective and efficient was the program format in assisting the clients in achieving their outcomes?

One such specific program evaluation procedure was developed by Connolly (1981, 1984). This procedure has been validated on a variety of programs and leads to useful evaluative data for the purpose of program review and revision. The procedure focuses on both the process and content of program delivery. As such, it is helpful in refining the focus of intervention programs, and in measuring client outcomes.

Client Evaluation and Client Outcomes

Client evaluation implies that the focus will be on whether the client outcomes targeted in the initial treatment plan have been accomplished. The focus will be on the end result of the intervention designed on behalf of the client, and is one part of patient care monitoring (Sheehan, 1992). For the most part, client evaluations will be conducted on an individual basis (for example, as progress notes or discharge and referral summaries), although these individual evaluations may be synthesized later into grouped data that addresses larger program evaluation concerns. Again, the achievement of client outcomes may be highly interrelated to the achievement of program outcomes.

The targeted client outcomes will vary based on the different client needs and varied purposes of the programs. In non-outcome-based programs, the focus of client evaluation may be the number of times the client attended a program or the level of client enjoyment. While these are sometimes important, when therapeutic recreation services are delivered as planned interventions, different client outcomes usually are expected. In intervention programs, the focus of service provision is client behavior or functional change as a direct, proven result of the program, and the focus of client evaluations becomes one of measuring and documenting those changes. "Outcome measurements become especially important if we view TR [therapeutic recreation] as an agent of change, as a means to modify behavior, attitudes or skills. This is important because the outcome measurements that we specify . . . will indicate what the client is expected to achieve during treatment" (Sheehan, 1992, p. 178). That is, specialists must target goals for client change that are expected to come about as a result of a well-planned and well-designed program. Typical questions concerning client outcomes include: Did the client achieve the targeted outcome within the planned program? If not, what prevented the client from achieving this end? Did the client learn a skill? change a behavior?

change an attitude? Other specific questions may exist according to the treatment plan established for and with the client.

Client outcomes are dependent on well-designed programs in which clients are placed systematically, and in which interventions are delivered for a specific purpose. In essence, client outcomes, like program outcomes, rely on all previous parts of the Intervention Model being in place and being conceptually cohesive. Several sources (cf., Dunn, Sneegas and Carruthers, 1991; Shank and Kinney, 1991; Sheehan, 1992) supply examples and methods for measuring client outcomes.

Quality Improvement and Efficacy Research

The most common method of evaluating therapeutic recreation services at the comprehensive program level is through quality assurance or quality improvement mechanisms (Huston, 1987; Wright, 1987). A parallel activity, that may or may not be a separate function, is efficacy research (Shank, Kinney and Coyle, 1993). Both of these activities are intended to provide useful data to document and improve the standard of care delivered to clients.

Quality assurance (now termed quality improvement or continuous quality improvement) is defined as a "wide spectrum of activities ranging from determining an appropriate definition of care to establishment of actual standards of practice, that, if implemented, will result in acceptable levels of service" (Riley, 1991a, p. 54). Quality assessment is defined as a systematic process of collecting targeted data, analyzing and comparing data against predetermined standards, taking appropriate action if necessitated, and optimally managing the entire quality review operation (Riley, 1991a, p. 54; Wright, 1987, p. 56). Both of these functions focus on the quality and appropriateness of service delivery (Navar, 1991).

Quality improvement tends to focus on four areas: "good professional performance, efficient use of resources, reduction of risk, and patient/family satisfaction" (Navar, 1991, p. 6).

These four areas can help the specialist to focus evaluative efforts and provide direction in defining the purpose of data collection. That is, they help establish the "content focus" of the evaluation process.

The quality improvement process, as outlined by the Joint Commission on Accreditation of Healthcare Organizations, involves 10 steps that are to be used by all healthcare providers in delivering and evaluating quality and appropriate services. These steps help provide the "process" to be used in improving quality service delivery. The reader should be aware that other sources are available that explain in greater detail the application of quality improvement activities to therapeutic recreation services (cf., Riley, 1987b, 1991b; Winslow and Halberg, 1992).

In a similar vein, efficacy research also focuses on the outcomes, benefits or results of service delivery (Shank, Kinney and Coyle, 1993). It involves systematic data collection and analysis, with an aim of documenting service effectiveness, specifically client-based outcomes, for a particular group or groups of clients. While it does have distinct purposes and actions separate from quality improvement, it also shares some similar goals and professional benefits. In addition, it can be accomplished only through a careful and systematic analysis of program delivery factors. A particularly useful resource for more information about efficacy research is Shank, Kinney and Coyle (1993).

Key Points to the Intervention Model

The purpose of the Therapeutic Recreation Intervention Model is to show the interrelationships between different tasks of providing intervention programs to clients. As such, several concepts are worth mentioning.

1. **In order to provide intervention, therapeutic recreation specialists must be aware of and competent in each task or type of documentation depicted in the Therapeutic Recreation Intervention Model.**

It is the responsibility of every therapeutic recreation professional to become well-versed in the various aspects of providing therapeutic recreation intervention. This means increasing competencies in all accountability activities, such as protocols, client assessments, and quality improvement activities. The therapeutic recreation literature and conference offerings are becoming richer with resources to help specialists increase understanding of and competencies in improving program accountability. It is each specialist's responsibility to make sure he or she understands and can apply these concepts to practice.

2. **In order to produce client outcomes, therapeutic recreation specialists must conceptualize the interrelationships between program design, delivery and evaluation.**

In the past, it was acceptable to be satisfied with providing Type I programs. In the vast majority of healthcare settings, this is no longer the case. Providing quality programs is not enough; we must be able to produce client outcomes—especially those that make a difference in the lives of clients and are valued by other healthcare providers. We can only address this change in service provision through recognizing that all parts of program delivery and documentation must align with one another. It is no longer acceptable to, for example, have a client assessment that gathers useless information (and dust!). We now acknowledge that all parts of the accountability system must match and follow a logical, interconnected pattern.

3. **The connection between components must be clear and logical.**

Again, the purpose of this Model is to provide a visual context that allows the specialist to view the entirety of service provision. Descriptors, such as systematic, interrelated, alignment, and connections, are crucial to ensuring that service provision be outcome-based. Literally every component box on the Model could be connected with every other box, because one action or decision affects all other actions or decisions. If one part of the Model, for example, client assessment, is not in alignment with other components, then being able to provide intervention is highly unlikely. The connections must be clear and logical.

4. **We need to take the guesswork out of "providing the right patient with the right service [at] the right time in the right setting at the right intensity and for the right duration" (Navar, 1991, p. 5).**

One aim of the Model is to help specialists become more systematic in delivering programs to clients. Therapists need to discover and document what works and what does not. We need better, more comprehensive "systems" for service provision. Each piece of the Model plays a vital part in conceptualizing and improving the accountability of therapeutic recreation programs. Systematic research and data collection will improve our ability to predict and deliver consistent client outcomes.

Summary

For nearly a decade, the profession of therapeutic recreation has focused on the production of client outcomes. Following mandates established by external accreditation bodies, health insurance companies, and other professions, the profession has made strides in upgrading the quality and appropriateness of service delivery.

The Therapeutic Recreation Intervention Model (TRIM) is provided as one avenue for describing the process used to design, implement, and evaluate quality intervention programs. It is intended that practicing professionals use it as a diagnostic tool in evaluating their program operations and that preservice professionals use it as a conceptual learning aid. It is offered with the intention of helping us design and provide quality programs that make a difference in the lives of clients.

References

Anderson, S. B., Ball, S., Murphy, R. T., and Associates. (1975). *Encyclopedia of educational evaluation.* San Francisco, CA: Jossey-Bass.

Carter, M. J., Van Andel, G. E., and Robb, G. M. (1995). *Therapeutic recreation: A practical approach* (2nd ed.). Prospect Heights, IL: Waveland Press, Inc.

Connolly, P. (1981). *Analysis of a formative program evaluation procedure for therapeutic recreation services.* Unpublished doctoral dissertation, University of Illinois at Urbana-Champaign.

Connolly, P. (1984). Program evaluation. In C. A. Peterson and S. L. Gunn (Eds.), *Therapeutic recreation program design: Principles and procedures* (2nd ed., pp. 136–179). Englewood Cliffs, NJ: Prentice-Hall, Inc.

Connolly, P., and Keogh-Hoss, M. A. (1991). The development and use of intervention protocols in therapeutic recreation: Documenting field-based practices. In B. Riley (Ed.), *Quality management: Applications for therapeutic recreation* (pp. 117–136). State College, PA: Venture Publishing, Inc.

Dunn, J. K. (1983). Improving client assessment procedures in therapeutic recreation programming. In G. Hitzhusen (Ed.), *Expanding horizons in therapeutic recreation XI* (pp. 146–157). Columbia, MO: Curators University of Missouri.

Dunn, J. K. (1984). Assessment. In C. A. Peterson and S. L. Gunn (Eds.), *Therapeutic recreation program design: Principles and procedures* (2nd ed., pp. 267–320). Englewood Cliffs, NJ: Prentice-Hall, Inc.

Dunn, J. K. (1987). Establishing reliability and validity in evaluation instruments. *Journal of Park and Recreation Administration, 5*(4), 61–70.

Dunn, J. K. (1989). Guidelines for using published assessment procedures. *Therapeutic Recreation Journal, 23*(2), 59–69.

Dunn, J. K. (1991, September). *Integrating client assessment into therapeutic recreation practice.* Paper presented at the Client Assessment Workshop, St. Peters, MO.

Dunn, J. K., Sneegas, J. J., and Carruthers, C. A. (1991). Outcome measures: Monitoring patient progress. In B. Riley (Ed.), *Quality management: Applications for therapeutic recreation* (pp. 107–115). State College, PA: Venture Publishing, Inc.

Ferguson, D. (1992, July). *Recreation therapy protocols.* Paper presented at the International Conference on Leisure and Mental Health, Salt Lake City, UT.

Huston, A. D. (1987). Clinical application of quality assurance in the therapeutic recreation setting. In B. Riley (Ed.), *Evaluation of therapeutic recreation through quality assurance* (pp. 67–96). State College, PA: Venture Publishing, Inc.

Kelland, J. (1995). *Protocols for recreation therapy programs.* State College, PA: Venture Publishing, Inc.

Knight, L., and Johnson, A. (1991). Therapeutic recreation protocols: Client problem centered approach. In B. Riley (Ed.), *Quality management: Applications for therapeutic recreation* (pp. 137–147). State College, PA: Venture Publishing, Inc.

Navar, N. (1984). Documentation in therapeutic recreation. In C. A. Peterson and S. L. Gunn (Eds.), *Therapeutic recreation program design: Principles and procedures* (pp. 212–266). Englewood Cliffs, NJ: Prentice-Hall, Inc.

Navar, N. (1991). Advancing therapeutic recreation through quality assurance: A perspective on the changing nature of quality in therapeutic recreation. In B. Riley (Ed.), *Quality management: Applications for therapeutic recreation* (pp. 3–20). State College, PA: Venture Publishing, Inc.

Peterson, C. A., and Gunn, S. L. (1984). *Therapeutic recreation program design: Principles and procedures* (2nd ed.). Englewood Cliffs, NJ: Prentice-Hall, Inc.

Riley, B. (1987a). Conceptual basis of quality assurance: Application to therapeutic recreation service. In B. Riley (Ed.), *Evaluation of therapeutic recreation through quality assurance* (pp. 7–24). State College, PA: Venture Publishing, Inc.

Riley, B. (Ed.). (1987b). *Evaluation of therapeutic recreation through quality assurance.* State College, PA: Venture Publishing, Inc.

Riley, B. (1991a). Quality assessment: The use of outcome indicators. In B. Riley (Ed.), *Quality management: Applications for therapeutic recreation* (pp. 53–67). State College, PA: Venture Publishing, Inc.

Riley, B. (Ed.). (1991b). *Quality management: Applications for therapeutic recreation.* State College, PA: Venture Publishing, Inc.

Russoniello, C. V. (1991). "Vision statements" and "mission statements:" Macro indicators of quality performance. In B. Riley (Ed.), *Quality management: Applications for therapeutic recreation* (pp. 21–28). State College, PA: Venture Publishing, Inc.

Scalenghe, R. (1991). The Joint Commission's "agenda for change" as related to the provision of therapeutic recreation services. In B. Riley (Ed.), *Quality management: Applications for therapeutic recreation* (pp. 30–42). State College, PA: Venture Publishing, Inc.

Shank, J., and Kinney, T. (1987). On the neglect of clinical practice. In C. Sylvester, J. L. Hemingway, R. Howe-Murphy, K. Mobily, and P. A. Shank (Eds.). *Philosophy of therapeutic recreation: Ideas and issues.* Alexandria, VA: National Recreation and Park Association.

Shank, J. W., and Kinney, W. B. (1991). Monitoring and measuring outcomes in therapeutic recreation. In B. Riley (Ed.), *Quality management: Applications for therapeutic recreation* (pp. 69–82). State College, PA: Venture Publishing, Inc.

Shank, J. W., Kinney, W. B., and Coyle, C. P. (1993). Efficacy studies in therapeutic recreation research: The need, the state of the art, and future implications. In M. J. Malkin and C. Z. Howe, (Eds.), *Research in therapeutic recreation: Concepts and methods* (pp. 301–335). State College, PA: Venture Publishing, Inc.

Sheehan, T. (1992). Outcome measurements in therapeutic recreation. In G. Hitzhusen, L. Jackson and M. Birdsong (Eds.), *Expanding horizons in therapeutic recreation XIV* (pp. 17–22). Columbia, MO: Curators University of Missouri.

Stumbo, N. J. (1991). Selected assessment resources: A review of instruments and references. *Annual in Therapeutic Recreation, 2,* 8–24.

Stumbo, N. J. (1992). Rethinking activity interest inventories. *Illinois Parks and Recreation, 23*(2), 17–21.

Stumbo, N. J. (1993/94). The use of activity interest inventories in therapeutic recreation assessment. *Annual in Therapeutic Recreation, 4,* 11–20.

Stumbo, N. J. (1994/95). Assessment of social skills for therapeutic recreation intervention. *Annual in Therapeutic Recreation, 5,* 68–82.

Stumbo, N. J. (1996). A proposed accountability model for therapeutic recreation services. *Therapeutic Recreation Journal, 30*(4), 246–259.

Stumbo, N. J. (1997). Issues and concerns in therapeutic recreation assessment. In D. Compton (Ed.), *Issues in therapeutic recreation: Toward a new millennium* (2nd ed., pp. 347–372). Champaign, IL: Sagamore Publishing, Inc.

Winslow, R. M., and Halberg, K. J. (Eds.). (1992). *The management of therapeutic recreation services.* Arlington, VA: National Recreation and Park Association.

Wright, S. (1987). Quality assessment: Practical approaches in therapeutic recreation. In B. Riley (Ed.), *Evaluation of therapeutic recreation through quality assurance* (pp. 55–66). State College, PA: Venture Publishing, Inc.

Chapter Two

Issues and Concerns in Therapeutic Recreation Assessment

Over 15 years ago, Witt, Connolly and Compton (1980) called for an increased sophistication in therapeutic recreation assessment:

> It seems improbable that any professional in the field would deny the importance of assessment within therapeutic recreation services. On the other hand, there appears to be some confusion over the purpose, approach and use of the assessment process in our services. (Witt, Connolly and Compton, 1980, p. 5)

The call for sophistication of client assessment is as appropriate today as it was in 1980, since confusion and misuse remain as professional concerns.

The purpose of this chapter is to explore some of the assessment concerns and issues that are likely to occur when providing therapeutic recreation intervention. These concerns and issues affect the quality of daily practice of therapeutic recreation specialists. To set the stage for this discussion, a case will be made for examining closely the relationship between client assessment and program design and implementation. A seven-step assessment model, adapted from Dunn (1984), will be used to review the accountability issues that affect the day-to-day operations of many therapeutic recreation departments. Assessment *decision points,* such as selecting, administering, interpreting and utilizing client assessment information, provide the structure for the seven-step model.

Connection Between Client Assessment and Program Delivery

Client assessment is "a systematic procedure for gathering select information about an individual for the purpose of making decisions regarding that individual's program or treatment plan" (Dunn, 1984, p. 268). Assessment is the initial step in establishing a meaningful baseline of the client's leisure-related interests, abilities, knowledge level, and/or attitudes. These baseline results provide the essential information for

Chapter Two is adapted from Stumbo, N. J. (1997). Issues and concerns in therapeutic recreation assessment. In D. Compton (Ed.), *Issues in therapeutic recreation: Toward the new millennium* (2nd ed., pp. 347–372). Champaign, IL: Sagamore Publishing, Inc. Reprinted with permission of Sagamore Publishing, Inc.

placing clients into the "right" intervention programs, and also provide the foundation for later determining the outcomes of therapeutic recreation intervention (Stumbo, 1996). Horvat and Kalakian (1996, p. 9) stated: "Assessment is the critical link in the testing process that renders worthwhile the time spent gathering data. Assessment also provides the basis for what instruction should follow."

Client assessment and program design and delivery are strongly linked in those programs which are considered intervention. Perschbacher (1995, p. 1), in discussing the need for accurate and timely assessments in long-term care, stated: "Resident assessments are the first step in understanding individuals. Assessments viewed as mere paperwork miss the point at which the activity program can make real differences in individual lives."

Intervention programs are intended to bring about some behavioral change in the client as a direct result of participation and involvement. The focus of intervention programs is on producing client outcomes; that is, some specific change in the client's behavior, skills, attitudes and/or knowledge. On the other hand, nonintervention or purely recreational programs are designed and delivered with the intent of providing fun and entertainment for participants. Client assessment is crucial to intervention programs, and cursory to nonintervention programs. An important task for therapeutic recreation specialists is to determine the overall intent of their programs and the assessments used to place clients into programs.

As therapeutic recreation services move further toward intervention and outcome-based service provision, the need for systematic and meaningful assessments increases. The connection between client assessment, intervention and client outcomes is a strong one and has been noted throughout the therapeutic recreation literature (Dunn, Sneegas and Carruthers, 1991; Navar, 1991; Olsson, 1992; Riley, 1991; Sheehan, 1992; Stumbo, 1996). Shank and Kinney (1991) noted that client outcomes are observable changes in the client's status as a direct result of the specialist's interventions and interactions. Riley (1991) discussed these as "measurable changes" and stated that "the causal relationship between the process of care (intervention) and the outcomes of care (change in patient behavior) is crucial" (p. 59).

Both of these thoughts about the connection between intervention and outcomes *assumes* that a valid and reliable baseline of information is gathered in order to later "prove" the change in behavior or status. That is, the client assessment collects the baseline information on the needs, strengths, limitations and current status of the client. This information provides the framework from which systematic intervention programs are designed, provided, and prescribed for individual clients. An "end-of-services" summary (perhaps the assessment readministered as a post-test) may provide the evaluative data to determine whether the appropriate client outcomes have been achieved at the conclusion of the intervention or the client's length of stay. This evaluative measurement allows for conclusions about the achievement of client outcomes to be made. Thus, the alliance between the assessment, the intervention and the measurement of outcomes is of paramount importance.

Decisions About Client Placement Into Programs

Outcome-based service delivery. Systematic. Connection. Intervention. Causal relationship. Paramount importance. These words are but a few that are used to illustrate the relationship between program design and delivery, client assessment, and client outcomes. This relationship is addressed through the concepts of validity and reliability. These concepts have been presented elsewhere in the therapeutic recreation literature (see specifically Dunn, 1983, 1984, 1987, 1989; Horvat and Kalakian, 1996; Howe, 1984, 1989; Sneegas, 1989; Stumbo, 1991, 1992a, 1992b, 1993/94, 1994/95, 1996), and will not be thoroughly reviewed here. However, Navar's (1991) presentation of appropriateness of services helps explain these concepts simply. Navar stated that the *appropriateness* of therapeutic recreation services hinged on whether the specialist is "providing the right patient with the right service [at] the right time in the right setting at the right intensity and for the right duration" (p. 5). The right client cannot be placed into the right program unless the assessment contains the right information (valid) and is refined to the point that placement is accurate (reliable).

The client assessment and program placement (CAPP) decision matrix in Figure 1.1 (page 5) helps to illustrate these concepts further. Outcome-based intervention programming needs dependable client assessment results—such as in Quadrants I and IV. These are correct decisions. The client's placement into programs

(or not) is based on need and the proven ability of the program to meet that need. Assessment results that lead to correct program placement have higher validity and reliability—as well as "appropriateness."

On the other hand, incorrect decisions from assessments, such as in Quadrants II and III, are less likely to be valid and reliable—and are usually very inappropriate to meet client need. Services in Quadrants II and III tend to put the client in jeopardy.

Figure 2.1 provides a different view of the way in which program content may or may not match assessment content. In the top example, program content differs greatly from the information collected on the assessment. The mismatch will produce assessment results that will

---

Figure 2.1. Examples of When Assessment Content Does and Does Not Match the Content of the Program.

Program Content	Assessment Content
Leisure Awareness	Personal History
Leisure Attitudes	Leisure Activity Preferences
Self-Awareness	Functional Abilities
Leisure Barriers	
Social Skills	
Conversational Skills	
Assertiveness Skills	
Problem-Solving Skills	
Leisure Resources	
Community Resources	
Community Reintegration	

Poor Example: The content of the assessment does not match the content of the program.

Program Content	Assessment Content
Leisure Awareness	Leisure Awareness
Leisure Attitudes	Leisure Attitudes
Self-Awareness	Self-Awareness
Leisure Barriers	Leisure Barriers
Social Skills	Social Skills
Conversational Skills	Conversational Skills
Assertiveness Skills	Assertiveness Skills
Problem-Solving Skills	Problem-Solving Skills
Leisure Resources	Leisure Resources
Community Resources	Community Resources
Community Reintegration	Community Reintegration

Better Example: The content of the assessment does match the content of the program.

be difficult to use in client placement into programs. The assessment results will probably be shelved while the specialist is left to devise client goals and a treatment plan based solely on professional judgment. In the second example, where program content and assessment content align, it will be easier to use assessment results to place clients into programs in a consistent and meaningful manner.

Therapeutic Recreation Intervention Model

Although the Therapeutic Recreation Intervention Model (TRIM) was discussed in Chapter One, it is reviewed briefly here to reiterate the importance of the multiple connections between programs, assessments and client outcomes (see Figure 1.2, page 7). Essentially the TRIM attempts to provide graphically an explanation of the whole of therapeutic recreation intervention programming. It is of great importance to note that the content and style of programs offered (as determined through program design and activity analysis) match the needs of clients (as determined through reviewing characteristics and gathering client information). Although other steps are involved, it is the connection between these two, and the foundation they provide, that increases the likelihood that the programs will be delivered as intervention and will produce measurable client outcomes. Note that client and program outcomes, and quality improvement and efficacy research efforts all provide feedback information for the improvement of the entire program delivery system. In other words, every component of the therapeutic recreation program delivery system is interrelated and provides feedback and direction for the improvement of other components and the entire system. Therapeutic recreation specialists who understand and utilize these relationships are most likely to provide the highest quality therapeutic recreation programs.

Issues in Implementing the Assessment Process

In the previous section, the direct relationship between therapeutic recreation intervention programming and client assessment was illustrated. This section will focus on the factors that influence the *assessment process,* from selection of assessment procedures to utilizing the assessment results. This framework will be used, not to address necessarily *how* this process works, but the *issues* that must be considered while implementing it. The structure for this discussion is provided by the seven-step Assessment Process Model found in Figure 2.2. The seven steps include: (a) selecting or developing an assessment tool or procedure; (b) understanding and practicing the assessment procedure; (c) administering the assessment; (d) determining the results or score; (e) interpreting the results and making client placement decisions; (f) documenting the placement and/or treatment plan in the client record; and (g) reassessing as necessary to show client progression or regression.

Step 1: Select or Develop an Assessment Tool or Procedure

The first step of selecting or developing an assessment has three major considerations: (a) the purpose of the assessment; (b) the content of the assessment; and (c) other selection criteria (Dunn, 1984). Each consideration will be reviewed and then discussed in terms of the concerns or issues that arise.

The first step in the selection process is determining the purpose of the assessment (Witt, Connolly and Compton, 1980). Client assessment generally serves four functions: (a) screening; (b) identifying the problem(s); (c) narrowing the problem(s); and (d) reassessing or monitoring progress. *Screening* serves as a generalized sorting function and may be given to all clients upon admission (Horvat and Kalakian, 1996). For example, an assessment that is used as a screening device may have a dozen basic questions to determine whether or

Figure 2.2. The Seven-Step Assessment Process (adapted from Dunn, 1984).

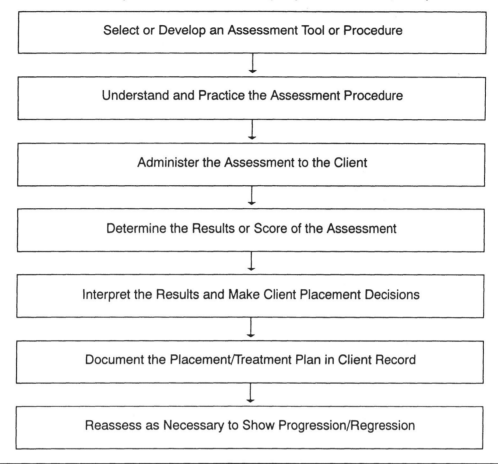

Select or Develop an Assessment Tool or Procedure

↓

Understand and Practice the Assessment Procedure

↓

Administer the Assessment to the Client

↓

Determine the Results or Score of the Assessment

↓

Interpret the Results and Make Client Placement Decisions

↓

Document the Placement/Treatment Plan in Client Record

↓

Reassess as Necessary to Show Progression/Regression

not an individual is appropriate for therapeutic recreation services (Does the person need social skills training?). *Identifying the problem(s)* requires more in-depth questioning that aids in program placement, and may be given to those individuals who were identified as needing further assessment from the screening device. For example, an assessment may help identify problems that can be worked on during therapeutic recreation services (What kinds of social skills does the person lack? interpersonal conversational skills? body space and proximity issues? hygiene?).

Assessments involved with *narrowing the problem(s)* provide the most in-depth information, and can be most useful for providing direction for working with clients on an individualized basis (What kinds of interpersonal skills does the person lack? eye contact? initiating conversations? maintaining conversations? ter-

minating conversations?). These assessments have the most utility in programs where clients participate for a considerable amount of time (adequate to work on in-depth problems) and where specific outcomes are targeted.

Assessments can also serve the purpose of *evaluating or monitoring client progression or regression.* If the assessment is of high quality and provides both valid and reliable results, then there is no better device to reassess a client to determine if outcomes have been achieved (Perschbacher, 1995). Those familiar with research techniques will equate this with pre- and post-testing, in which the same instrument is used both before and after a designated intervention. This aids in increasing the reliability of comparison results.

As mentioned previously, the content of the assessment must coincide with the content of the program:

While assessment clearly provides the foundation for individual program planning, its relationship to the program's conceptual foundation is as critical. The theory or philosophy which drives the program should be reflected in the assessment procedures. If the program seeks to build a client's repertoire of leisure skills in certain areas then an appropriate skill or activity-oriented inventory is needed. If the intent of the program is to increase the client's perceived competence or effectiveness in leisure, an instrument which measures levels of learned helplessness . . . or perceived leisure competence . . . may be needed. (Stumbo and Rickards, 1986, p. 3)

In addition to purpose and content, other factors influence the selection or development of a client assessment. For example, the agency's and department's philosophy, the population characteristics, documentation and accountability needs, staff resources and competence, and mandates for assessment all play a role in the selection process (Perschbacher, 1995; Stumbo and Rickards, 1986). That is:

> . . . it should be expected that assessments used in therapeutic recreation:
>
> - fulfill their intended purpose;
> - have the ability to gather specified information;
> - gather that information accurately;
> - utilize an appropriate method;
> - are appropriate for clients; and
> - are appropriate for the agency and the situation. (Dunn, 1983, p. 63)

Specialists must consider both the purpose and content, as well as other factors, before selecting or developing an assessment procedure. If a commercially available assessment can be located that meets the purpose and content needed in the assessment, then purchase is logical. However, this is relatively rare in that

therapeutic recreation programs, because they are based on unique factors such as community resources, agency mission, resources, and the like (Peterson and Gunn, 1984), are not uniform across the country or, in fact, any state. Many professionals, then, must rely on developing assessments to meet their department's needs.

The major concern, regardless of whether the assessment is purchased or developed, is that professionals often fail to consider the purpose or function of the assessment, and the necessity to match the content of the assessment with the content of the program. This match requires that the professional use comprehensive program design to create programs and that these areas be translated into assessment content. Failure to consider the link between program placement and assessment data results in poor decisions in Quadrants I and III (Figure 1.1, page 5). This means that the link between the assessment results and the placement into programs is likely to be faulty and lack validity. If this link is not established, the content of the assessment will tend to be haphazard and not lead to appropriate program placement decisions. This, obviously, is a major concern in therapeutic recreation assessment and program delivery.

Step 2: Understand and Practice the Assessment Procedure

In this step, the specialist is responsible for preparing to administer a client assessment. All assessments, whether commercially sold or self-developed, should be accompanied by adequate documentation that includes information on the development of the tool as well as standardized procedures for its use, analysis and interpretation. For example, documentation should include the conceptual development of the tool, the validity and reliability statistics of validation studies and pilot tests, and resources needed to perform all steps of the assessment. Additionally, documentation should include standardized procedures for training (both staff and interns), preparing the assessment environment (including supplies), and administering, scoring and interpreting the procedure. Dunn (1987, 1989) provides excellent guidelines for using or creating the necessary documentation to accompany assessments.

The major concern of this step is that both commercially available and self-developed assessments rarely have adequate accompanying documentation. The lack of this documentation decreases the opportunities for standardized (and hopefully, valid and reliable) procedures across staff and units. This means that results will be interpreted and reported based on the fluctuating perceptions of individual staff members. The lack of uniform implementation of assessments, even within a single department, reduces the likelihood of correct and consistent placement decisions. This lack of precision weakens the assessment process and increases the likelihood of incorrect program placement decisions—another important concern for the profession.

Step 3: Administration of the Assessment to the Client

In this step, the specialist implements the procedures that were outlined and reviewed in the last stage. Assessments in therapeutic recreation tend to be of three kinds: (a) interviews (with clients and/or their families) (see Ferguson, 1983); (b) observations (see Stumbo, 1983); and (c) record reviews. Each type collects unique information and has its own advantages and disadvantages. Types may be used in combination to strengthen the validity of the results. With interviews and observations, protocol is followed in order to establish rapport with the client (or family), and convey information about the purpose of the assessment, its relationship to future treatment, and expected outcomes. This step gathers information that is pertinent to placing clients directly into therapeutic recreation programs, and as such, relies on the specialist paying close attention to the tasks and concerns in the first two steps.

The primary concern with administration is that it is often inconsistent between departments (no two departments administer the assessment in the identical way), between specialists (no

two specialists administer the assessment in the identical way) and within specialists (each specialist is not consistent from one administration to the next). These inconsistencies greatly affect the outcome of the assessment, thus affecting the placement of clients into programs. Again, incorrect decisions may be made, jeopardizing the likelihood that clients will receive needed treatment and will achieve the desired or intended outcomes. Adequate and uniform documentation, training and guidelines would assist in alleviating this weakness.

An additional concern is the differing abilities of clients on singular or multiple units. Since administration needs to be consistent, when client abilities differ greatly (some clients who cannot read, some with cognitive disabilities, some with visual or hearing impairments), the assessment(s) must be designed to meet these varying needs and must be administered as consistently as possible when these conditions are present.

The point is that assessments need to be administered consistently to the fullest extent possible. That means that the assessment needs a specific protocol that is consistent across: (a) units (if programs are similar); (b) specialists; (c) administrations by an individual specialist; (d) clients; and (e) assessment environments. Deviations from these consistencies lower the confidence that can be placed in the results and program placement decisions.

Step 4: Determining the Results or Scoring the Assessment

Following the established protocol for scoring the assessment, the specialist, in this step, summarizes the information collected on the assessment in a clear and concise manner. Also referred to as *data reduction,* this summary condenses quantitative (numbers) and/or qualitative (words) data, into an understandable and cohesive picture of the client.

Like previous steps, the major concern here is one of consistency. The vast majority of therapeutic recreation assessments do not have adequate protocols for reliable scoring. In fact, many, because they rely on purely qualitative or open-ended data, are difficult to "score" due to the lack of an agreed-upon, congruent method of gathering and synthesizing information. For example, asking "How do you spend your leisure time?" as an open-ended question with no established categories for marking an answer, is likely to result in a diversity of answers that are difficult to categorize after the fact.

Indeed, it is probably this step that has been one of the most problematic for therapeutic recreation specialists. Because standardized scoring procedures are all but nonexistent (especially for agency-specific assessments), the specialist often is forced to rely on personal judgment for summarizing the results (and this may fluctuate based on many superfluous reasons, such as mood, need to fill programs, personal preference, and the like). That is, the specialist *collects* assessment data (perhaps largely because of external or agency mandates), but then ignores any systematic procedure to score the results, and later places clients into programs based on personal preferences or the need to fill certain programs, or worse yet, every client is placed in every program. This inconsistent, unreliable "method" of program placement results in faulty decisions and the inability to produce client outcomes. As such, it jeopardizes the entire programming process and threatens the quality of therapeutic recreation program delivery.

Step 5: Interpreting the Results and Making Client Placement Decisions

The goal of the fifth step is to make objective, consistent and correct decisions for placing clients into therapeutic recreation programs. These placements should be based on the results of the assessment process obtained in the fourth step. If the results were obtained through a valid and reliable process, the interpretation of the results and placement decisions also are more likely to be valid and reliable. If two clients have similar scores or results on the assessment and they are placed in similar programs,

as indicated as necessary from the assessment, then these "right" individuals are likely to be receiving the "right" service. On the other hand, if two clients have similar scores or results on the assessment, and they are placed in dissimilar programs, then the process is probably not producing valid or reliable results and are resulting in faulty interpretation and placement decisions.

Obviously, this step is closely related to the previous step. If data reduction is problematic, then interpretation of the data similarly will be problematic. Often specialists rely too heavily on personal judgment, and their placement of clients into programs is imprecise. This results in either clients not receiving necessary services (Quadrant II, Figure 1.1, page 5) or clients receiving unnecessary services (Quadrant III, Figure 1.1, page 5).

Step 6: Documenting the Placement and Treatment Plan in the Client Record

While the format of client records often are decided at the agency or company level, the content that professionals enter into the record usually is decided by the department's staff, in consultation with other disciplines. The content to be reported from the results of the assessment is determined by the content of the programs, and in turn, the content of the assessment.

One of the frustrations, if the previous five steps have been done incorrectly or incompletely, is that the specialist has little valuable or unique information to report. When prior assessment steps have not followed a logical, consistent and justifiable sequence or if programs are not based in a systematic analysis of client needs, the information provided by therapeutic recreation specialists may not differ greatly from other disciplines or may not contribute to the client goals.

For example, a therapeutic recreation specialist may be providing valuable intervention programs with the *content* of (a) leisure awareness; (b) social interaction skills; and (c) community leisure resources. These are well-designed, outcome oriented intervention programs that appear to be successful and complement the treatment programs of the other disciplines. However, the assessment *content* includes (a) personal history; (b) past leisure interests; and (c) future leisure interests. How well does the content of the assessment match the content of the program? What can the specialist say about client placement into programs? How will the "right" clients be placed systematically into the "right" programs? How will the link be translated in the client record?

The answer is that client placement into the correct programs is unlikely and the specialist will have little of value to report in the client record or to the treatment team. As a beginning, the specialist needs the assessment to reflect the program content of (a) leisure awareness; (b) social interaction skills; and (c) community leisure resources. Other information may have little value, and be regarded poorly by other members of the treatment team. Figure 2.1 (page 17) provided a schematic of this idea.

Step 7: Reassessing as Necessary to Show Progression or Regression

The final phase of reassessment was mentioned previously. Whenever the status of a client needs to examined, conducting a reassessment using the same tool as the initial assessment appears logical. This reassessment may be necessary to write progress notes or discharge and referral summaries. If the original assessment tool produces results that are valid and reliable, then no better tool exists to determine the progression or regression of a particular client. This does mean that the original assessment must have the precision (reliability) to determine sometimes small increments of movement. For example, if it is determined from the original assessment that a client lacks social interaction skills (and, therefore, the client is placed into a social skills program), the assessment must measure these skills with enough accuracy to determine if change has been made during or at the completion of the program. If the assessment provides rough or "crude" estimates of ability, then reassessment will be difficult, if not

impossible. If this is the case, the specialist will have an extremely difficult time "proving" that the client achieved the intended outcomes of the therapeutic recreation program.

All seven steps show the need for the assessment process to be both valid and reliable, and this requires a great deal of specialist expertise, competence, and effort. This discussion shows that each step is intricately linked and that poor decisions in one phase result in mistakes or poor execution in other steps.

Other Concerns in Therapeutic Recreation Assessment

In addition to how the assessment process is executed, there are several other issues and concerns in therapeutic recreation assessment. Among these are (a) specialist expertise and attitude; (b) lack of assessments; (c) lack of appropriate assessments; (d) complexities of measurement; and (e) lack of assessment resources. Although these are connected with and impact the concerns mentioned in the previous section, these issues will be discussed separately.

Specialist Expertise and Attitude

Sneegas (1989), among others, identified the need for specialists to be better trained in assessment, research methods and leisure behavior, and called for better communication between "investigators and practitioners" to conduct needed research (p. 233). Horvat and Kalakian (1996) identified several qualifications for professionals conducting assessments. Among these are:

a. knowledge of measurement principles, including validity, reliability and objectivity;
b. knowledge of potentials and limitations of test interpretations;
c. competence in the administration and interpretation of specific tests;

d. competence in assessment validation procedures; and

e. knowledge of procedures to avoid undue discrimination, such as age, gender or cultural biases.

The National Council for Therapeutic Recreation Certification (NCTRC) (1997) has completed a new job analysis. This job analysis included knowledge areas that provide the foundation for the national certification examination. These knowledge areas include:

a. purpose;
b. domains:
   1. cognitive (e.g., memory, problem solving, attention span, orientation, safety awareness),
   2. social assessment (e.g., communication and interactive skills, relationships),
   3. physical (e.g., fitness, motor and sensory functioning),
   4. emotional (e.g., attitude toward self, expression),
   5. leisure (e.g., barriers, interests, attitudes, patterns and skills, knowledge), and
   6. background information (e.g., demographics, diagnoses, prior medical history);
c. procedures:
   1. behavioral observations,
   2. interview,
   3. functional skills testing,
   4. current therapeutic recreation/leisure assessment instruments,
   5. other inventories and questionnaires, and
   6. other sources of assessment data (e.g., records, other professionals);
d. process:
   1. selection (e.g., reliability, validity, practicality, availability),
   2. implementation, and
   3. interpretation.

It should be noted that assessment was among the highest rated areas of the job analysis, meaning that assessment is one of the most important and frequent functions of the Therapeutic Recreation Specialist.

These competencies require that education about assessments become a lifelong process for the specialist, who needs to continue to learn about improving client assessment procedures throughout his or her career. Howe (1989) in summarizing a book chapter on assessment stated:

But, what [this chapter] cannot give is the thorough and complete education needed to use assessment instruments or procedures well, mindful of both their strengths and their weaknesses. That training requires either formal degree work or continuing professional education. It takes time and study to gain the insight and skills to validate instruments, let alone to practice one's skills at assessment design, quantitative and qualitative data collection and analysis, and the interpretation and application of results. So, in that sense, any assessment is only as good as the TRS [Therapeutic Recreation Specialist] conducting it. (p. 219)

Students and specialists alike must make the commitment to learn as much as possible about assessment as it is one of the most powerful decision points in the therapeutic recreation intervention process. As knowledge and use of assessments improve, so too will the quality of intervention programs and the success of therapeutic recreation within the healthcare arena.

Lack of an Adequate Number of Assessments

For a profession as large and diverse as therapeutic recreation, there are few quality instruments commercially available for use. Two difficulties exist: (a) most commercially available instruments lack adequate testing and validation for use by specialists in different settings working with varied populations; and (b) there are not enough instruments to meet the demands of the diverse programming of therapeutic recreation professionals. There are not enough commercial instruments that have the content to reflect the content of programs offered within therapeutic recreation services—meaning that most of the instruments available are not valid for the programs with which specialists would like to use them.

This presents three further problems. First, the specialist may buy instruments that are not appropriate (valid, reliable or usable) for the purpose for which he or she would like to use them. The specialist then encounters the problem of not being able to make proper programming placement decisions (Quadrants II and III, Figure 1.1, page 5). Second, the specialist may "borrow" an assessment from a related field, such as adapted physical education. This may seem fairly attractive, and some therapeutic recreation textbooks advocate this approach. However, if the content of the assessment does not match the content of the therapeutic recreation program, the results will likely lead to random program placement, again resulting in faulty program placement decisions and lack of client outcomes. Third, the specialist may develop an assessment specifically for use within his or her agency. Given the problems noted in the previous section with Therapeutic Recreation Specialist expertise, this option can be problematic (Dunn, 1984; Kinney, 1980; Stumbo, 1991; Touchstone, 1975). To counteract these pitfalls, the specialist needs to develop considerable expertise in assessment, and more and better assessments need to be developed and marketed.

Lack of Standardized and Valid Assessments

The available assessment instruments that are non-agency-specific are still sketchy, still evolutionary, and still conceptually cloudy. The tension between the applied and theoretical dimensions of the assessment process continues, es-

pecially with the continual proliferation of agency-specific assessment devices that are little more than interest inventories but are incorrectly used and touted for purposes way beyond those of such inventories. (Howe, 1989, p. 217–218).

The problems specifically with activity interest inventories and similar instruments have been outlined elsewhere in the literature (Stumbo, 1992b, 1993/94), and these problems remain in practice today. Stumbo (1991) stated that since activity interest inventories and other similar tools contain a relatively narrow *activity* definition of services, they miss the mark in helping understand the broader *leisure behavior* and *functional independence* focus of most therapeutic recreation programs. As such they may provide little help in understanding client behavior. "A frustrating outcome of this misguided use of assessment as measurement is the realization that the results derived from an irrelevant assessment instrument are of little informative value in providing program direction and may totally misdirect program decisions" (Witt, Connolly and Compton, 1980, p. 6). In other words, without adequate standardization and validation of client assessment tools, improper program placement decisions (Quadrants II and III, Figure 1.1, page 5) will be made.

Complexities of Measurement

Citing work completed by Dunn (1984), Howe (1984), and Stumbo and Thompson (1986), Sneegas (1989, p. 226) noted that "there are few instruments designed to obtain assessment information related to leisure behavior which demonstrate adequate reliability, validity, and practical utility." Leisure behavior and functional independence are complex entities and their measurement is fraught with measurement dangers:

. . . the measurement of leisure behavior in individuals with disabilities and in special populations is not as simple as it might appear on the surface. The current state of the art for assessing leisure behavior is relatively undeveloped because obtaining valid and reliable measures of the leisure behavior of anyone (not even considering any additional problems presented by disability) is a complex process. (Sneegas, 1989, p. 224)

For instance, Sneegas (1989) discusses problems with how leisure is defined (time, activity or state of mind), and therefore, measured through assessments. Sneegas (1989) also warns of simplistic or univariate studies, and those that lack richness or contextual and/or qualitative information. In addition, this contribution to the literature examined some of these difficulties in light of assessing individuals with disabilities and special needs. For example, Katsinas (1992) made the case that most therapeutic recreation assessment tools are not refined enough to measure low levels of functioning or regressed behavior, and are not sensitive enough to measure small increments of behavioral change. Howe (1989, p. 217) noted that most therapeutic recreation assessments lacked the ability to measure "richness" and "complexity" of the individual client.

The lack of ability to measure the complexities of human behavior—especially individuals with disabilities, illnesses and/or special needs—is a major concern for therapeutic recreation assessment. The field needs more and better research describing and measuring the leisure behavior of clients. This, in turn, will improve the ability to standardize and validate tools to measure baseline and progressive information.

Lack of Assessment Resources

Another area for concern with therapeutic recreation assessment is the difficulty that most specialists have in locating information about available and usable assessments. Keeping abreast of current information about assessments and related issues is essential, although largely a difficult and fragmented enterprise. This area has improved, but warrants continued attention:

Several shifts in the provision of therapeutic recreation services, including the emphasis on program accountability and the measurement of client outcomes (Olsson, Shearer and Halberg, 1988), the increasing sophistication of therapeutic recreation specialists, and the increasing number of cottage industry publishers, have improved this bleak outlook considerably in the past five years. More and better instruments are being produced and validated, client assessments are conducted more frequently and at a higher level of quality and the availability of instruments is greater than ever. (Stumbo, 1991, p. 9)

Specialists must take responsibility to expend (sometimes great) effort to locate, read, and understand the published assessment literature. Authors need to continue to write and publish quality articles and books on assessment that are of high value to practice. Professional organizations and publishers need to continue to create avenues to provide easy access to the newest information. Educators need to ensure that the latest techniques and tools are an integral part of therapeutic recreation curricula. Only as each group continues to take responsibility for its part of the information chain, will better and more timely assessment information be widely available to all who desire it.

The Challenge

Therapeutic recreation assessment will advance rapidly and issues will be minimized greatly only when each student and specialist meets the challenge of improving the future state of the art in assessment. To meet this end, the reader is challenged to answer the following questions:

a. What *specific actions* will you take to improve your personal knowledge of validity, reliability and usability as measurement characteristics that affect the quality of therapeutic recreation assessments? What articles, chapters or books will you read?

b. What *specific actions* will you take to better understand the crucial link between program design and client assessment in therapeutic recreation assessment? How can you use the two models (CAPP and TRIM) discussed in this chapter?

c. What *specific actions* will you take to improve your ability to implement assessments through observations, interviews, or record reviews? Will this include practice sessions under peer review?

d. What *specific actions* will you take to remain informed about new developments and literature concerning therapeutic recreation assessments? Does this plan include reading periodicals, journals and books? attending conferences and workshops? developing assessments through research and cooperative partnerships?

Summary

The intent of this chapter is to provide a starting point for discussion about the improvement of therapeutic recreation assessment. The challenges outlined, including issues about selecting and implementing assessments; specialist expertise; and instrument validity, standardization, and availability, point to the continued need to improve the current state of the art of therapeutic recreation assessment. This will happen only when each student and professional in the field meets the challenge of improving his or her own knowledge, skills and understanding of assessment and its crucial link to intervention programming. Are you up to the challenge?

References

Dunn, J. K. (1983). Improving client assessment procedures in therapeutic recreation programming. In G. L. Hitzhusen (Ed.), *Expanding horizons in therapeutic recreation X* (pp. 61–84). Columbia, MO: University of Missouri.

Dunn, J. (1984). Assessment. In C. A. Peterson and S. L. Gunn (Eds.), *Therapeutic recreation program design: Principles and procedures* (2nd ed., pp. 267–320). Englewood Cliffs, NJ: Prentice-Hall, Inc.

Dunn, J. K. (1987). Establishing reliability and validity of evaluation instruments. *Journal of Park and Recreation Administration, 5*(4), 61–70.

Dunn, J. K. (1989). Guidelines for using published assessment procedures. *Therapeutic Recreation Journal, 23*(2), 59–69.

Dunn, J. K., Sneegas, J., and Carruthers, C. A. (1991). Outcome measures: Monitoring patient progress. In B. Riley (Ed.), *Quality management: Applications for therapeutic recreation* (pp. 107–116). State College, PA: Venture Publishing, Inc.

Ferguson, D. (1983). Assessment interviewing techniques: A useful tool in developing individual program plans. *Therapeutic Recreation Journal, 17*(2), 16–22.

Horvat, M., and Kalakian, L. (1996). *Assessment in adapted physical education and therapeutic recreation* (2nd ed.). Madison, WI: Brown & Benchmark.

Howe, C. (1984). Leisure assessment instrumentation in therapeutic recreation. *Therapeutic Recreation Journal, 18*(2), 14–24.

Howe, C. Z. (1989). Assessment instruments in therapeutic recreation: To what extent do they work? In D. Compton (Ed.), *Issues in therapeutic recreation: A profession in transition* (pp. 205–221). Champaign, IL: Sagamore Publishing Co.

Katsinas, R. P. (1992). Social skills assessment for long-term care residents who have cognitive and multiple impairments. In G. Hitzhusen and L. T. Jackson (Eds.), *Expanding horizons in therapeutic recreation XIV* (pp. 193–224). Columbia, MO: University of Missouri.

Kinney, W. B. (1980). Clinical assessment in mental health settings. *Therapeutic Recreation Journal, 14*(4), 39–45.

National Council for Therapeutic Recreation Certification (NCTRC). (1997). *Job analysis of the job of therapeutic recreation specialists.* Thiells, NY: Author.

Navar, N. (1991). Advancing therapeutic recreation through quality assurance: A perspective on the changing nature of quality in therapeutic recreation. In B. Riley (Ed.), *Quality management: Applications for therapeutic recreation* (pp. 3–20). State College, PA: Venture Publishing, Inc.

Olsson, R. H., Jr. (1992). Assessment and progress note writing: Skills needed for treatment documentation. In G. Hitzhusen and L. T. Jackson (Eds.), *Expanding horizons in therapeutic recreation XIV* (pp. 167–176). Columbia, MO: University of Missouri.

Olsson, R. H., Shearer, T. W., and Halberg, K. J. (1988). The effectiveness of a computerized leisure assessment system for individuals with spinal cord injuries. *Journal of Expanding Horizons, 3*(3), 35–40.

Perschbacher, R. (1995). *Assessment: The cornerstone of activity programs.* State College, PA: Venture Publishing, Inc.

Peterson, C. A. and Gunn, S. L. (1984). *Therapeutic recreation program design: Principles and procedures* (2nd ed.). Englewood Cliffs, NJ: Prentice-Hall, Inc.

Riley, B. (1991). Quality assessment: The use of outcome indicators. In B. Riley (Ed.), *Quality management: Applications for therapeutic recreation* (pp. 53–68). State College, PA: Venture Publishing, Inc.

Shank, J. W., and Kinney, W. B. (1991). Monitoring and measuring outcomes in therapeutic recreation. In B. Riley (Ed.), *Quality management: Applications for therapeutic recreation* (pp. 69–82). State College, PA: Venture Publishing, Inc.

Sheehan, T. (1992). Outcome measurements in therapeutic recreation. In G. Hitzhusen and L. T. Jackson (Eds.), *Expanding horizons in therapeutic recreation XIV* (pp. 177–192). Columbia, MO: University of Missouri.

Sneegas, J. J. (1989). Can we really measure leisure behavior of special populations and individuals with disabilities? In D. Compton (Ed.), *Issues in therapeutic recreation: A profession in transition* (pp. 223–236). Champaign, IL: Sagamore Publishing Co.

Stumbo, N. (1983). Systematic observation as a research tool for assessing client behavior. *Therapeutic Recreation Journal, 17*(4), 53–63.

Stumbo, N. J. (1991). Selected assessment resources: A review of instruments and references. *Annual in Therapeutic Recreation, 2*(2), 8–24.

Stumbo, N. J. (1992a). *Leisure education II: More activities and resources.* State College, PA: Venture Publishing, Inc.

Stumbo, N. J. (1992b). Rethinking activity inventories. *Illinois Parks and Recreation Magazine, 23*(2) 17–21.

Stumbo, N. J. (1993/94). The use of activity interest inventories in therapeutic recreation assessment. *Annual in Therapeutic Recreation, 4,* 11–20.

Stumbo, N. J. (1994/95). Assessment of social skills for therapeutic recreation intervention. *Annual in Therapeutic Recreation, 5,* 68–82.

Stumbo, N. J. (1996). A proposed accountability model for therapeutic recreation services. *Therapeutic Recreation Journal, 30*(4), 246–259.

Stumbo, N. J. (1997). Issues and concerns in therapeutic recreation assessment. In D. Compton (Ed.), *Issues in therapeutic recreation: Toward the new millennium* (2nd ed., pp. 347–372). Champaign, IL: Sagamore Publishing, Inc.

Stumbo, N. J., and Rickards, W. H. (1986). Selecting assessment instruments: Theory into practice. *Journal of Expanding Horizons in Therapeutic Recreation, 1*(1), 1–6.

Stumbo, N. J., and Thompson, S. R. (1986). *Leisure education: A manual of activities and resources.* State College, PA: Venture Publishing, Inc.

Touchstone, W. A. (1975). The status of client evaluation in psychiatric settings. *Therapeutic Recreation Journal, 14*(4), 166–172.

Witt, P., Connolly, P., and Compton, D. (1980). Assessment: A plea for sophistication. *Therapeutic Recreation Journal, 14*(4), 3–8.

Chapter Three

An Examination of the Logical Assumptions Underlying the Use of Activity Interest Inventories in Therapeutic Recreation Assessment

One of the many responsibilities facing therapeutic recreation specialists in clinical facilities is the mandate to measure client outcomes as the direct result of interventions (Riley, 1991; Shank and Kinney, 1991). This mandate has evolved through the upgrading of quality improvement and management mechanisms, the power of external accreditation bodies, and the call for accountability from within the therapeutic recreation profession (Scalenghe, 1991).

According to Riley (1991, p. 59), "In direct application to therapeutic recreation, outcomes would be defined as the measurable change in clients' health status or well-being after receiving therapeutic recreation intervention. The concepts of *measurable change* and *relationship* are critical to this definition." He continues to note that measurements are required both before and after treatment to prove a causal relationship between the process of care and the outcomes of care. That is, before outcomes of intervention can be measured, an initial baseline of information about the patient must be obtained. This requires that appropriate, accurate and meaningful information be gained from client assessments.

However, client assessment continues to be a problematic area for therapeutic recreation professionals. Several authors have noted that general problems include (a) lack of assessment tools in general; (b) limited content, scope and intent of assessment tools; (c) lack of psychometric adequacy; (d) lack of specialists' expertise; and (e) lack of availability of usable resources (Dunn, 1983, 1984; Ellis and Witt, 1986; Howe, 1984, 1989; Sneegas, 1989; Stumbo, 1991; Witt, Connolly and Compton, 1980). The totality of these problems indicates that much is awry in trying to obtain baseline information on clients and proving causal relationships between therapeutic recreation interventions and client outcomes.

One specific problem that has plagued therapeutic recreation for some time is the continued use of activity interest inventories for collecting baseline information. Howe (1984) defined activity interest inventories or leisure interest finders as:

> Those devices that allow individuals to check off activities about which they are curious, already involved in, "like"

Chapter Three is adapted from Stumbo, N. J. (1993/94). The use of activity interest inventories in therapeutic recreation assessment. *Annual in Therapeutic Recreation, 4,* 11–20.

or are skilled at, depending on the exact focus of the instrument. Some are used to determine leisure preferences. But all are framed in terms of recreational activity selection. They are useful to the therapeutic recreator in determining activities about which the client may be aware, interested, already engaged in or wanting to pursue in the future. (p. 22)

Over a decade ago, Witt, Connolly and Compton (1980, p. 7) noted that:

Much of the current state of the art reveals a dominant emphasis on interest inventories and profiles related to leisure activity involvement. Additionally, current assessment efforts seem to be largely agency-specific, focused on isolated developments in assessment procedures to address unique agency needs or services.

In 1985, Beddall and Kennedy conducted a study on the attitudes and practices of professionals and concluded that the same problem continued. "This study revealed that therapeutic recreation practitioners were more inclined to utilize in-house forms, checklists and inventories for the purpose of client assessment . . . rather than using specific instruments which have been described in the literature" (p. 68). The problem was again highlighted by Sneegas (1989) who stated:

. . . identifying and measuring participation in various activities is alone not a valid and sufficient measure of the full spectrum of leisure behavior. In order to obtain more meaningful information, the antecedents and consequences of activity involvement—that is the preexisting needs and subsequent effects of leisure involvement . . . as well as the subjective experiences of the individual—need to be examined. (p. 225)

Despite the accumulation of literature for almost two decades arguing against the use of activity interest inventories, many therapeutic recreation professionals continue to use them in practice. This chapter will provide a logical argument for discontinuing the heavy reliance on activity inventories, especially in times of increasing accountability and in light of the increased availability of more appropriate instruments. While activity interest inventories are quick and easy, the information they provide may be undermining therapeutic recreation professionals' efforts to provide viable healthcare services:

. . . assessment instruments are too often selected for their ease of use or because they lead to seemingly concrete analyses of human functioning. The imminent pitfall in this area is in selecting tests and instruments that are readily available regardless of their *conceptual relevance* [emphasis added] to our area of service. A frustrating outcome of this misguided use of assessment as measurement is the realization that the results derived from an irrelevant assessment instrument are of little informative value in providing program direction and may totally misdirect program decisions. (Witt, Connolly and Compton, 1980, p. 6)

Prior to examining reasons that activity inventories may be "conceptually irrelevant," several underlying assumptions will be discussed. These include assumptions about client characteristics, definitions of leisure, therapeutic recreation programs and client assessment tools.

Assumptions About Clients and Intervention Services

There are at least three major assumptions that can be made about clients in clinically-based settings where therapeutic recreation programs are implemented. The first major assumption is that clients within a facility or unit have similar problems that need some form of intervention. Some authors have called this *problem clusters* meaning that individuals with similar diagnoses or problems usually are grouped according to those diagnoses (Peterson and Gunn, 1984). For example, large general hospitals usually have units for physical rehabilitation, chemical dependency, geriatrics, and the like, where clients with similar problems are categorized by diagnoses. That is, clients on a particular unit are recognized as individuals, but tend to have similar problems (problem clusters) and needs for treatment (thus, *treatment clusters*).

This practice of treatment clustering can be both helpful and problematic for therapeutic recreation specialists. Having clients with similar needs on one unit is convenient both programmatically and administratively. A potential problem, however, arises when clients are not assessed specifically enough to determine individual needs and problems, and thus, are placed in large group programs regardless of real needs. Labeled as *Type I* (Dunn, 1991) or *cafeteria-style* (Stumbo, 1992) programming, this type reflects a lack of comprehensive program design and results in poor assessment selection and decisions.

The second assumption is that the clients have significant problems or deficits in social, cognitive, physical and/or emotional domains that can be reduced or alleviated through some form or process of treatment. That is, healthcare professionals, such as physicians, social workers and nurses, plan a course of treatment directed at reducing the "presenting problem." The outcome of overall healthcare for the client is a reduction of the problem for which he or she was admitted. Each professional discipline plans a part of the client's treatment based on its specialty of service. Each professional is assuming that there is a relationship between the treatment and the client outcomes, and that the treatment can produce measurable change (Riley, 1991).

Very closely related to this is the third assumption that clients may benefit from the pro-

vision of therapeutic recreation as a specific type of intervention service. As part of the treatment team, therapeutic recreation professionals specifically design a course of action to reduce the client's problem and/or increase his or her overall health and wellness, leading to an independent leisure lifestyle. The assumption is that provision of therapeutic recreation services adds a unique, but complementary, contribution to the overall treatment of the client. As above, a therapeutic recreation professional provides services based on a presumed relationship between treatment and outcomes, resulting in measurable change in the client's leisure knowledge, attitude, behavior or skills. To some, this assumption is tenuous, at best, because of the lack of empirical research demonstrating the contributions therapeutic recreation makes to healthcare and rehabilitation (Shank and Kinney, 1991).

All three of these assumptions about clients and general service provision impact the types of intervention people receive while in a healthcare system. They influence and are influenced by related assumptions about leisure and specific therapeutic recreation service provision.

Assumptions About Definitions of Leisure

Professionals' definition(s) of, or assumptions about, leisure also play a large role in client assessment and programming (Sneegas, 1989; Witt, Connolly and Compton, 1980). Defining leisure and leisure behavior is problematic because of the complex nature of the leisure experience (Sneegas, 1989). Simply stated, leisure has been defined as an activity, a space of time, or a subjective state of mind. The definition chosen by the therapeutic recreation professional impacts program conceptualization and implementation. For example, if one prefers the activity definition, then most of the therapeutic recreation program is built upon the development of clients' leisure skills. The overall goal would be for clients to maximally participate in a variety of activities. If one selects the time definition, then helping the individual recognize and develop blocks of time separate from work and maintenance may be the focus of therapeutic recreation services. If leisure is viewed as a state of mind then the subjective, individualistic nature of leisure must be accepted and explored through programs that focus on the development and expression of leisure attitudes, values, perceptions, motivations, and the like, as well as social and leisure-related skills (Sneegas, 1989; Witt, Connolly and Compton, 1980). The professional's definition or concept of leisure impacts how services are designed and implemented for client consumption. These fundamental assumptions lay the foundation for all programming and related decisions that follow.

Assumptions About Therapeutic Recreation Programs

Therapeutic recreation programs are created and operationalized based on the designer's ideas about clients, leisure and the overall purpose of therapeutic recreation services. The primary assumption about therapeutic recreation programs is that they are based on client needs and directly contribute to the overall recovery or health of the client through focusing on the leisure perspective.

In order to meet this basic assumption, the clinician has to develop a comprehensive program plan that takes into account the general characteristics of the community, the agency, the therapeutic recreation department, and the clients (Peterson and Gunn, 1984). Community factors include general descriptors such as overall economic level, religious influences, other healthcare services in the area, and demographics. Characteristics of the agency, including mission (e.g., detoxification versus recovery, or medical stability versus rehabilitation, or for-profit versus nonprofit), resources (e.g., budget, facilities and areas, transportation), and total staffing plan, help define the boundaries of the services provided and impact all healthcare

professionals, including therapeutic recreation specialists.

Characteristics of the department, such as the presence of other related professionals, total number and qualifications of staff, and hours of operation, also affect the types and quality of services that can be provided. General characteristics of the clients play a major role in service provision, because the categories of diagnoses, socioeconomic background, family support networks, and the like, impact the types of services that are appropriate and meaningful.

All four of these (community, agency, department and clients) must be taken into consideration when first beginning comprehensive program development (Navar, 1980; Peterson and Gunn, 1984; Stumbo and Rickards, 1986). Departmental goals that later guide specific program provision must be developed so that services can truly impact client outcomes, and so that other administrative functions, such as quality management, can be conducted (Dunn, Sneegas and Carruthers, 1991). Without comprehensive program goals, it is extremely easy for the program to "go astray" and offer a cafeteria-type program that has no meaningful aim and does not impact client outcomes.

Once the departmental service goals are documented, specific program areas must be developed that meet the intent of these goals. For example, if one of the overall goals is to improve the social skills of the clients, then appropriate specific programs must be designed to meet the social skills deficits of the clients. Thus, specific programs on appropriate dress, negotiating conflicts, and communication skills, may be necessary to meet the needs of the clients. Two assumptions are operational here: First, that these areas for specific programs are selected because they are typically problem areas for the clients, and second, that direct intervention must be provided to impact client outcomes for successful independence in the community.

It is also important to note that the departmental goals and specific programs directly impact the type of client assessment that is selected. Dunn (1984) and Stumbo and Rickards

(1986) provide useful models to explain these relationships. Using the example of social skills, if the problem area is communication skills, then the assessment tool must measure these skills. In fact, to be useful both as a placement device (to put clients into programs) and as an evaluation device (to later measure client outcomes from the intervention) (Dunn, 1984; Kinney, 1980; Stumbo and Rickards, 1986; Wehman and Schleien, 1980), the assessment tool must be able to measure very specific communication skills. That is, the assessment must be able to distinguish the clients who are in need of and will benefit from specific communication skills programs. If it does not, then clients may be placed inappropriately into programs, and outcomes cannot be measured at discharge.

Dunn (1991) delineates two general types of therapeutic recreation programs. Type I programs are those which "all the clients on the unit attend whatever has been planned for the day. There is no provision which matches his or her unique treatment goals. All clients are essentially seen as having the same treatment needs and thus receive the same services" (p. 3). The only differentiation between clients may be in the interaction between the therapist and individual clients. Type I programming does little to distinguish between or meet the needs of individual clients. Assessment results are not particularly useful because all clients receive similar services, regardless of diagnostic need. The second type of programs, Type II, focuses on the individual needs of clients, typically through smaller groups or one-to-one services. These programs are structured to achieve goals on the clients' treatment plans and require adequate assessment to identify client problem areas and needs (Dunn, 1991). Type II programs are more likely to be oriented to intervention (that is, have a relationship between the intervention program and desired outcomes) and be able to produce desirable changes in the clients.

It is clear to see from the above discussion and example, that assumptions about the client, comprehensive program design and specific programs greatly influence the assessment(s)

that should be selected for use (Dunn, 1984, 1989; Navar, 1980; Stumbo and Rickards, 1986). However, these assumptions are violated fairly frequently by therapeutic recreation specialists. For whatever reason, many continue to use inappropriate assessments and are left being unable to measure client outcomes.

Assumptions About Client Assessments

Assumptions about assessments are related to and follow from the assumptions about clients and the therapeutic recreation program. The first is that the information gained from the assessment must have meaning:

> A test in itself is not important, but how it is used. Test results alone will seldom, if ever, provide complete answers of individual problems, deficiencies and weaknesses. The values of testing are in determining strengths and weaknesses for utilizing strengths and for devising programs, approaches and techniques to help individuals overcome or cope with identified problems and deficiencies. (Krug, 1979, p. 42)

The questions on the assessment and the information gained from it must be able to describe something about the client's behavior that is useful. Again, that usefulness depends on the contribution the assessment makes to decisions about client placement into programs and the measurement of client outcomes from intervention (Kinney, 1980; Touchstone, 1984). For example, asking clients about past leisure interests is not appropriate if the information is not used to put clients into programs, it is not used during programs, there is no program that addresses this area, or that outcomes cannot be measured at some later point. When meaningless information is on the assessment, specialists often become disillusioned with the client assessment process and begin to disregard it, placing clients into programs based on personal judgment, or even worse, no judgments are made and all clients attend all programs. An assessment that does not produce meaningful information is often filed away, without the specialist ever making reference to it for decisions about clients.

The meaning or value of the information gained from an assessment relates to the concept of validity. Validity "refers to the extent to which the results of an evaluation procedure serve the particular uses for which they are intended" (Gronlund, 1981, p. 65). If the information is useless or is skewed in some fashion, then the decisions that can be made from the results are not valid. Say, for example, that an activity interest inventory has the activities of sledding, snowmobiling and downhill skiing. If the assessment is administered to someone in a warmer climate, the results are very likely unusable for programming purposes. The results would not serve the use for which the assessment was intended.

Validity depends on the specialist making informed decisions about selecting assessments based on the needs of the clients, the comprehensive program design, specific program intervention and the targeted client outcomes. If the assessment is not selected based on these four factors, then the value and usefulness of the results are negligible.

Reliability is important in that it indicates the degree of consistency of the assessment results (Dunn, 1989). Reliability indicates how much error is present in the results. Error can be introduced through changes in the client's fatigue or motivation level, the client's reading ability, two specialists administering an assessment in different ways, and the like. Establishing and reporting reliability of an instrument or procedure is important so that the results received are as reflective as possible of the clients' true abilities, knowledge or interests. Measures of validity and reliability indicate how much confidence can be placed in the results of an assessment tool or procedure.

While the content of the assessment is extremely important, so too is the process used to collect the information (Stumbo and Rickards,

1986). Regardless of whether the specialist is using a standardized or agency-specific tool, or whether the data is collected through interview, observation or another method, the process used to gather the information must be standardized (Dunn, 1989). Every specialist should be collecting information in the same way and under the same conditions, asking the questions in the same manner and/or recording information in the same fashion. One of the biggest violators of this assumption are interviews with open-ended question formats (e.g., "Tell me about your past interests"). Some specialists may use prompts, some may use different phrasing, some may help supply example answers. If the information is not gathered in a systematic, consistent and accurate way, then the results are probably not going to be meaningful, reliable or useful. Too much "garbage" variance may be introduced based on differences between the specialists, the environments, and the way questions are asked. Helpful strategies for using standardized assessment instruments (Dunn, 1989), observational instruments (Levy, 1982; Stumbo, 1983) and interview procedures (Ferguson, 1983; Malik, 1990; Malik, Ashton-Shaeffer and Kleiber, 1991) are found elsewhere in the therapeutic recreation literature. Dunn (1987, 1989) also provides a comprehensive set of guidelines for establishing reliability and validity in a variety of assessment tools.

Decisions about using client assessment procedures, then, depend on several factors or assumptions. The procedure or tool must:

a. be used in the manner in which it was intended to be used;
b. match the comprehensive program design, goals and specific programs in the department in which it is being used;
c. have meaning and be able to fully and accurately describe the client's problems or status;
d. be administered and interpreted in a consistent fashion by all who use it;
e. be able to help place clients into appropriate intervention programs, based on the results; and

f. be able to aid in measurement of outcomes from involvement in programs or services.

If these factors or assumptions are ignored, the time spent on assessment has been an exercise in futility.

Assumptions About Activity Interest Inventories

All of the preceding discussion has been a prologue to the case against activity interest inventories. The use of logical assumptions and sound program decisions is necessary to lay the foundation for realizing that activity interest inventories are probably the most abused and least understood types of assessments conducted by therapeutic recreation specialists. The remaining portion of this chapter will discuss the problems associated with interest inventories and highlight some of the assumptions underlying their use.

The first underlying assumption is that a client's leisure interests automatically translate into leisure skills and participation. If a client says or signals he or she is interested in bowling, the specialist assumes that he or she wants to either learn the skills, or already has the skills and wants to get better; that is, the person wants to participate in the activity to some degree (Joswiak, 1980; Navar, 1980). However, the assumption is a faulty one because a person may be *interested* in hypnosis, but neither wants to be hypnotized nor be a hypnotist. Some individuals find lots of things in life interesting, but do not necessarily want to gain the skills or participate in them. Each person may have a myriad of interests in which he or she has no intention of ever gaining skills or participating, so to assume the opposite, that interests reflect skills and participation, can be misleading. Witt and Groom (1979), in discussing a proposed relationship between needs, wants and interests, concluded that expressed interests may be more

related to cultural and nurtured values, social desirability, and motivation than actual participation patterns. Individuals may state an interest in certain activities because they believe that it is valued, the specialist wants them to, or their friends participate in it. However, their behavior may not match their stated intentions or participation rates.

Also, many tools ask questions that are too simplistic about past participation in leisure activities. Often these tools may ask about frequency of participation (daily, weekly, monthly, seasonally) or time passed since last participation. Many hidden variables (not on the assessment) may account for the answers to these questions. Perhaps the client used to live next to a shopping mall, so shopping was a frequent activity. Perhaps a close friend, who recently moved, loved to go to old movies, so the client often went too. Asking about participation assumes that the activity is the most important motivator, but this approach often overlooks the intrinsic motivation behind the choice (Fain and Shank, 1980). Typically, leisure choices are based on social interaction with friends and family, a sense of achievement, a chance to take risks, and other factors that are unaccounted for by simply looking at interest or participation in the activity itself.

The activity is often a means for the client to gain something else, but the activity itself is often unimportant. According to Witt and Groom (1979), "individuals may select activities on the basis of their ability to satisfy social needs as opposed to characteristics such as location, time or energy expenditure. Whom one participates with is viewed as more critical than what one participates in" (p. 27). Activity interest inventories then "do not give the professional insight into the meaning of the activity for the client" (Howe, 1984, p. 22), unless accompanied by careful, systematic questioning.

Another commonly held belief is that *more* interests and skills are needed by the client. Some specialists have taken the idea of leisure lifestyle (of having a diverse set of leisure interests and skills) to the extreme. Most typical individuals, adults and adolescents alike, tend to focus on a few special leisure interests (e.g., watching sports, collecting antiques, reading, playing Nintendo) to satisfy their needs. This focus often is necessary to become good at something, to become involved to the point where the interest can deliver intrinsic satisfaction. While having only one narrow interest is not the intention, more is not necessarily better (Navar, 1980).

Another assumption is that old (premorbid) skills always need to be adapted and new skills need to be learned. The specialist may assume that if the client gained pleasure or satisfaction from the activity prior to the onset of the disability or illness, the activity can be adapted to satisfy the same needs after the onset of the condition. Two examples may illustrate this point. On a chemical dependency unit, a person may have gone bowling with friends several times a week, where they usually drank for several hours each night. The assumption would be that, minus the alcohol consumption, the activity can be "adapted" for future participation. The second illustration is an individual with quadriplegia on a physical medicine unit who used to play tennis. The adaptation to play tennis after discharge may be to use special handle modifications that do not require finger grasp. However, in both these examples, not only has the activity changed, but so perhaps has the *reason* or *motivation* for participation. Any amount of modification may not make these two examples pleasurable and satisfying again for the individual. While modifications are important for those clients who truly want and need them, the point made here is that surveying past interests does not necessarily help the client in establishing a future leisure lifestyle. Witt and Groom (1979) warn not only of measurement problems with substitutability of activities, but also with discounting the factors of complementary activities (shopping because it's close to home) and desire to be with significant others.

Other assumptions are made about the instrument used to collect the interest information. The first is that activities can be neatly categorized into packages of similar activities. Such instruments often have headings of Out-

door Activities, Sports, Collections, and the like. This may be due to our human nature that makes us classify large amounts of information so that it can be more readily digested and viewed. However, activities across categories may often have more in common than those under the same heading. For example, sports spectating (usually under Sports) may be more like watching television (usually under Passive Activities), than like playing rugby (also under Sports). On further thought, if activities were easily categorized, then only one classification system would be needed and that would have probably been developed long ago. The important point to recognize, again, is that by using categories, valuable information is often overlooked, people's interests may be placed in the wrong categories, and faulty decisions about interests and participation made.

A closely related assumption is that a listing of activities, under the major headings, can be comprehensive enough to match all clients' interests. Few instruments list as many as 50 activities, but even 50 activities could not encompass the diversity of interests of most client groups. It may be impossible to list all conceivable activities, but if the client's interests are not represented, then the information is not likely to be useful for placement into programs. Back to the previous discussion, the activity interest inventory may not have validity because it does not cover the important aspects of the client's behavior. Some instruments try to overcome this limitation by having blanks to fill in at the end, but a problem occurs whenever either the specialist forgets to ask the question, or the client forgets an activity. This problem would make the instrument then less reliable or accurate.

The final assumption about activity interest inventories is that they are used for programming. From the previous beginning discussion, it was brought out that the content of the assessment must reflect the content of the program. That is, the assessment must have "conceptual relevance" (Witt, Connolly and Compton, 1980, p. 6) to both the program content and clients' needs. The assessment results provide the vital link, placing the clients, based on needs, into the most appropriate program to meet these needs.

Activity interest inventories present an interesting situation. If a client expresses an interest in an activity, then this information is used to place the client into an appropriate program that teaches or provides that activity. It seems safe to assert, however, that few departments could program for all the interests on any given inventory. Four options then exist for the specialist: (a) create a new program based on this interest; (b) place the client into a program for different, but similar interests; (c) ignore the interest; and (d) supply resource information for participating at another facility or organization. The last option may seem the most reasonable, as new programs based on individual interests would proliferate out of control, and the middle two options do not meet the needs of the client and do not provide measurable outcomes. This being the case, a major goal of a department that uses activity interest inventories may be client referral to other activity-based programs.

Appropriate Uses of Activity Inventories

A logical process has been used to examine some of the problems associated with using activity interest inventories as the basis for client assessment in intervention programs. Most persons using interest inventories have not thought about the underlying assumptions on which they arc basing their decisions about clients. This practice cannot only put clients in jeopardy of receiving less than adequate treatment services, it, in turn, can lead to the inability to be accountable for services rendered on a larger scale. With that said, the author is not attempting to advocate the total abolishment of activity inventories for all cases nor to discount client activity preferences in programming. In fact, they are quite useful for some areas of service provision.

An appropriate use of activity inventories is when: (a) the client has choice about participat-

ing in programs; (b) the client has the ability to make informed decisions; (c) the services offered can be determined by the wishes of the individuals; (d) intervention is not the intent of the program; and/or (e) they are used to collect client history or background that is supplementary to an intervention program. Many commercial, private and public facilities and agencies successfully use activity inventories under the first four conditions. A smorgasbord of activities can be offered, frequently changing based on the wants and needs of the individuals in the program. Individuals may register or attend based on their own choices and decisions they make; they have expressed interests and they come to programs to fulfill these interests.

Within therapeutic recreation services, this model is often used in long-term or total care residential facilities. Therapeutic recreation programs in these facilities may be broadly classified into intervention and diversional orientations. While the activity interest surveys would not be appropriate for intervention programs within these facilities, they may help specialists target programs that are offered as diversional in nature. Since these agencies must often fulfill the individuals' total leisure lifestyle, diversionary programs may be necessary to meet the needs and interests of the clients, and activity inventories may be the best way to assess these interests. Having an assessment that includes an interest inventory is justified based on the fact that it matches the overall comprehensive program design (a combination of intervention and diversion).

Another exception is noted by Dattilo (1988); Certo, Schleien and Hunter (1983), and Wehman and Schleien (1980). These authors advocate determining the leisure preferences and skill levels of individuals with severe developmental disabilities to allow for maximal choice and increased freedom. While they do not suggest the use of traditional checklists or inventories, they promote a variety of procedures to ensure that activity preferences of individuals with severe disabilities are determined in order to reduce further barriers to leisure opportunities. This allows the personal activity preferences of individuals to be known, but a change in client outcomes through intervention is not necessarily the goal.

The third exception is therapeutic recreation programs in community-based agencies. Client participation is often based on choice, and a variety of programs can be offered to meet the clients' interests. While skill development may be a major intent of these services, intervention in the form of treatment programs is often not within the mission or scope of the agency. Direct intervention is not a major component of the comprehensive program design. The programs within these agencies could be well-served by activity interest inventories that include a wide range of interests.

And last, it should be noted that the use of activity inventories may be appropriate in intervention situations in which information about the clients' past or present leisure interests is used to supplement or augment other parts of directed intervention. In some situations, knowing the clients' leisure interests or involvement may help to illuminate past behavior, the

strength of habits, and the like. While the information is not used as primary data to create a treatment plan, it may be used as secondary data within programs to aid the clients' treatment.

Summary

The intent of this chapter has been to review the assumptions that therapeutic recreation specialists make about clients, programs and assessments. What is often discovered is that these assumptions have not been closely examined, and specialists often fall into the trap of using activity interest inventories because they are easy to construct, administer and score. However, the argument is made that they often do not provide useful information for intervention programs and do not lead to measurable client outcomes. The information is provided to challenge specialists to examine the logical assumptions regarding their choices of client assessments and to improve the accountability and measurability of their services.

References

Beddall, T., and Kennedy, D. W. (1985). Attitudes of therapeutic recreators toward evaluation and client assessment. *Therapeutic Recreation Journal, 19*(1), 62–70.

Certo, N. J., Schleien, S. J., and Hunter, D. (1983). An ecological assessment inventory to facilitate community recreation participation by severely disabled individuals. *Therapeutic Recreation Journal, 17*(3), 29–38.

Dattilo, J. (1988). Assessing music preferences of persons with severe disabilities. *Therapeutic Recreation Journal, 22*(2), 12–23.

Dunn, J. K. (1983). Improving client assessment procedures in therapeutic recreation programming. In G. Hitzhusen (Ed.), *Expanding horizons in therapeutic recreation XI* (pp. 146–157). Columbia, MO: Curators University of Missouri.

Dunn, J. K. (1984). Assessment. In C. A. Peterson and S. L. Gunn (Eds.), *Therapeutic recreation program design: Principles and procedures* (2nd ed., pp. 267–320). Englewood Cliffs, NJ: Prentice-Hall Inc.

Dunn, J. K. (1987). Establishing reliability and validity in evaluation instruments. *Journal of Park and Recreation Administration, 5*(4), 61–70.

Dunn, J. K. (1989). Guidelines for using published assessment procedures. *Therapeutic Recreation Journal, 23*(2), 59–69.

Dunn, J. (1991, September). *Integrating client assessment into therapeutic recreation practice.* Paper presented at the Client Assessment Workshop, St. Peters, MO.

Dunn, J. K., Sneegas, J. J., and Carruthers, C. A. (1991). Outcome measures: Monitoring patient progress. In B. Riley (Ed.), *Quality management: Applications for therapeutic recreation* (pp. 107–115). State College, PA: Venture Publishing, Inc.

Ellis, G. D., and Witt, P. A. (1986). The Leisure Diagnostic Battery: Past, present and future. *Therapeutic Recreation Journal, 20*(4), 31–47.

Fain, G. S., and Shank, J. W. (1980). Individual assessment through leisure profile construction. *Therapeutic Recreation Journal, 14*(4), 46–53.

Ferguson, D. D. (1983). Assessment interviewing techniques: A useful tool in developing individual program plans. *Therapeutic Recreation Journal, 17*(2), 16–22.

Gronlund, N. E. (1981). *Measurement and evaluation in teaching* (4th ed.). New York, NY: Macmillan.

Howe, C. Z. (1984). Leisure assessment instrumentation in therapeutic recreation. *Therapeutic Recreation Journal, 18*(2), 14–24.

Howe, C. Z. (1989). Assessment instruments in therapeutic recreation: To what extent do they work? In D. Compton (Ed.), *Issues in therapeutic recreation: A profession in transition* (pp. 205–222). Champaign, IL: Sagamore Publishing Company.

Joswiak, K. F. (1980). Recreation therapy assessment with developmentally disabled persons. *Therapeutic Recreation Journal, 14*(4), 29–38.

Kinney, W. B. (1980). Clinical assessment in mental health settings. *Therapeutic Recreation Journal, 14*(4), 39–45.

Krug, J. L. (1979). A review of perceptual motor/sensory integrative measurement tools. *Therapeutic Recreation Journal, 13*(2), 41–43.

Levy, J. (1982). Behavioral observation techniques in assessing change in therapeutic recreation/play settings. *Therapeutic Recreation Journal, 16*(1), 25–32.

Malik, P. B. (1990). Leisure interests and perceptions of group home residents. *Annual in Therapeutic Recreation, 1*, 67–73.

Malik, P. B., Ashton-Shaeffer, C., and Kleiber, D. A. (1991). Interviewing young adults with mental retardation: A seldom used research method. *Therapeutic Recreation Journal, 25*(1), 60–73.

Navar, N. (1980). A rationale for leisure skill assessment with handicapped adults. *Therapeutic Recreation Journal, 14*(4), 21–28.

Peterson, C. A., and Gunn, S. L. (1984). *Therapeutic recreation program design: Principles and procedures* (2nd ed.). Englewood Cliffs, NJ: Prentice-Hall Inc.

Riley, B. (1991). Quality assessment: The use of outcome indicators. In B. Riley (Ed.), *Quality management: Applications for therapeutic recreation* (pp. 53–67). State College, PA: Venture Publishing, Inc.

Scalenghe, R. (1991). The joint commission's "agenda for change" as related to the provision of therapeutic recreation services. In B. Riley (Ed.), *Quality management: Applications for therapeutic recreation* (pp. 30–42). State College, PA: Venture Publishing, Inc.

Shank, J. W., and Kinney, W. B. (1991). Monitoring and measuring outcomes in therapeutic recreation. In B. Riley (Ed.), *Quality management: Applications for therapeutic recreation* (pp. 69–82). State College, PA: Venture Publishing, Inc.

Sneegas, J. J. (1989). Can we really measure leisure behavior of special populations and individuals with disabilities? In D. Compton (Ed.), *Issues in therapeutic recreation: A profession in transition* (pp. 223–237). Champaign, IL: Sagamore Publishing Company.

Stumbo, N. J. (1983). Systematic observation as a research tool for assessing client behavior. *Therapeutic Recreation Journal, 17*(4), 53–63.

Stumbo, N. J. (1991). Selected assessment resources: A review of instruments and references. *Annual in Therapeutic Recreation, 2,* 8–24.

Stumbo, N. J. (1992). Rethinking activity inventories. *Illinois Parks and Recreation Magazine, 23*(2), 17–21.

Stumbo, N. J. (1993/94). The use of activity interest inventories in therapeutic recreation assessment. *Annual in Therapeutic Recreation, 4,* 11–20

Stumbo, N. J., and Rickards, W. H. (1986). Selecting assessment instruments: Theory in practice. *Journal of Expanding Horizons in Therapeutic Recreation, 1*(1), 1–6.

Touchstone, W. (1984). A personalized approach to goal planning and evaluation in clinical settings. *Therapeutic Recreation Journal, 18*(2), 25–31.

Wehman, P., and Schleien, S. J. (1980). Relevant assessment in leisure skill training programs. *Therapeutic Recreation Journal, 14*(4), 9–20.

Witt, P. A., Connolly, P., and Compton, D. M. (1980). Assessment: A plea for sophistication. *Therapeutic Recreation Journal, 14*(4), 5–8.

Witt, P. A., and Groom, R. (1979). Dangers and problems associated with current approaches to developing leisure interest finders. *Therapeutic Recreation Journal, 13*(1), 19–31.

Leisure Awareness Activities

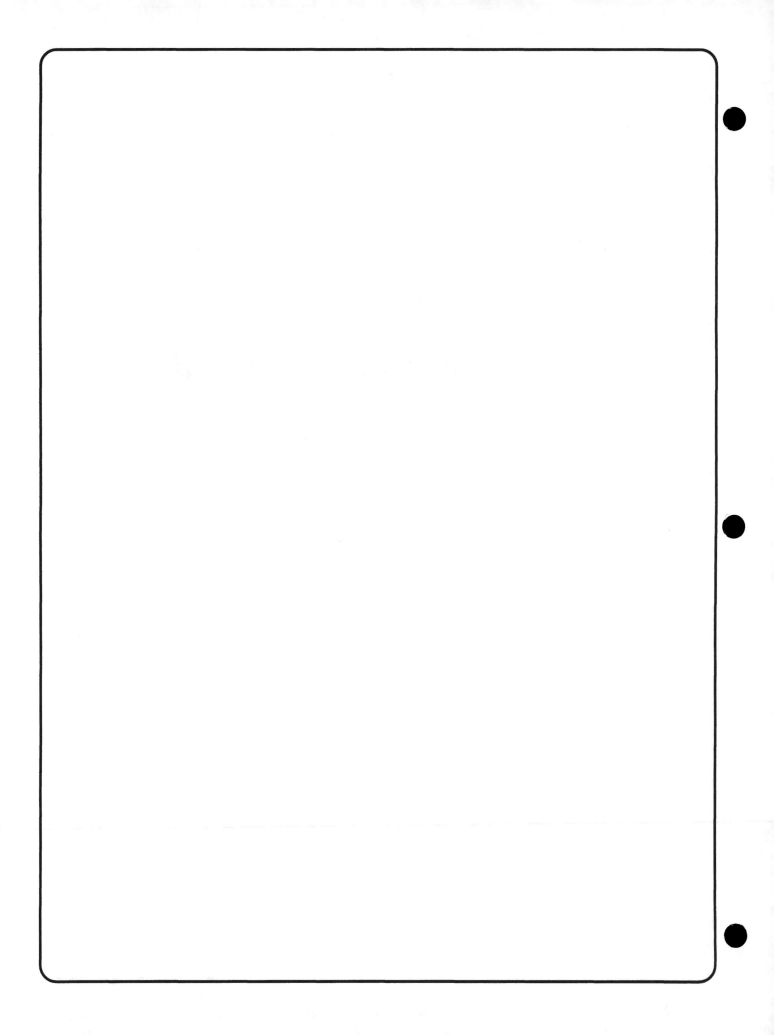

Leisure Jeopardy

Space Requirements: Classroom or activity room

Equipment/Resource Requirements: Construction paper, markers, tape, prepared game pieces and play money (see preparation instructions)

Group Size: Small group or large group

Program Goals:
1. To increase participants' awareness of leisure activities.
2. To test participants' knowledge of different leisure activities or information.

Program Description:

Preparation:

Develop five categories (e.g., Sports, Parks, Entertainment, Table Games, Special Events) and five questions relating to each category. The five questions from each category should range in degree of difficulty from easy to difficult (e.g., Sports Category—Question 1: A "spare" is a term used in which sport? Answer: Bowling).

Write these questions on construction paper. Fold the paper over, so the question cannot be seen and write the answer on the back (see diagram).

Tape the categories and questions to a wall. Each question is designated a money amount, from $10 to $50, with $10 being the easiest and $50 the most difficult.

Introduction:

Explain to the group the rules of the game. They must be told to raise their hands to answer questions. This game is very similar to the game show "Jeopardy" on TV.

Activity Description:

Establish which participant will go first. This person will choose a category and dollar amount. If the person guesses correctly, he or she will receive that amount of play money. If the person answers incorrectly, the other participants have a chance to answer the question. If that person answers correctly, he or she gets the dollar amount, and if not, another player gets a chance. This continues until the question is answered or there are no more players. Whoever answers correctly selects the next category and dollar amount. If no one can answer a question correctly, the last person to answer a question correctly chooses the next category and dollar amount.

Play continues until all questions are answered.

At the end of the game, each participant will total his or her money. The person with the highest dollar amount wins the game. Review purpose and goals of the activity.

Debriefing Questions/Closure:
1. Discuss how leisure encompasses all of the categories and questions.
2. Name two facts about leisure activities that you did not know before you played this game.
3. Why is it important to know information about leisure activities?
4. What are some topics or categories that you would enjoy learning more about?

Leadership Considerations:
1. The leader must be familiar with regular "Jeopardy."
2. Allow adequate planning time to develop categories and questions.
3. An extra person is helpful in order to recognize who raised his or her hand first.

Variations:
1. The leader can change questions and categories to meet the needs of the group.
2. Provide "Double Jeopardy" questions.

Creators: Lisa Scherer, CTRS, and David Griggs, CTRS, Choate Mental Health and Developmental Center, Anna, Illinois.

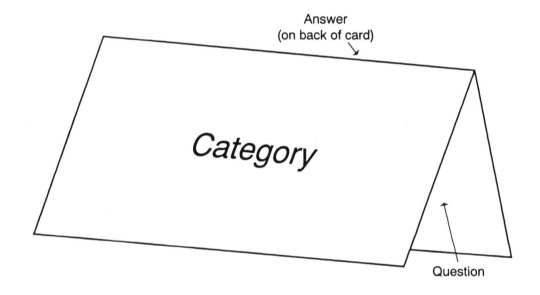

Spin and Write

Space Requirements: Classroom or activity room

Equipment/Resource Requirements: Spinner, paper to write on, pens or pencils

Group Size: Small group

Program Goals:
1. To evoke participants' memories of past leisure experiences.
2. To increase participants' awareness of attitudes related to leisure.
3. To improve participants' awareness of self in leisure.

Program Description:
Preparation:
Prepare spinner (see diagram). The spinner is divided into three equal sections, corresponding with the listed subjects the participants are to write about.

Introduction:
The group should begin by discussing the meaning of leisure and previous leisure experiences.

Activity Description:
Hand each person a blank sheet of paper and a pencil. Place spinner in the middle of the group. Each participant spins the spinner, which points to one of three topics. Each participant writes about the topic on which he or she landed. Allow three to five minutes for the participants to complete their answers. The participants are then to share what they wrote about with the other participants.

The participants are to spin again. If a participant lands on the same space as before, he or she should switch with another participant or spin again. Each participant should write about the new subject. When the writing is done, the participants should share what they wrote.

The following are the subjects on which the participants should write:

1. Describe one leisure activity you have always wanted to do, but never have done, why you want to do it, and why you have not done it.
2. Describe one fond memory of yourself in leisure, who this was with, and why it is such a fond memory.
3. Describe how leisure fits into your life, with whom you enjoy participating in leisure, and what you could do to enhance the level of leisure in your life.

Debriefing Questions/Closure:
1. How did writing about these experiences make you feel?
2. Have you noticed anything about your leisure through this activity? If so, what?
3. What did you learn about other participants' experiences?

Leadership Considerations:
1. Numbers should be assigned to each of the experiences to write about and correspond with the numbers on the spinner. Colors could be used in the same way.
2. Allow enough time for each participant to write as much as he or she feels is necessary.
3. Participants may need more paper than they are given. Extra paper should be provided.

Variations:
1. The participants have to spin and discuss whichever topic the spinner lands on instead of writing about the subject.
2. The subjects could be changed to contain all past experiences, current experiences, or desired future experiences.
3. The subjects could all be changed to involve experiences with friends, family, or by oneself.

Creator: Julie Keil, CTRS, Illinois State University, Normal, Illinois.

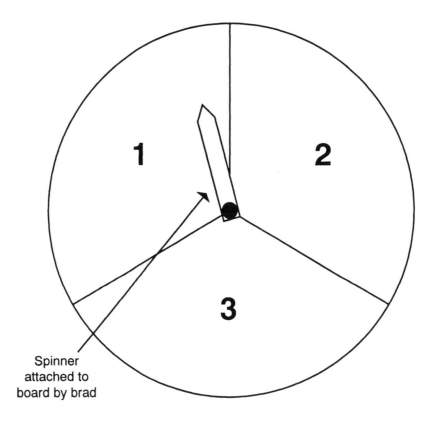

Spinner
attached to
board by brad

By Any Stretch of the Imagination

Space Requirements: Classroom or activity room

Equipment/Resource Requirements: None required

Group Size: Small group

Program Goals:
1. To increase participants' awareness of leisure activities and opportunities.
2. To improve participants' physical flexibility through gentle stretching exercises.

Program Description:
Preparation:
None required.

Introduction:
The purpose of this activity is to help participants become familiar with leisure activities and opportunities in a fun and creative way, while stretching or limbering up (perhaps for another activity). Explain the procedures of the activity to the participants.

Activity Description:
Have participants stand at arm's length from each other in an open area. The leader will spell out a word one letter at a time (for example "l-e-i-s-u-r-e") and participants are to stretch to *form* the letter (think of the "YMCA" song). Participants are to move slowly and reach as far as possible as they form the letters. Go through one practice round, say with the word "p-l-a-y."

Add another component to the stretch. As the leader calls out a letter, he or she also will call out the name of a participant, who will then name a leisure activity or opportunity that begins with that letter. For example, the leader says "L, Bob." Then Bob must say an activity or opportunity that begins with the letter *L*—such as "lounging" or "laughing at a comedy movie" or "lap swimming." The group continues to stretch to form the letter while Bob says the leisure activity name.

This continues until all letters of the word have been completed. Continue with as many words as there is time or until the participants feel stretched out.

Close with a discussion about leisure activities and opportunities.

Debriefing Questions:
1. What are some of your favorite leisure activities?
2. How often are you able to participate in these activities?
3. How many activities were named today that you were unaware of?
4. How might you use this activity on your own when you need to stretch?

Leadership Considerations:
1. This is a fun activity any time you want an audience to stretch. Great for workshops and long classes!

Variations:
1. Instead of letters, have participants move to the names of their favorite animals, making the same movements the animals might.
2. Go through the letters of the alphabet instead of spelling words.

Creator: Norma J. Stumbo, Ph.D., CTRS, Illinois State University, Normal, Illinois.

Leisure Awareness Box

Space Requirements: Classroom or activity room

Equipment/Resource Requirements: Shoebox with lid (one for each participant), construction paper, magazines, markers, scissors, glue, several blank slips of paper

Group Size: Small group

Program Goals:
1. To increase participants' ability to follow directions.
2. To improve participants' ability to identify leisure activities that the participant finds enjoyable.
3. To increase participants' awareness of why activities were chosen.

Program Description:

Preparation:
Cut paper into small slips. Prepare leader's example of box. Prepare boxes and materials for participants.

Introduction:
The tables in the room should be prearranged with the materials in the center of each table. The clients should be asked not to touch the materials on the table until directed to do so. The specialist should have a sample box to show to the group prior to the start of the activity.

Activity Description:
Each participant will be asked to choose a shoebox. The participants are then to use the construction paper to cover the outside of the box so that any writing cannot be seen. The inside of the box should remain open. The lid to the box should then be covered, using the same material, so that any writing cannot be seen. The lid should still fit over the top of the box.

The participants then cut a hole in the center of the lid of the box. The hole should be approximately one-half-inch wide by four-inches long. (The specialist may show the sample box as an example.) Holes can also be cut prior to the activity to save some time.

Once the hole has been cut, the participants will be asked to spend the next 20 minutes looking through magazines to find images of leisure activities that they enjoy, would like to try, would like to learn, that they like to do with others or by themselves. Once these images are found, the participants may cut the photos out of the magazine. If an image is not found, the participants may write the activity on the outside of the box or locate printed words.

Once the images or words have been cut out, the participants may glue the images to the outside of the box. After about 20 minutes have passed, the participants need to take a blank slip of paper for each image or word pasted on the outside of the box (15 images = 15 blank slips).

For each of the activities pasted on the outside of the box, the participants must list three reasons why that activity was chosen. When the blank slips have been completed, the sheets are placed inside of the box. (If time runs out, participants may complete their blank slips at a later time.)

At the end of the session, the participants are asked to clean their work area, leaving behind the magazines, scissors, glue and construction paper. The participants are asked to bring their boxes to the next group session.

At the next group session, participants are asked to choose three activities pasted on the outside of the box. Each participant will read the slips of paper to the group, for each of the three activities chosen. When all of the participants have had the opportunity to share, the group will have a discussion about the activity and leisure awareness.

Debriefing Questions/Closure:
1. How did this activity increase your awareness of your leisure interests?
2. Name additional reasons why you chose the activities you did.
3. What about this activity did you enjoy?
4. What about this activity did you not enjoy?
5. What could be changed to make this activity more enjoyable?

Leadership Considerations:
1. Leader should have a sample box available while describing the activity.
2. Leader may want to precut the holes in the lids to avoid any potential injuries from working with the scissors.
3. Leader should check on participants during the activity to ensure that the directions are being followed and to answer any questions.
4. Plan on spending two group sessions to complete this activity.

Variations:
1. Leisure Benefits Box—photos of activities on outside and list benefits on slips of paper.
2. Positive Message Box—photos of activities enjoyed on outside and positive messages from other group members on inside.
3. Chemical Dependency Box—box divided into two sides, one for barriers to leisure when using and one for benefits of leisure when sober; photos on outside, slips of paper on the inside.

Creator: Theresa M. Connolly, CTRS, Illinois State University, Normal, Illinois.

Top 10 Countdown

Space Requirements: Classroom or activity room

Equipment/Resource Requirements: Accompanying form, pens or pencils, ideas for topics

Group Size: Small group

Program Goals:
1. To increase participants' awareness of leisure activities and opportunities.
2. To increase participants' awareness of options for participation in various situations.

Program Description:

Preparation:

Make copies of the accompanying form, one for each participant. Prepare Top 10 ideas.

Introduction:

The purpose of this activity is to help participants think, in creative ways, of options for leisure participation in various situations. Adapted from David Letterman's Top 10 lists, the idea is to help participants creatively come up with options, and share these with other participants. Explain the procedures of the activity to the group.

Activity Description:

Hand each participant a copy of the accompanying form and a pencil. Give the participants the first topic as a practice run. Allow just one or two minutes for them to come up with 10 things for that topic. Have participants share what was on their lists. Perhaps ask participants to vote for the most creative but realistic idea for that topic.

Go to the second topic. Again, allow only two to three minutes for them to develop a list of 10 things for that topic. Either discuss at this point or go to next list and discuss when all are done. Continue with six topics.

Ideas for topics:

Things to do on the beach
Things to do on a Saturday afternoon
Things to do for under $5.00
Opening lines when meeting strangers
Crafts involving yarn
Things to do at a park
Ways to eat ice cream
Benefits from exercise
Songs to whistle while you play
Skills to learn for leisure
Places to go on your birthday
Things to do with people you do not know very well

Pets that can be kept in the house
Where you can go within an hour
What to do while you are waiting
Books to read for fun
Ways to make new friends
Places to meet new people
Dishes to take to a potluck dinner
Ways to serve chicken
Games to play with a Nerf ball
Ways to get exercise for free
Things to do at the library

Close with discussion questions, and refocus on the goals of the activity.

Debriefing Questions:
1. How creative were you in coming up with options?
2. How easy or difficult was it to come up with 10 options for each list?
3. What ideas might you use from yours or other people's lists?
4. Where can you get ideas for leisure involvement if you run out?
5. How do you go about thinking of new things to do when you are bored?

Leadership Considerations:
1. May have a demonstration example so participants get the idea of what is expected of them.
2. Try to keep their ideas realistic so they are usable for options.

Variations:
1. Change the topics according to the needs and interests of the participants.

Creator: Patti Tanner Florez, CTRS, Chestnut Health Systems, Bloomington, Illinois.

Top 10 Countdown

Topic: _____   Topic: _____

  1. _____   1. _____
  2. _____   2. _____
  3. _____   3. _____
  4. _____   4. _____
  5. _____   5. _____
  6. _____   6. _____
  7. _____   7. _____
  8. _____   8. _____
  9. _____   9. _____
10. _____   10. _____

Topic: _____   Topic: _____

  1. _____   1. _____
  2. _____   2. _____
  3. _____   3. _____
  4. _____   4. _____
  5. _____   5. _____
  6. _____   6. _____
  7. _____   7. _____
  8. _____   8. _____
  9. _____   9. _____
10. _____   10. _____

Topic: _____   Topic: _____

  1. _____   1. _____
  2. _____   2. _____
  3. _____   3. _____
  4. _____   4. _____
  5. _____   5. _____
  6. _____   6. _____
  7. _____   7. _____
  8. _____   8. _____
  9. _____   9. _____
10. _____   10. _____

Where Is My Playground?

Space Requirements: Classroom or activity room

Equipment/Resource Requirements: Chalkboard and chalk, magazine photos of leisure locations (large, blown up in size)

Group Size: Small group

Program Goals:
1. To increase participants' awareness of past and present locations where they have participated in leisure.
2. To increase participants' ability to identify benefits of locations where they have participated in leisure.
3. To increase participants' knowledge of potential locations for future leisure.

Program Description:
Preparation:
The therapist should set out several photographs (blown up in size) of various locations where individuals participate in leisure.

Introduction:
The therapist introduces the activity by asking the group members to name the places shown in the photographs. The therapist then should explain that the activity is going to focus on leisure locations and the clients' awareness of the various locations.

Activity Description:
The therapist will take one of the photographs from the table and ask, "Who has ever gone to a place similar to this picture?" "When did this happen?" "For what reason were you at this location?"

The therapist, following the responses of the clients, will allow the clients to share their stories related to the location in the picture. (Try for two to three stories per picture.) Ask the clients to list the benefits of each location as a site for leisure.

The therapist will follow the same process for each of the photographs. When all of the photographs have been discussed, ask the clients to brainstorm a list of alternative locations for leisure not including those in the photos. Ask the clients again to list the benefits of the locations mentioned.

Close the activity by addressing the purpose and goals, using the debriefing questions that follow.

Debriefing Questions/Closure:
1. How did this activity increase your awareness of past and present locations where you participated in leisure?
2. How did this activity increase your ability to identify the benefits of the locations discussed?
3. List the locations that you plan to use in the future when participating in leisure, and why you plan to use the locations.

Leadership Considerations:
1. Allow all participants to share stories or activities done at the locations discussed, but keep an eye on the clock and allow enough time to complete the activity.
2. Keep the focus of the activity on the positive aspects of the locations and try to keep clients from sharing negative experiences or stories.
3. Consider using other props besides the photographs, e.g., fishing pole, football, book, picnic basket, swimming suit, music.

Variations:
1. Allow the clients to share in the responsibility and take turns leading the session and discussion.
2. Ask the participants to bring three photographs or props to the session and share their experiences at the locations related to the photos or props.
3. Once clients have discussed past and present locations, allow the clients to develop their ideal future leisure location, as a group or individually, to be shared at the next group meeting.

Creator: Theresa M. Connolly, CTRS, Illinois State University, Normal, Illinois.

The Wall of Leisure

Space Requirements: Classroom or activity room

Equipment/Resource Requirements: Large sheet of white paper (six-feet long by three-feet wide, large white butcher paper works best), scissors, glue, magazines, markers or colored chalk

Group Size: Small group

Program Goals:
1. To increase participants' awareness of their personal definitions of leisure.
2. To assist participants in identifying leisure activities.

Program Description:

Preparation:
Tape sheet of paper to the wall. At the top center of the paper write "The Wall of Leisure." Draw large bricks on the sheet of paper to represent a brick wall. Gather magazines for participants to use during the activity. Set out resources needed for the activity.

Introduction:
Begin the group activity by discussing the importance of leisure, and words the group members might associate with leisure. Encourage the participants to identify the activities in which they participate during their leisure time. Explain to the group members that they will be using the wall to communicate their ideas about what leisure is, and what activities they consider to be leisure activities.

Activity Description:
Participants are instructed to either draw, write or cut out words and pictures that represent ideas they associate with leisure (e.g., fun, risky, pleasurable, relaxing), and different leisure activities (e.g., reading a book, riding a horse, playing soccer). Each of these words or pictures are to be drawn or glued on the bricks of the Wall of Leisure.

After participants have completed the Wall of Leisure, lead a discussion on the personal definitions of leisure, and what activities they consider to be leisure activities.

Debriefing Questions/Closure:
1. What do your pictures on the wall represent?
2. What words or ideas do you most associate with leisure?
3. How would you define leisure—what is leisure to you?
4. How do you feel about your leisure?
5. What activities do you consider to be leisure?
6. When is an activity considered leisure and when is it not?

Leadership Considerations:
1. Cut out pictures of healthy leisure activities prior to the group's meeting to help the group identify with positive leisure time pursuits.
2. Encourage each participant to explain his or her contributions to the wall.

Variations:
   1. Create a variety of themes for the wall activity, for example, Wall of Community Leisure Resources or the Leisure Barrier Wall.

Creator: Shelley A. Vaughan, CTRS, St. John's Hospital, Springfield, Illinois.

Magic Leisure Box

Space Requirements: Classroom or activity room

Equipment/Resource Requirements: Small box covered with construction paper or gift wrap

Group Size: Small group

Program Goals:
1. To increase participants' awareness of their leisure priorities.
2. To have participants identify one item they consider of great value to their leisure.

Program Description:
Preparation:
Wrap box in construction paper or gift wrap.

Introduction:
Have participants form a circle, either seated on the floor or in chairs. Introduce the activity's purpose and goals to the participants. Discuss the importance of being able to identify priorities in order to make sure that they happen. Often, with leisure, it is easy to let priorities slip and spend time on something else—like only work.

Activity Description:
Place the Magic Leisure Box in the middle of the circle of participants. Tell participants that the box is indeed magic, and each participant will be able to make the box change into one thing related to leisure. It can be just about anything, but must represent the person's highest priority if he or she could only have *one* leisure-related thing. For example, someone might make it a baseball bat in order to play in the World Series, someone else might make it a packet of seeds to grow a flower garden, someone might make it a cruise ship in order to travel, someone might make it a park for all to enjoy. Participants are not limited as to options (as long as they relate to leisure), but it may help for them to think of this as the only item they will ever receive.

Allow time for participants to think of what their priorities would be. Ask one participant to start, by picking up the Magic Leisure Box, and explaining to the group what thing he or she selected, and why it was selected.

When that person is finished, the box should be passed to the left, and the next person is to identify his or her object to the group, along with an explanation of why it was chosen and why it is a priority. Continue until all group members have been able to explain what is in their Magic Leisure Box.

Review the items mentioned by group members, as well as the purpose and goals of the activity. Include the following debriefing questions.

Debriefing Questions/Closure:
1. Why might it be difficult for you to select just one item?
2. Would you agree that this is a priority for you in your leisure?
3. How did your item differ from everyone else's?
4. How does this differ from what you might have selected five or 10 years ago?
5. Do you think you will select the same item five to 10 years from now?

Leadership Considerations:
1. Make sure to give creative examples so that participants are creative.
2. Allow adequate time for participants to think of their items.
3. Make sure participants know that there are no right or wrong answers—all are acceptable.

Variations:
1. Instead of a box, pass around a balloon, ball, or toy and have participants explain what uses they could find for these items.

Up and Down

Space Requirements: Classroom or activity room

Equipment/Resource Requirements: Accompanying poem, chairs in circle

Group Size: Small group

Program Goals:
1. To improve participants' awareness of leisure activities.
2. To increase participants' ability to identify leisure activities.

Program Description:

Preparation:
This activity is similar to musical chairs. Place chairs in a circle facing out. Use one less chair than there are participants. Have group stand in large circle outside of the chairs. Participants will walk to the left outside the circle of chairs.

Introduction:
Introduce purpose and goals of this activity. Ask each participant to identify one leisure activity he or she enjoys or has heard of, to let the group begin thinking about types of leisure activities. Explain the rules of the activity.

Activity Description:
Ask participants to start walking around the outside of the circle of chairs. Begin reading the Up and Down poem. When a leisure activity is read, the participants must sit in a chair as quickly as possible. The person without a chair must stand inside the circle of chairs. Remove one chair from the circle.

Begin reading again as the participants walk outside the circle of chairs. Repeat that the person left standing goes to the center of the circle. Repeat until one player is left.

If someone sits down prematurely, before an activity is read, this person also goes to the center of the circle.

When one person remains, either start a new round (if the poem is not finished), or ask participants to put chairs back into circle, this time facing in, for discussion and closure.

Debriefing Questions/Closure:
1. Which of the activities in the poem were familiar to you?
2. Which of the activities in the poem were new to you?
3. In which of these activities would you like to participate?
4. Where might you go to participate in these activities?

Leadership Considerations:
1. This activity could accommodate a fairly large group of participants.
2. Monitor that people remain polite during this activity.
3. If used more than once with one group, change the leisure activities mentioned in the poem.

Variations:
1. Consider making poems that are seasonal or contain activities that are of special interest to the participants.
2. Instead of chairs, participants can sit on the floor, and the last one to sit goes to the center.
3. Ask the participant who most recently went to the center of the circle to read the poem for a turn, so he or she can continue to participate.

Up and Down

Spring time is the best, no, I like the fall.

But, summer brings fun, with **swimming** and all.

Each season of the year brings its own special **games.**

Now listen to the rhyme

Can you tell me their names?

Let's start with fall when the weather is cool

And it's time for everyone to head back to school.

Hup one, hup two, **football** is here.

And for our favorite team we will certainly cheer.

Outdoor camping is another great sport

Now let's try our luck at the **basketball** court.

The weather is chilling, our season is changing

Winter's a good time to learn the art of **flower arranging.**

Or we can bundle up warmly and go outside.

Hurry! It's time for the big **sleigh ride!**

Spring time is here, a warm breeze is blowing,

Let's go plant a **garden** since everything is growing.

Yes, spring is the season which brings a special kind of fun.

You'll often hear the question, **tennis** anyone?

The weather is hotter, summer is here.

Let's go **fishing** down at the pier.

Decorations and goodies we'll be creating,

It's the Fourth of July **party** that we're celebrating.

Leisure is fun and can be found throughout the year.

You may have to **travel,**

Or it could be quite near.

You're sure to enjoy whatever you chose,

It doesn't even matter if you win or lose.

Leisure Scattergories

Space Requirements: Classroom or activity room

Equipment/Resource Requirements: Accompanying form, pens or pencils

Group Size: Small group

Program Goals:
1. To increase participants' awareness of leisure activities and opportunities.
2. To increase participants' awareness of options for participation in various situations.

Program Description:

Preparation:
Make copies of accompanying form, one for each participant. Have 15 ideas prepared for topics.

Introduction:
The purpose of this activity is to help participants increase their awareness of leisure activities and opportunities, and to help develop ideas and options for participation. Ask participants to name a few of their favorite leisure activities. What other options are there for their leisure participation? Explain procedures of the activity to the participants.

Activity Description:
Hand each participant a copy of the accompanying form and a pencil. Explain that participants will be given a topic, and they are to come up with five answers that begin with the letter of the alphabet on the work sheet. The specialist may want to give an example or have question 1 be a practice round.

For example, for topics 1, 6 and 11, their answers have to start with the letters *a, b, c, d,* and *e.* If topic 1, is "Things to do at home," the answers can be something like: a–artwork; b–bake cookies; c–cook a meal; d–develop a positive attitude; and e–exercise.

Examples of topics:

Leisure activities to do on the beach	Adjectives to describe summer
Leisure activities to do in the winter	Things to see in a museum
Places to go on vacation	Things to see at a fine arts event
Leisure activities to do in the city	Board games you can play with friends
Places to go camping	Things you would see in the mall
Things you could do on a weekend	Adjectives that describe leisure
Things you would see in a park	Things to do in town for free
Leisure activities to do at home	Places to go with your family

Continue through topics 1 through 15. After all are completed, have participants read their answers aloud. Any that are mentioned by someone else, get crossed off the list. Any that are unique, earn one point. The person with the most points wins. (The leader can decide whether to make the game competitive.)

Close with a discussion, using the following debriefing questions.

Debriefing Questions/Closure:
1. How many unique ideas did you have?
2. How did you go about coming up with answers to fit the letters and topics?
3. How many creative, yet realistic options did you have?
4. How did this help you to see that there are many leisure options out there?
5. What did you learn that you can use in the future?
6. How will this help you brainstorm for leisure activity ideas in the future?

Leadership Considerations:
1. Have an example ready so they understand the directions to the work sheet.
2. *X* has been deleted from this work sheet, because there are few words that begin with this letter.

Variations:
1. Change the topics to meet the needs and interests of the participants.

Creator: Jennifer Harz-Morgan, CTRS, Elmhurst Memorial Hospital, Elmhurst, Illinois.

Leisure Scattergories

1		6		11	
A	_____		_____		_____
B	_____		_____		_____
C	_____		_____		_____
D	_____		_____		_____
E	_____		_____		_____

2		7		12	
F	_____		_____		_____
G	_____		_____		_____
H	_____		_____		_____
I	_____		_____		_____
J	_____		_____		_____

3		8		13	
K	_____		_____		_____
L	_____		_____		_____
M	_____		_____		_____
N	_____		_____		_____
O	_____		_____		_____

4		9		14	
P	_____		_____		_____
Q	_____		_____		_____
R	_____		_____		_____
S	_____		_____		_____
T	_____		_____		_____

5		10		15	
U	_____		_____		_____
V	_____		_____		_____
W	_____		_____		_____
Y	_____		_____		_____
Z	_____		_____		_____

Mime or Go Fish

Space Requirements: Classroom or activity room

Equipment/Resource Requirements: Prepared game cards with leisure activities on them

Group Size: Small group

Program Goals:
1. To increase participants' awareness of leisure activities.
2. To increase participants' ability to identify leisure activities.
3. To increase participants' ability to work cooperatively with peers.

Program Description:

Preparation:
Prepare deck(s) of leisure cards (number of decks depends on number of small groups). Using three-by-five-inch index cards or something similar, make two of each kind of activity card. For example, if the leisure activity is swimming, write the word swimming on the top and bottom of the card and draw or place a picture of swimming in the middle of the card. Prepare two of these cards per activity. Prepare several sets, depending on the cognitive ability of the participants.

Introduction:
Introduce the activity's purpose of helping participants increase their awareness of leisure activities. Explain the rules of the game. Ask if there are any questions. This activity is similar to Go Fish.

Activity Description:
Divide the participants into groups of four. Each group gets one deck of cards, containing several sets of activities. Have each group shuffle the deck of cards well. Each person in the group gets dealt four cards. The remaining cards are placed faced down in the middle of the table.

One participant in each group is selected to start. This person points to another member in the group. The first person mimes the leisure activity that he or she wants for a card, and the other person guesses the leisure activity. If that person has the card, he or she must surrender it to the person who mimed the activity. If the person does not have that card, he or she tells the person who mimed to "Go Fish" and that person draws from the deck in the middle of the table. If a pair (two cards with the same activity) is made at either time, the player places the pair on the table in front of him or her.

This process is repeated, rotating to the left. The first person to have complete sets on the table and no cards in his or her hand is the winner.

Debriefing Questions/Closure:
1. How many leisure activities were identified in this game?
2. How difficult or easy was it to match pairs of activities?
3. Which leisure activities were new to you?
4. In which of the activities have you participated?
5. Which of these activities would you like to try?

Leadership Considerations:
1. Make sure an adequate number of cards and sets are prepared prior to the start of the activity.
2. Encourage discussion about leisure activities during the game.
3. Allow adequate time for both playing the game and discussion.

Variations:
1. If participants are available, perhaps one activity session might be to make the cards, and the next activity session then uses the cards.
2. Leisure resources can be used on the cards in place of the leisure activities.
3. Social skills can be used on the cards in place of the leisure activities.

Story Time Tag

Space Requirements: Classroom or activity room

Equipment/Resource Requirements: Accompanying story

Group Size: Small group

Program Goals:
1. To increase participants' awareness of leisure activities.
2. To increase participants' ability to act out leisure activities in front of a group.

Program Description:
Preparation:
Use Story Time Tag story or prepare one more suitable to participants.

Introduction:
Introduce the purpose of the activity and explain the rules.

Activity Description:
Select two participants to begin acting out the story. Begin reading the story. Whenever a third group member calls "freeze," action stops. The third participant comes to the front and tags one of the two other participants. The tagged person sits down with the rest of the group. The person who tagged then begins acting and the story continues.

At any time, a participant from the audience can tag one of the actors. The acting should be confined to the story line. Allow each person to tag at least once.

The acting continues until the story is finished. Bring the group to closure with the following discussion and debriefing questions.

Debriefing Questions/Closure:
1. How many leisure activities in the story can you recall?
2. In how many of these activities have you participated or do you participate?
3. Which of the activities are ones you might be interested in learning?
4. What would be the advantages of having diverse leisure interests?
5. What would be the advantages of having several friends or playmates?
6. How comfortable did you feel acting out the story in front of the group?

Leadership Considerations:
1. The leader may have to set some time parameters if participants are tagging too frequently.
2. The leader may have to establish some system for tagging if participants are not tagging enough.
3. Make the story challenging for and appropriate to the participants.
4. While reading the story, pause in places where the actors need time to act out the scene.
5. Ensure that all participants have acted before one participant is allowed a second turn to act.
6. The leader should read the story slowly enough that participants have adequate time for acting out the situation.

Variations:

1. In one session, have the participants write the story or stories to be acted out, and then in the next session, act them out.
2. Change the content of the story to match the needs of the participants.

Creator: Norma J. Stumbo, Ph.D., CTRS, Illinois State University, Normal, Illinois.

Story Time Tag

Once upon a time, there was a young girl, named Sally, who was very active. She liked to play with her next-door neighbor, Rudolph. They liked to play games together, such as tag and catch. Often after school, they would catch butterflies in her backyard, or go to the park and play on the swings. At the park, they also liked to take their bikes and ride along the trail that went up and down small hills, and around sharp corners. Sometimes, Sally took her skateboard on the trail and did fancy footwork tricks. Sally and Rudolph always had a good time together when they played, and they made sure they shared toys and took turns.

On some Saturdays, Sally's cousin, Amanda came to her house. They liked to play with dolls and bake cookies. Of course one of the best parts about baking cookies, was sitting at the kitchen table and eating them! One of Amanda's other favorite treats was playing with Sally's dog, named Pokie. Pokie was a fun pet because he knew many tricks and would fetch small balls that Amanda threw. Amanda thought she would like a pet of her own to take care of some day.

In the summer, Sally's parents would take her and her big brother, Chris, on vacation, often in long trips in the car. Her parents made sure they brought lots of toys, games, and food for the long ride. This helped Sally and Chris be able to enjoy the ride and look forward to where they were going. The family went sightseeing to places like the mountains, the ocean, or to national parks. Sometimes they went to professional baseball games or to amusement parks. Those were lots of fun! It was great to eat hot dogs and cotton candy! And both Sally and Chris loved to ride the tallest roller coaster and Ferris wheel!

Sally had many favorite leisure activities that she shared with her best friend, Tawny. They liked to read mystery books, put together model cars, and collect sports cards. Sometimes they had so many interests that it was hard to choose which ones to do together! They liked to learn new things, and go to new places, so they were glad they had lots of interests from which to choose. Of course, they took Pokie with them, whenever they could. They were sure they were going to be best friends forever, and next year planned to take tennis and golf lessons together.

Leisure Hangman

Space Requirements: Classroom or activity room

Equipment/Resource Requirements: 25 to 50 index cards with one leisure activity written on each one, dry erase board, dry erase marker

Group Size: Small group or large group

Program Goals:
1. To increase participants' awareness of leisure activities.
2. To increase participants' ability to identify activities of interest to them.

Program Description:
Preparation:
The leader should prepare 25 to 50 index cards with one leisure activity written on each card, e.g., Rollerblading.

Introduction:
Explain the purpose and rules of the activity.

Activity Description:
Select one participant to start the activity. This person chooses one card from the deck, and draws the number of lines on the dry erase board that represent the number of letters. For example, Rollerblading would be _ _ _ _ _ _ _ _ _ _ _ _ _ . This person also draws the basic hangman scaffold to start this round.

The other participants begin guessing the letters in the word, one at a time. For each letter that is guessed correctly, the person places the letter in its correct position on the dashes. Incorrect letter guesses recorded as "body parts" on the hangman scaffold (in order: head, body, right arm, left arm, right leg, left leg—to allow for six incorrect guesses). Incorrect letters also are written in the corner of the board, so participants do not re-guess the same letter.

Letter guessing continues until participants are able to guess the leisure activity. The word is then filled in, and a new round starts with a new person at the board. Play continues until all index cards are used or the time ends.

Close with debriefing questions.

Debriefing Questions/Closure:
1. Which of the activities mentioned are new to you?
2. Which of these activities have you tried before?
3. Which activities mentioned today would you like to try?
4. How easy or difficult was it to guess the activities?

Leadership Considerations:

1. Give the hint to guess vowels first.
2. Keep rules to a minimum to keep focus on the leisure activities.
3. Ask questions related to the activities as play continues, such as "When was the last time you were involved in that activity?"
4. Make sure the group members are old enough to understand the concept of the hangman game.
5. Mix both challenging and easy activities in the card deck.

Variations:

1. All the words on the cards may have a common theme, like summer activities, holiday activities, activities done alone, low-cost activities, or activities done at the facility.
2. May increase the number of body parts that are drawn (like mouth, eyes, nose) to increase the number of times participants can guess incorrectly.
3. The difficulty can be increased by completing phrases instead of just words. For example, shopping at the mall would be _ _ _ _ _ _ _ _ _ _ _ _ _ _ _ _ _ .
4. Divide the group into teams and play competitively.
5. Have participants develop the cards in one session, and then play Leisure Hangman in the next session.
6. Once the activity has been guessed correctly, ask the participants to describe how to participate in or play the activity, to promote increased leisure awareness.

Creator: Bonnie Beasley, CTRS, Orchard Place Child Guidance Center, Des Moines, Iowa.

Leisure Memory

Space Requirements: Classroom or activity room

Equipment/Resource Requirements: Deck of prepared cards, with leisure activities on them

Group Size: Small group

Program Goals:
1. To improve participants' awareness of leisure activities.
2. To aid participants in improving concentration skills.

Program Description:

Preparation:

Prepare a deck of about 50 leisure cards. These can be prepared on three-by-five-inch index cards. Each card in the deck is one of a pair or has a match (such as two cards with "tennis" written on them or one card with "tennis," and one card with "tennis racket"). This game is similar to the card game "Concentration."

Introduction:

Explain the purpose and rules of this activity to the participants.

Activity Description:

Participants can either play individually or in pairs. Cards are to be shuffled. Cards are laid face down on the table (for example five rows of 10 cards each) in random order. Participants are not to see the faces of cards as they are laid on the table.

The first participant will turn over two cards. If the cards match, the participant takes the two cards out of play and sets them on his or her side of the table, and takes another turn at revealing two cards. If the cards do not match, the next player takes a turn. If the cards match, that player places them on his or her side, if not, play returns to the other person.

Players should be reminded to pay attention to the placement or location of cards, as the object of the game is to pair as many cards as possible.

Play continues until all matches are made. The player with the most matches or cards on his or her side wins.

The activity closes with the following discussion questions.

Debriefing Questions/Closure:
1. What types of activities were on the cards?
2. In which of these activities have you participated?
3. How difficult or easy was it to make matches?
4. What did you learn by participating in this activity?
5. How difficult or easy was it to concentrate on and remember the placement of the cards?

Leadership Considerations:
1. Matches may be color-coded to help participants recognize pairs.

Variations:

1. Reduce or increase the number of cards, depending on the cognitive level of participants.
2. Have the cards represent themes, such as activities done in the home, done with family, or done within the state.
3. Vary the content of the activity by having the pair of cards represent the activity and the piece of equipment that goes with it (tennis, tennis racket), or the activity and the location of the activity (canoeing, lake).
4. Have participants create the cards in one session, and play Leisure Memory in the next session.

Creator: Jennifer Matkowich, Illinois State University, Normal, Illinois.

Leisure Perceptions and Well-Being

Space Requirements: Classroom or activity room

Equipment/Resource Requirements: Accompanying form, pencils

Group Size: Small group

Program Goals:
1. To improve participants' awareness of the importance of leisure experiences to their well-being.
2. To examine participants' awareness of their freedom to choose experiences that enhance their well-being.
3. To help participants' identify their perceptions of benefits gained from their leisure experiences.

Program Description:

Preparation:

Make copies of the Leisure Perceptions and Well-Being form, one for each participant.

Introduction:

Leisure experiences have varying values and benefits. A particular experience may have differing impacts. Each participants' leisure lifestyle is unique. Change in any major life function impacts each of the other elements of well-being including leisure. We become more sensitive to the value of our leisure experiences in relation to well-being by contemplating factors that influence our perceptions and leisure awareness.

Explain the purpose and directions of the activity.

Activity Description:

In column 1, participants are to list leisure experiences participated in routinely, at least once per week, that contribute to their well-being.

In column 2, participants are to prioritize from highest to lowest (one being highest) the importance to their well-being of each experience listed in column 1.

In column 3, the participants are to determine the degree to which they freely choose to participate in each experience listed in column 1 by using *I* for Internal or primarily selected by the participant, or *E* for External or primarily selected because someone else wanted the person to participate. Column 3 should, therefore, have either *I* representing internal locus of control or *E* representing external locus of control listed for experiences in column 1.

In column 4, participants are to consider the benefits gained from participating in each experience listed in column 1. They are to use *A* to rate those experiences perceived to be of greatest benefit. They are to use *B* for those believed to be somewhat beneficial and a *C* for the experiences having minimal benefit to their well-being.

After allowing participants adequate time to provide information in the columns, ask them to discuss their answers. Close with the following debriefing questions.

Debriefing Questions/Closure:
1. Who influences the choices you make about your leisure participation, you (*I* responses in column 3) or someone else (*E* responses)?
2. Which experiences contribute most to your well-being and why (refer to the importance ratings in column 2)?
3. How do the experiences with high importance ratings (e.g., column 2) contribute most to your well-being (benefits in column 4)?
4. Are the most beneficial experiences (column 4) also those that you freely choose (column 3)?
5. What patterns are evident among the ratings (are the most important experiences also freely chosen and highly beneficial)?

Leadership Considerations:
1. Have participants list their leisure experiences for an average week or month in the first column before requesting them to respond to the importance column.
2. Discuss factors that contribute to well-being (e.g., satisfaction, family, companionship) during the introduction.
3. Explain the concept of internal and external locus of control during the introduction.

Variations:
1. List leisure experiences that occur only in particular seasons of the year or for a specific time period (e.g., one day or week).
2. Add a column that would gain input from others about the participants' perceptions.

Creator: Marcia Jean Carter, Re.D., CLP, CTRS, Ashland University, Ashland, Ohio.

Leisure Perceptions and Well-Being

Column 1	Column 2	Column 3	Column 4
Leisure Experiences	Importance (Numerical Rating High to Low)	Freedom to Choose (I = Internal E = External)	Benefit (Estimate: Greatest = A to Least = C)

1. _____

2. _____

3. _____

4. _____

5. _____

6. _____

7. _____

8. _____

9. _____

10. _____

11. _____

12. _____

13. _____

14. _____

15. _____

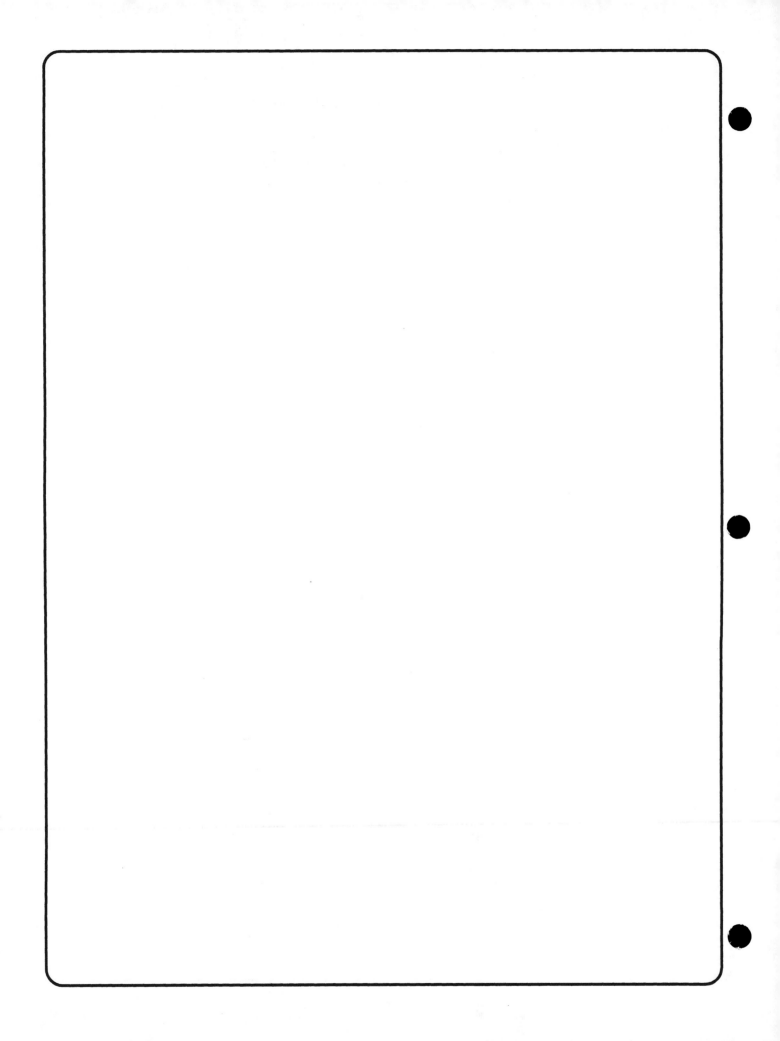

Leisure Outburst

Space Requirements: Classroom or activity room

Equipment/Resource Requirements: Leisure Outburst cards, paper and pencils, two-minute timer

Group Size: Small group

Program Goals:
1. To increase participants' awareness and understanding of leisure.
2. Depends on topics on Leisure Outburst cards.

Program Description:
Preparation:
Prepare Leisure Outburst cards. See accompanying list for ideas for cards. Place one topic on each card. Prepare 20 to 40 cards, depending on the size of the group and cognitive ability of the participants.

Introduction:
Begin introduction with discussion of leisure pursuits. Discuss the variety of activities available, how each person can choose his or her own leisure, and how leisure improves our lives. Review the purpose and goals of the activity. Explain the rules of play. This activity is much like the regular game of "Outburst."

Activity Description:
Divide groups into two teams or play as one large team. Have the first team draw a card. Start the two-minute timer. Members of that team (or everyone) shouts out the possible answers to the topic. Points are awarded for answers that are identical or nearly identical to the responses on the card. One point is awarded for each correct response, within the two-minute time limit.

Have the other team draw a card. Members of that team shout out responses, and are awarded one point for every correct answer within the two-minute time limit.

Play continues until the cards are all used or the session time ends. Close with discussion which includes the following debriefing questions.

Debriefing Questions/Closure:
1. What did you learn from this activity?
2. How did responses for group members help you think of new options?
3. Also ask questions specific to the content of the cards, for example:

   • What were the benefits of leisure your team listed?
   • What types of activities for under $5.00 did your group name?
   • What different things can you do with a tennis ball?
   • Where in the community can you go with a friend?

Leadership Considerations:
1. Be familiar with the regular game of "Outburst."
2. Address topics most fitting for the participants.
3. Focus on the topics, not the competition.

Variations:
1. Cards can be changed to any topic of interest to the group.
2. Have participants come up with the cards for the other team.

Creator: Stacey Zimmerman, CTRS, Mission Nursing Home, Plymouth, Minnesota.

Leisure Outburst

Example topics for cards:

Activities for Under $5.00
1. Strolling in the park
2. Walking
3. Reading a short story
4. Completing a crossword puzzle
5. Eating an ice cream cone
6. Watching the sunset
7. Walking along the beach
8. Talking to your next door neighbor
9. Reading the newspaper
10. Playing cards

Things You Can Do With a Tennis Ball
1. Play tennis
2. Play fetch with a dog
3. Play catch with a child
4. Practice your golf swing
5. Juggle
6. Balance it on your nose
7. Throw it against a wall
8. Toss it in the air
9. Leave it on the floor as a cat toy
10. Dress it up for Halloween

Where in the Community You Can Go With a Friend
1. Park
2. Shopping mall
3. Movie theater
4. Bowling
5. Video store
6. Ice cream store
7. Restaurant
8. Book store
9. Coffee shop
10. Fitness center

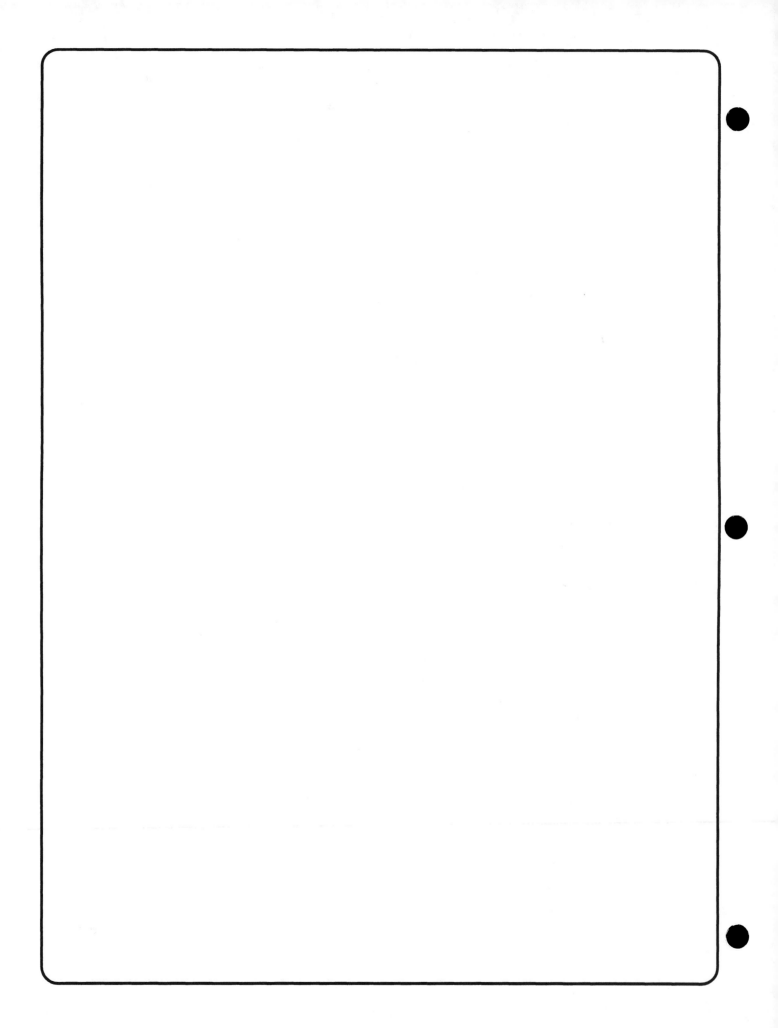

Recipe for the Perfect Leisure Day

Space Requirements: Classroom or activity room with tables

Equipment/Materials: Accompanying recipe cards, pencils or pens

Group Size: Small group

Program Goals:
1. To increase participants' awareness of the characteristics and values that they treasure in their leisure and play time.
2. To increase participants' self-assessment of how many activities they know to do in their leisure and play time.
3. To increase participants' ability to make decisions regarding the use of their leisure and play time.
4. To increase participants' awareness of what others value in their leisure and play time.

Description/Procedure:
Preparation:
Make copies of Recipe for the Perfect Leisure Day card, one for each participant.

Introduction:
Participants should be seated in a circle around a table. Hand each participant the Recipe for the Perfect Leisure Day card.

Begin the session by discussing the importance of leisure and play time. The leader may ask participants some of their favorite activities. Are they individual or group activities? indoors or outdoors? active or passive? The purpose of this activity is to determine what activities each person likes to do and how each person is responsible for making his or her own leisure choices.

Activity Description:
Each person is to complete the Recipe for the Perfect Leisure Day card for having a perfect leisure day. What activities should be included? How long would each activity take? Are other people required? Is equipment required? How are choices made?

The leader should allow 10 to 15 minutes for participants to complete their Recipe for the Perfect Leisure Day card. Neatness is not important, as each person is to keep his or her own Recipe for the Perfect Leisure Day card.

When each participant is finished with his or her Recipe for the Perfect Leisure Day card, the leader facilitates a discussion on the perfect leisure day. Discussion may focus on similarities and differences between participants, as well as how each person thinks he or she makes personal choices for leisure.

Realistic expectations and self-awareness are important considerations for this activity.

Discussion/Debriefing Questions:
1. How was your perfect day of leisure spent? What types of activities were there?
2. Was there a schedule to the day? beginning? ending?
3. Who else was involved or required? Why?
4. Was any equipment necessary? How would you go about getting it?
5. What factors were important to your choices?
6. How many days have you spent like the one you described?
7. What is needed to make this type of day happen in the future?

Leadership Considerations:
1. Emphasize that people's expectations and definitions of leisure and play may differ.
2. Emphasize what each person might change in his or her schedule to create better leisure and play time.
3. Emphasize that making choices is an important part of a leisure lifestyle.
4. Do not let discussion focus on the negative aspects of people's current leisure.

Variations:
1. Change the content of the activity from leisure awareness to one most beneficial to the participants.

Creator: Norma J. Stumbo, Ph.D., CTRS, Illinois State University, Normal, Illinois.

Recipe for the Perfect Leisure Day

From the file of _____

Ingredients:

_____

_____

_____

_____

_____

_____

_____

_____

_____

_____

Recipe Directions:

_____

_____

_____

_____

_____

_____

_____

_____

_____

_____

_____

_____

_____

_____

_____

_____

_____

Leisure Activity Bull's-Eye

Space Requirements: Classroom or activity room

Equipment/Resource Requirements: Accompanying form, magazines, markers, glue or tape, scissors

Group Size: Small group

Program Goals:
1. To increase participants' ability to identify their favorite leisure activities.
2. To increase participants' ability to prioritize their favorite activities.

Program Description:

Preparation:
Make copies of accompanying Leisure Activity Bull's-Eye form, and gather necessary materials.

Introduction:
Participants will be informed that the purpose of the activity is to help them identify their favorite leisure activities and then place them in priority order. Ask participants what some of their favorite activities are, as a starting point for this activity.

Activity Description:
Distribute magazines and scissors or have pictures precut from the magazines and placed into packets.

Ask participants to select pictures either from the magazines or packets that represent their favorite activities. Have each participant select anywhere from five to 15 activities. Allow 15 to 20 minutes for participants to locate these pictures.

When enough pictures are located, hand each participant a copy of the Leisure Activity Bull's-Eye form. Distribute markers and glue.

Ask participants to place the activities on the table in order of how much they like to participate in them. For example, the most preferred activity is at their left, and the least preferred is at their right—the remaining activities are ranked somewhere in between the most left one and the most right one.

Explain the idea of a bull's-eye if necessary. Ask participants to place their most favorite activity in the center of the bull's-eye and glue or tape it there. Other activities are placed in a loosely descending order on the larger circles of the bull's-eye. The outermost ring should have their least favorite activities.

Ask each participant to individually share his or her bull's-eye with the group. Facilitate a discussion about individual preferences, chosen leisure activities, how decisions were made, and the like. Debriefing questions follow. Reiterate the goals of the activity to provide closure.

Debriefing Questions/Closure:
1. How many activities were you able to identify?
2. How difficult was it to rank your activities, when all started as your "favorites"?
3. How often do you get to do your most favorite activity?
4. What did you learn about your preferences by completing this activity?
5. What did you learn about other members of the group?
6. How will you use this information in the future?

Leadership Considerations:
1. Have an adequate number of copies of the Leisure Activity Bull's-Eye forms.
2. Have an adequate variety of magazines and pictures.
3. Acknowledge that prioritizing may be difficult, given that all activities were identified as favorites.

Variations:
1. The bull's-eye idea might be used for benefits of leisure, leisure locations, or leisure partners.

Creator: Beth Turner, Illinois State University, Normal, Illinois.

Leisure Activity Bull's-Eye

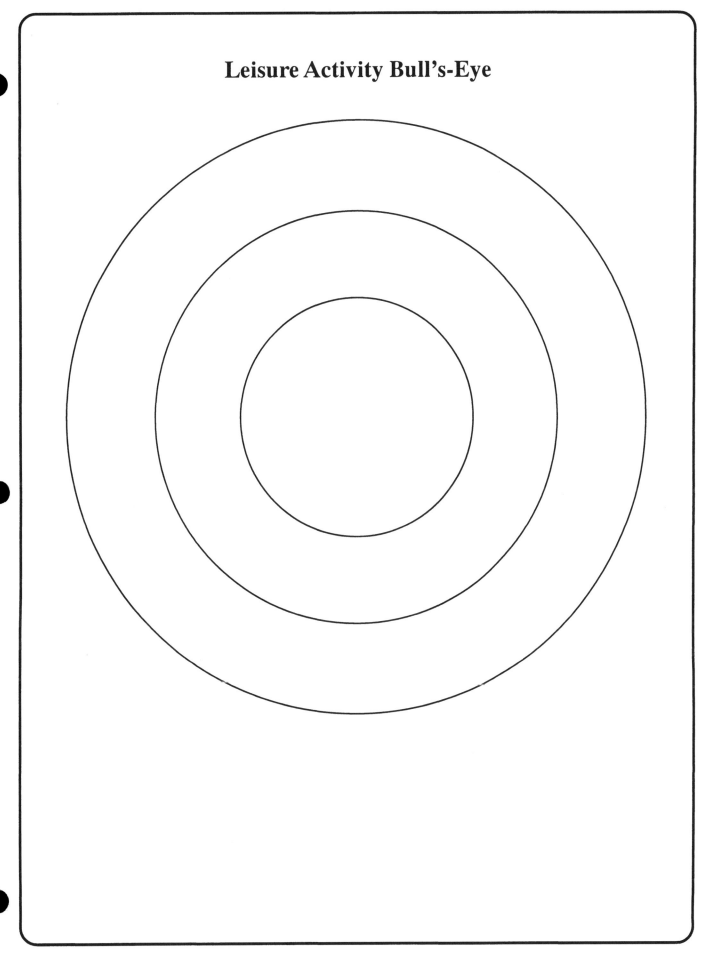

Mini-Vacation

Space Requirements: Classroom or activity room

Equipment/Resource Requirements: Travelogues and brochures, yellow pages telephone book, cookbook, library, ethnic stores and shops, clubs, radio station, local festivals

Group Size: Small group

Program Goals:
1. To teach participants how to access information about different cultures and locations.
2. To help participants explore a culture of interest.

Program Description:

Preparation:
Gather travel brochures and other materials from travel agencies, bookstores, newspapers, and the like.

Introduction:
Introduce the purpose and goals of this activity. Introduce the subject of travel and novelty. Ask participants where they have always wanted to go or think they might enjoy traveling. Give some examples of famous places, different cultures, and points of interest.

Activity Description:
Distribute the travel brochures, yellow pages phone book, ethnic cookbooks, and any other resources on different places or cultures. Explain to the group members that while they may not always be able to afford to travel to different locations, they can still learn and experience what a place has to offer without actually going there.

Ask each participant to identify a location or culture he or she would like to explore. Explain how the group members might use travel brochures, cookbooks, the yellow pages, and ethnic stores to learn more about the location. Ask each participant to find information about the location in which he or she is interested, using these resources or others he or she might find useful. Allow sufficient time for participants to gather this information. Share information within the group.

Review the purpose and goal of the activity, using the following debriefing questions.

Debriefing Questions/Closure:
1. What did you learn about the location or culture in which you were interested?
2. What did you learn about other locations and cultures from other participants?
3. If you were going to travel to this location, how would you prepare?
4. What did you learn about gathering information on another culture?

Leadership Considerations:
1. Have adequate resources available for a variety of interests.
2. Allow sufficient time for participants to gather and understand the information they have accumulated.

Variations:
    1. Instead of a country, offer information on a trip to the beach, mountains, or a farm.

Creator: Linda Traylor, CTRS, VA Medical Healthcare System, Fort Howard, Maryland.

Leisure Around the World

Space Requirements: Classroom or activity room

Equipment/Resource Requirements: Accompanying form, construction paper, paints, cutout doll shapes (make your own or order from a craft supply company), paintbrushes, glue, scissors, yarn for hair, markers, hole punch, and pin tabs to hold all the dolls together, information about the leisure habits of four countries' cultures (can be found in books in the library).

Group Size: Small group

Program Goals:
1. To increase participants' awareness of various leisure activities around the world.
2. To increase participants' understanding of various leisure pursuits in various countries.

Program Description:

Preparation:
Leader must go to the library and research four countries' (e.g., Australia, Canada, Japan, Africa) leisure activities. Make copies of the doll body (see accompanying form) on construction paper. Make drawings of particular clothing styles, based on cultures, or let participants develop their own patterns during the activity. Gather equipment and materials needed for participants to complete the leisure dolls.

Introduction:
Present to the group information about the leisure habits of each of the four countries. Have participants choose which country they are going to represent with their dolls, as well as one leisure skill from that country.

Activity Description:
Distribute outlined bodies and tell the participants to cut out the outlined bodies. Distribute the construction paper, paints, glue and yarn and have them decorate their leisure dolls. Tell them to make their doll represent one of the four countries they just learned about. Tell them to make their doll holding a piece of equipment that represents a leisure activity from that country.

After all dolls are completed, go around the room and have each participant show his or her doll and tell which country it represents and what leisure activity was chosen for the doll to represent, based on that doll's culture.

Then take the hole punch and punch holes on the end of the hands of each doll, and link with pin tabs to form a chain. Hang chain in hallway or activity room.

Debriefing Questions/Closure:
1. What was your favorite country and why?
2. Would you like to spend time in that country learning new leisure skills?
3. Explain the leisure habits of your doll.
4. How has this activity helped you to develop a larger perspective of leisure around the world?

Leadership Considerations:
1. Make sure your group is old enough to understand the concepts in this activity.
2. Make sure the leader has done background research on the leisure habits of various countries.
3. This activity works best with eight to 10 participants.
4. Make copies of outlined body of the doll ahead of time.
5. Be organized in the presentation and distribution of the materials.

Variations:
1. Have the group work in pairs to complete the activity.
2. Bring to the group books on different countries and have participants research the various leisure habits of a culture.
3. Have the participants present the information they have found concerning their particular country.

Creator: Bonnie Beasley, CTRS, Orchard Place Child Guidance Center, Des Moines, Iowa.

Leisure Around the World

Time Capsule Keepsake

Space Requirements: Classroom or activity room

Equipment/Resource Requirements: Time capsule questions typed on colorful paper, pens or pencils

Group Size: Individual or small group

Program Goals:
1. To increase participants' awareness of self.
2. To increase participants' personal awareness of leisure interests.
3. To increase participants' awareness of other participants' leisure interests.

Program Description:

Preparation:
Copy the Time Capsule Keepsake form onto colored paper, one for each participant. Design a cover for the keepsake book, with "Time Capsule Keepsake" typed in bold letters. Include space for "written by" on cover. Each person will get to keep his or her own version of the book.

Introduction:
Introduce the idea of a time capsule keepsake by asking the group members to describe what a time capsule is (e.g., pictures, letters, or any item or memory preserved for others to view in the future). The purpose of the activity is to increase participants' awareness of self and how each person has different qualities and interests that are important. This activity will also help others to get to know the participant.

Activity Description:
Hand out one Time Capsule Keepsake page and cover to each individual. Instruct participants to answer each question, allowing approximately 30 minutes for completion. Facilitate the group as participants are completing the keepsake books, by asking participants if they have any questions about the activity or about their leisure interests.

When activity is completed, have group sit in a circle around table for discussion. Have each participant share answers to certain questions picked by the group leader.

The leader should note similarities and differences among responses. Discussion should focus on how each person has different qualities and how each quality is important and affects who each person is.

Debriefing Questions/Closure:
Wrap up discussion by having each participant name something he or she would like others to remember about himself or herself (e.g., qualities, interests). Conclude with talking about how a time capsule captures what we want others to know about ourselves and also may help us to better understand who we are as individuals.

Debriefing Questions:
1. What were the similarities you noticed among group members?
2. What were differences you noticed among group members?
3. Which group member are you most like? most different from?
4. What did you learn about yourself from this activity?
5. Who would you like to find your time capsule keepsake?

Leadership Considerations:
1. This activity may stand alone or be included as one segment of a larger leisure education program.

Variations:
1. Have participants design their own cover for book to allow participants a chance to express creativity.
2. Have each participant come up with own question for whole group to answer individually and can add questions to end of book or make up own book of questions.

Creator: Judy K. Hoogewerf, CTRS, Neighborhood Resources, Colorado Springs, Colorado.

Time Capsule Keepsake

1. What are the names of your parents? Do you have any brothers or sisters? If yes, what are their names?

2. Do you have or have you ever had any pets? What kind? What are their names?

3. Name five things you like to do.

4. Name three things you do not like to do.

5. What is your favorite food to eat? What is your least favorite food?

6. Name three things that describe yourself (such as nice, funny, patient).

7. What state were you born in? Where do you live now?

8. What is your favorite restaurant to go to? Do you go there often?

9. What color is your hair? What color are your eyes? How tall are you?

10. Do you play a musical instrument? If yes, what instrument do you play?

11. What sports do you play?

12. Name one thing that makes you happy.

13. Name one thing that makes you sad.

14. Name one thing that makes you angry.

15. Name one thing that makes you laugh.

16. If you could travel to any place in the word, where would you go? Why would you go there?

17. If you could do anything you wanted to, what would you do?

18. If you won a million dollars, what would you buy?

Share Something Wonderful

Space Requirements: Classroom or activity room

Equipment/Resource Requirements: Large star made of a durable material, music and playing device, chairs seated in a circle

Group Size: Small group

Program Goals:
1. To offer a nonthreatening method of sharing leisure interests.
2. To expand the participants' knowledge of another participant's recreational activities.
3. To explore participants' needs that can be satisfied through leisure.

Program Description:
Preparation:
Before participants enter room, arrange chairs in circle, with seats facing in.

Introduction:
This is an activity similar to musical chairs, however, no one is eliminated or loses. All participants are winners. Review with the participants the purpose and goals of this activity.

Activity Description:
Have the group sit in a circle. Explain how the activity is played. The participants will pass a large star until the music stops. When the music stops, the participant who is holding the star will stand up and share something wonderful he or she does in his or her leisure time. Ask each participant why he or she thinks the activity is wonderful. Review commonalties of activities and feelings.

Play continues until all group members have had an opportunity to share. Review the purpose and goals of the activity. Close the session by asking the following debriefing questions.

Debriefing Questions/Closure:
1. Why do the activities you named make you feel wonderful?
2. What were similarities and differences of leisure interests among group members?
3. When was the last time you were able to participate in the activity you named?

Leadership Considerations:
1. Select the music according to the age and interests of the participants.
2. If standing before the group seems to be too threatening for participants, allow them to remain seated.
3. It's important for the facilitator to remain energized!

Variations:
1. Select another topic for activity.
2. Replace the star with a seasonal object.

Creator: Susan Leifer Mathieu, M.S., CTRS, California State University–Dominguez Hills, Carson, California.

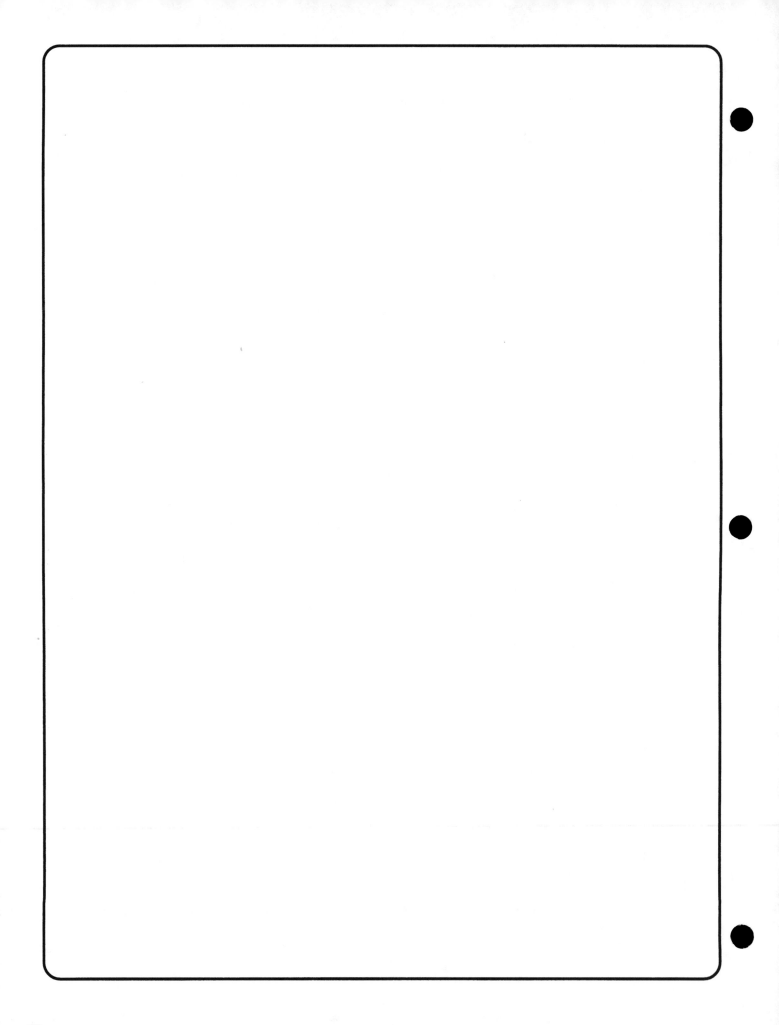

My Personal Newsletter

Space Requirements: Classroom or activity room

Equipment/Resource Requirements: Accompanying form, pencils or pens

Group Size: Individual or small group

Program Goals:
1. To increase participants' awareness of personal leisure interests.
2. To increase participants' awareness of future leisure interests.

Program Description:

Preparation:
Make copies of the My Personal Newsletter form, one for each participant.

Introduction:
The purpose of this activity is to increase the clients' awareness of personal leisure interests and future leisure interests.

Activity Description:
Explain to the participants that they will be creating their own personal newsletter by writing several "columns" relating to their personal leisure interests. Provide the participants with copies of the My Personal Newsletter form.

Allow time for participants to think of ideas and write columns under each heading. Allow from 20 to 30 minutes for completion of this part of the activity. Encourage participants to be creative, while being truthful.

After the newsletters are completed, ask participants to share their newsletters with the group. Close with a review of the purpose and goals of the activity and the following debriefing questions.

Debriefing Questions/Closure:
1. How did you choose what to write under each heading?
2. How often do you participate in your favorite activity?
3. Do you think leisure is a priority in your life?
4. Why have you not tried activities you are interested in?
5. What kinds of barriers do you have to your leisure?
6. What does the newsletter tell you about yourself?

Leadership Considerations:
1. Leader may want to give specific topic titles or let the client choose from a list.
2. Some subjects may be sensitive.
3. Ensure that topics are appropriate to the participant group.

Variations:
1. Use to relate leisure interests before and after a disabling injury.
2. Make the titles specific to injury (e.g., wheelchair sports).

Creator: Becky Klein, Illinois State University, Normal, Illinois.

My Personal Newsletter

My Most Favorite Leisure Activity

Leisure Barriers to Overcome

Forecasts of Future Leisure

My Next Leisure Outing:

Personal Life Priorities

Brand New Leisure Interests Developing on the Home Front

Future Vacation Plans

Spiral About Me

Space Requirements: Classroom or activity room

Equipment/Resource Requirements: Accompanying forms, pens or pencils

Group Size: Small group

Program Goals:
1. To increase participants' awareness of self in relation to leisure.
2. To increase participants' awareness of leisure interests.
3. To increase participants' awareness of leisure participation patterns.

Program Description:
Preparation:
Make copies of both Spiral About Me forms, one of each for each participant.

Introduction:
This activity begins with participants answering questions about themselves and then applying these answers to the spiral. The participants are to write about themselves. The questions are to aid in the writing.

Activity Description:
The participants should each be given the accompanying forms to complete. The first page of questions should be completed first. Allow about five minutes for completion of this part of the activity.

After the questions are complete, the second Spiral About Me page should be handed out to each participant. The participants should use the answers from the first page to fill in the spiral. On the spiral, participants should write any of the answers and any other words or phrases to describe themselves in relation to leisure. The participants' descriptions of themselves should fill the spirals. Allow about 10 minutes for this part of the activity.

Discussion should focus on participants' spirals, and what each says about the individual. Close with a discussion related to the purpose and goals of the activity, including the following debriefing questions.

Debriefing Questions/Closure:
1. What did this activity help you realize about yourself?
2. What did you discover about your leisure participation patterns?
3. What did you discover about your leisure interests?
4. What changes in your leisure would you like to make?
5. How can you make those changes?
6. What would motivate you to take action?

Leadership Considerations:
1. The different angles of the spiral can represent the different angles of the individual and portray that each individual is different.
2. The participants may have difficulty coming up with answers to some of the questions, so the leader should be prepared to give assistance.
3. Allow adequate time for each participant to fill in his or her spiral.
4. Have sample spiral completed and prepared as an example.

Variations:
1. The participants could fill in the spiral with leisure activities that they enjoy or in which they would like to participate.
2. The activities could be listed in order of most favorite to least favorite with the favorite activities being towards the center of the spiral.
3. The participants could write closest to the center about what they feel on the inside and farthest from the center about how they think others see them.

Creator: Julie Keil, CTRS, Illinois State University, Normal, Illinois.

Spiral About Me

1. I like myself because _____.

2. I am good at _____.

3. I enjoy participating in _____ leisure activities.

4. I contribute to others by _____.

5. I enjoy being with _____.

6. The activities I enjoy most are _____.

7. I would like to improve _____ about myself.

8. In leisure I see myself as _____.

9. In leisure others see me as _____.

10. In my dreams I am _____.

11. I would like to be more _____.

12. I am _____.

13. Some day I would like to _____.

14. The person I am closest to is _____.

15. I enjoy being with this person because _____.

16. I describe myself to others as _____.

17. Others see me as _____.

18. I would like others to see me as _____.

19. To change this I can _____.

20. In leisure I would like to be more or less _____.

Spiral About Me

3

2

1

4

5

Myself in Leisure

Space Requirements: Classroom or activity room

Equipment/Resource Requirements: Accompanying form, pens or pencils

Group Size: Small group

Program Goals:
1. To increase participants' awareness of self in relation to leisure.
2. To increase participants' ability to identify limitations to leisure.

Program Description:

Preparation:
Make copies of Myself in Leisure form, one for each participant.

Introduction:
The leader should first discuss the meaning of leisure with the participants. Participants should define what leisure means to each of them. Discuss the purpose and goals of the activity.

Activity Description:
Hand each client a copy of the Myself in Leisure form and a pen or pencil. Have each participant fill out the form. Allow 15 minutes for completion of this part of the activity.

Ask participants to share their answers with the group. After sharing answers in the group, the participants should expand one of the questions on the accompanying form. Have participants write down their answers.

Debriefing Questions/Closure:
1. What discoveries did you make about yourself?
2. What question did you branch off of?
3. Did you find this activity difficult? If so, why?
4. How does it make you feel to write down your responses?

Leadership Considerations:
1. Some participants may not feel comfortable sharing their responses. They should not be forced to share if they do not want to share.
2. Leader may discuss the meanings of each question with the participants.

Variations:
1. Participants may want to draw pictures to go with their responses.
2. The questions may be altered to ask specifically about leisure activities.

Creator: Julie Keil, CTRS, Illinois State University, Normal, Illinois.

Myself in Leisure

Directions: Answer each of the six numbered questions next to the corresponding number at the bottom of the work sheet.

1. What is your personal definition of leisure?
2. Describe how you think of yourself in leisure and its importance to you.
3. Describe how you think others see you in relation to leisure.
4. What types of leisure experiences do you enjoy?
5. What kinds of personal changes would you like to make about yourself that would affect your leisure?
6. What limits or prohibits your leisure?

1

2

3

4

5

6

What If . . .

Space Requirements: Classroom or activity room

Equipment/Resource Requirements: Accompanying form, pens or pencils

Group Size: Small group

Program Goals:
1. To increase participants' awareness of self in leisure.
2. To increase participants' creativity related to leisure.

Program Description:
Preparation:
Make copies of What If form, one for each participant.

Introduction:
Introduce participants to the concept of leisure. Have them share some leisure experiences from their own lives (either recent or in the past). Discuss what happened in these leisure experiences. Now think of what would have happened if something about that experience was altered or changed. Think of how this experience would have been changed. Review the purpose and goals of the activity with the participants.

Activity Description:
Hand each participant a copy of the What If form and a pen or pencil. Ask participants to fill out the accompanying form. The What If scenarios could be realistic possibilities or completely "off the wall" ideas. Allow 15 minutes for participants to complete this part of the activity.

When participants are finished writing their What If scenarios, ask them to share their experiences and What If scenarios. Lead a discussion about the experiences and scenarios.

Conclude with a discussion of the purpose and goals of the activity, including the following debriefing questions.

Debriefing Questions/Closure:
1. What kinds of scenarios did you think of?
2. How difficult or easy was it to think of the scenarios or the leisure events?
3. How did thinking of these scenarios make you feel?
4. What did the scenarios make you think of?
5. How realistic were most of your scenarios?
6. Describe how the What If scenarios could really happen.

Leadership Considerations:
1. Allow enough time for each of the participants to share at least one of their responses.
2. Provide examples for the participants to base their responses. Example: I was playing basketball and Michael Jordan came and joined my game. . . .
3. Do not make fun of anyone's response.

Variations:
1. Have participants describe what they would have liked to have happen in the leisure event.
2. Have participants write about upcoming leisure events they have not yet experienced, what they would like to have happen at these events, and how they could realistically achieve this.

Creator: Julie Keil, CTRS, Illinois State University, Normal, Illinois.

What If . . .

Choose at least four (4) ordinary leisure and recreation events that have occurred or will occur, and for each event write five (5) What If scenarios that would completely alter your life. With these What If scenarios, describe how each of them could realistically happen.

1. _____

_____

What If . . . _____

_____

_____

_____

2. _____

_____

What If . . . _____

_____

_____

_____

3. _____

_____

What If . . . _____

_____

_____

_____

4. _____

_____

What If . . . _____

_____

_____

_____

Realistic Possibilities

_____

_____

_____

_____

Positive Messages Box

Space Requirements: Classroom or activity room

Equipment/Resource Requirements: Shoebox with lid (one for each participant), construction paper, magazines, markers, scissors, glue, several blank slips of paper

Group Size: Small group

Program Goals:
1. To increase participants' ability to follow directions.
2. To increase participants' ability to give themselves positive messages.
3. To improve participants' ability to identify the positive aspects of other individuals participating in the group activity.

Program Description:

Preparation:
Make blank slips of paper, one for each participant. Prepare leader's box as example. Prepare boxes and materials for participants.

Introduction:
The tables in the room should be prearranged with the materials in the center of each table. The clients should be asked not to touch the materials on the table until directed to do so. The leader should have a sample box to show to the group prior to the start of the activity. The purpose and goals of the activity should be introduced to the participants.

Activity Description:
Each participant will be asked to choose a shoebox. The participants are then to use the construction paper to cover the outside of the box so that any writing cannot be seen. The inside of the box should remain open. The lid to the box should then be covered, using the same material, so that any writing cannot be seen. The lid should still fit over the top of the box.

The participants must then cut a hole in the center of the lid of the box. The hole should be approximately one-half-inch wide by four-inches long. (The leader may show the sample box as an example). Holes can also be cut prior to the activity to save some time. Each participant should write his or her name on the outside of his or her box.

The participants are asked to spend the next 20 minutes looking through magazines to find images or words that relay positive messages about themselves. Once these images or words are found, the participants may cut them out of the magazine.

Once the images have been cut out, the participants may glue the images to the outside of the box. If an image is not found, the participants may write the positive message on the outside of the box.

When the 20 minutes have passed, the participants need to take a blank slip for each member of the group. At their own pace, or on their own time, the participants must write a positive message to each member of the group. Reinforce that the messages must be positive and genuine.

Members of the group will be asked to keep their boxes in a general area of the facility so members may drop messages into one another's boxes at any time during the week (ask members not to write their name on the messages they send to others).

At the end of the session, the participants are asked to clean their work area, leaving behind the magazines, scissors, glue and construction paper. The participants are asked to bring their boxes to the next group session.

At the next group session, the participants are to bring their boxes, and share some of the messages from the other group members (only do so if comfortable sharing).

The participants will have a brief discussion on the Positive Messages Boxes.

Debriefing Questions/Closure:
1. Explain the positive messages you included about yourself.
2. How did you feel when you placed a message in the box of another group member?
3. How did it feel to receive a message from another group member?
4. What did these messages tell you about how others see you?

Leadership Considerations:
1. Leader should have a sample box available while describing the activity.
2. Leader may want to precut the holes in the lids to avoid any potential injuries from working with the scissors.
3. Leader should check on participants during the activity to ensure that the directions are being followed and to answer any questions.
4. Reserve the right to review the messages to ensure that the messages contain appropriate language and content.
5. Plan on spending two group sessions to complete this activity.

Variations:
1. Anger Control Box—the clients write coping methods for anger control and place those on the inside to refer to when they become angry.
2. The boxes can also be used as a type of mail box or theme box for messages during the various holidays.
3. Chemical Dependency Box—box divided into two sides, one for barriers to leisure when using and one for benefits of leisure when sober; photos on outside, slips of paper on the inside.

Creator: Theresa M. Connolly, CTRS, Illinois State University, Normal, Illinois.

Personal Leisure Values

Space Requirements: Classroom or activity room

Equipment/Resource Requirements: Accompanying form, pens or pencils

Group Size: Small group

Program Goals:
1. To improve participants' knowledge and understanding of leisure.
2. To improve participants' awareness of self in leisure.
3. To identify participants' leisure patterns and values.

Program Description:

Preparation:

Make copies of Personal Leisure Values form, one for each participant.

Introduction:

Discuss the goals of the activity with the participants. The leader should explain that this activity will help the participants understand the role that leisure plays in each of their lives. Pointing out that leisure may have a different role in each of their lives may be helpful to participants.

Activity Description:

Hand out a copy of the Personal Leisure Values form and a pen or pencil to each participant.

Have the participants answer each question on the form in order from one to 10. The participants should individually write down their answers and keep them to themselves. Participants can work at their own pace unless a time limit is set. Allow about 10 minutes to complete the questions.

When participants have completed the questions to their satisfaction, ask each participant to share his or her answers to the questions with the rest of the group. Review the purpose and goals of the activity. Use the following questions for debriefing and closure of the activity.

Debriefing Questions/Closure:
1. What is leisure?
2. What connections do you see between your values and your answers to these questions?
3. How do people value leisure differently?
4. What priority does leisure have for you?
5. Why is leisure important or unimportant to you?
6. What could be done to make leisure a more important part of your lives?
7. What, if any, participants' answers surprised you?
8. How many of you would like to have more leisure and why?
9. Why do you prefer active or passive leisure?
10. What are the similarities between any of the participants?
11. What is your perception of leisure and how it fits into your life now after completing this activity?

Leadership Considerations:
1. Be sure to allow enough time for the participants to answer the questions to their satisfaction.
2. Leader may have a discussion after each question to help the participants understand the meaning of each question.
3. Leader may give a time limit for answering the questions so the participants do not take too long answering them.
4. Leader may ask people to share their ideas while they are answering the questions to help those who are having trouble thinking of answers.

Variations:
1. The discussion questions could ask participants to identify leisure resources within the home or community based on the answers to the questions on the work sheet.
2. The questions on the work sheet could ask participants to identify leisure barriers.
3. Instead of concentrating on personal leisure values, emphasis in the discussion could be placed on the leisure activities the participants enjoy that were named on the work sheet and how to continue participation in these activities.

Creator: Julie Keil, CTRS, Illinois State University, Normal, Illinois.

Personal Leisure Values

1. Name one thing that you consider to be leisure.

2. On a scale of 1 to 10 (1 being low, and 10 being high), please rank the importance of leisure in your life.

3. How much leisure on average do you have per week?

4. Do you enjoy being alone in your leisure?

5. Is your leisure more enjoyable for you when it is shared with another person (such as a family member or friend)?

6. Is there anything you do for leisure on a daily or weekly basis and if so how important is it to you?

7. Do you prefer to be active or passive in your leisure?

8. Must you be doing something for you to consider it leisure or can leisure for you include doing nothing at all?

9. Would you be bothered if your amount of leisure per week were decreased to one hour per week, and why or why not?

10. Name anything you would like to change about your leisure, why you would like to make this change, and how you can make this change.

My Top Four Choices

Space Requirements: Classroom or activity room

Equipment/Resource Requirements: Paper, pens or pencils

Group Size: Small group

Program Goals:
1. To increase participants' ability to identify values related to leisure activities.
2. To increase participants' awareness of their personal values.
3. To increase participants' awareness of activities and leisure resources used in everyday life.

Program Description:
Preparation:
Make copies of the My Top Four Choices form, one for each participant.

Introduction:
This activity asks participants to look at what four things they value the most in four areas of their lives. Review the purpose and goals of the activity with the participants.

Activity Description:
Hand each participant a copy of the My Top Four Choices form and a pen or pencil. Instruct the participants first to list four activities which are most important to them. Next, the participants should list the four people which are most important to them. Third, the participants should list the four places which they feel are most important to them. Finally, the participants list four objects which they find most important to them.

Allow 10 to 15 minutes for participants to complete this part of the activity. After the lists are completed, pair the participants and have them discuss their answers. Instruct them to look for similarities, differences, unique answers, etc.

Ask the partners to report their findings back to the larger group. Review the purpose and goals of the activity through the following debriefing questions.

Debriefing Questions/Closure:
1. What did you feel were the four most important things under each category and why?
2. How often do you participate in your four most important activities?
3. How often do you see the four most important people on your list?
4. How often do you go to your four most important places?
5. Are these four most important places also your favorite places? If so, why and if not, why not?
6. How often do you use your four most important objects? Are these your favorite objects?
7. In leisure how are these values shown? What values are apparent in your leisure?

Leadership Considerations:
1. Participants may have difficulty understanding what types of items could go on their lists, so the leader should provide examples.
2. Make sure not to judge the participants on their choices.
3. Allow adequate time for the participants to complete the lists.
4. Ensure that items chosen are appropriate to the participant group.

Variations:
1. The participants could list under each category what they use the most often instead of what is most important.
2. A discussion could take place after each category instead of just at the end.
3. The participants could name their choices verbally instead of writing down their alternatives.

Creator: Julie Keil, CTRS, Illinois State University, Normal, Illinois.

My Top Four Choices

List four leisure activities which are most important to you.

1.

2.

3.

4.

List four people who are important to you.

1.

2.

3.

4.

List four places that are important to you.

1.

2.

3.

4.

List four objects that are important to you.

1.

2.

3.

4.

Barriers Busters

Space Requirements: Classroom or activity room

Equipment/Resource Requirements: Accompanying form, pens or pencils, prepared Barriers Busters index cards

Group Size: Small group

Program Goals:
1. To improve participants' ability to identify barriers to their leisure.
2. To improve participants' ability to identify ways to remove barriers to leisure participation.

Program Description:

Preparation:
Make copies of the Barriers Busters form, one for each pair of participants. Prepare Barriers Busters index cards (see examples).

Introduction:
The purpose of this activity is to help participants identify barriers they have toward leisure, and ways to remove those barriers. Oftentimes we have barriers to our leisure and do not problem solve to remove them so we can enjoy our leisure fully. Ask participants what *barrier* means. Barriers are different forces that inhibit leisure involvement. Ask participants to name two types of leisure barriers (e.g., financial, physical, architectural, lack of skill, attitudinal). Ask participants about leisure barriers they have experienced. Ask them to be specific and to give examples, and ask them what they did to overcome them (if they did anything). Proceed with the activity once participants have a good understanding of the concept of leisure barriers.

Activity Description:
Pass out one Barriers Busters card to each individual. Instruct individuals to find their partners by matching the barrier (Set A) with the examples (Set B).

For example:

Set A of cards	*Set B of cards*
Financial barriers	You want to go to the movies but do not have any money.
Lack of free time	You are working so much you do not take time for leisure.
Lack of leisure skills	You would like to play tennis but do not have the skills.
Physical ability	You have a disability that limits your leisure involvement.
Social skills	You would like to join a service group but are too shy to try.
Lack of knowledge	You do not know where to go for leisure in the community.
Attitude (self)	You do not value your leisure enough to plan for it.
Lack of leisure partners	You would like to go to the movies but do not know anyone.
Architectural barriers	You would like to go to a restaurant and it is not accessible.
Attitude (others)	You want to go skiing and your family does not think you should take the risk.

After each person has found a partner, give each set of partners one Barriers Busters work sheet and a pencil. The partners are to complete the work sheet together. Allow 10 to 15 minutes for completion.

Ask the partners to share their answers with the group for discussion. The leader should facilitate the discussion through asking questions such as those in the following debriefing section. Close with a summary of the purpose of the activity and what participants have learned.

Debriefing Questions:
1. How many of you experience similar barriers in your leisure?
2. What are some examples of the leisure barriers you have experienced?
3. What are some alternatives you came up with to offset the barrier?
4. What are some follow-up actions you would need to take?
5. What are ways to problem solve around barriers?
6. How much does a person's attitude affect being able to overcome barriers to leisure?
7. What is one leisure barrier that you need to face in the next two weeks?
8. What will you do to overcome that barrier? What actions will you need to take?
9. How can you use what you have learned in this activity in the future?

Leadership Considerations:
1. Be prepared to give an example, perhaps from personal experience.
2. Mention to participants that all individuals experience barriers to their leisure at one time or another.

Variations:
1. Change the content to meet the needs and interests of the participants.

Creator: Jennifer Harz-Morgan, CTRS, Elmhurst Memorial Hospital, Elmhurst, Illinois.

Barriers Busters

Leisure Barrier:

Leisure Barrier Situation:

Personal Barrier Similar to Above Situation:

Alternatives to the Barrier:

Actions to Implement the Alternatives:

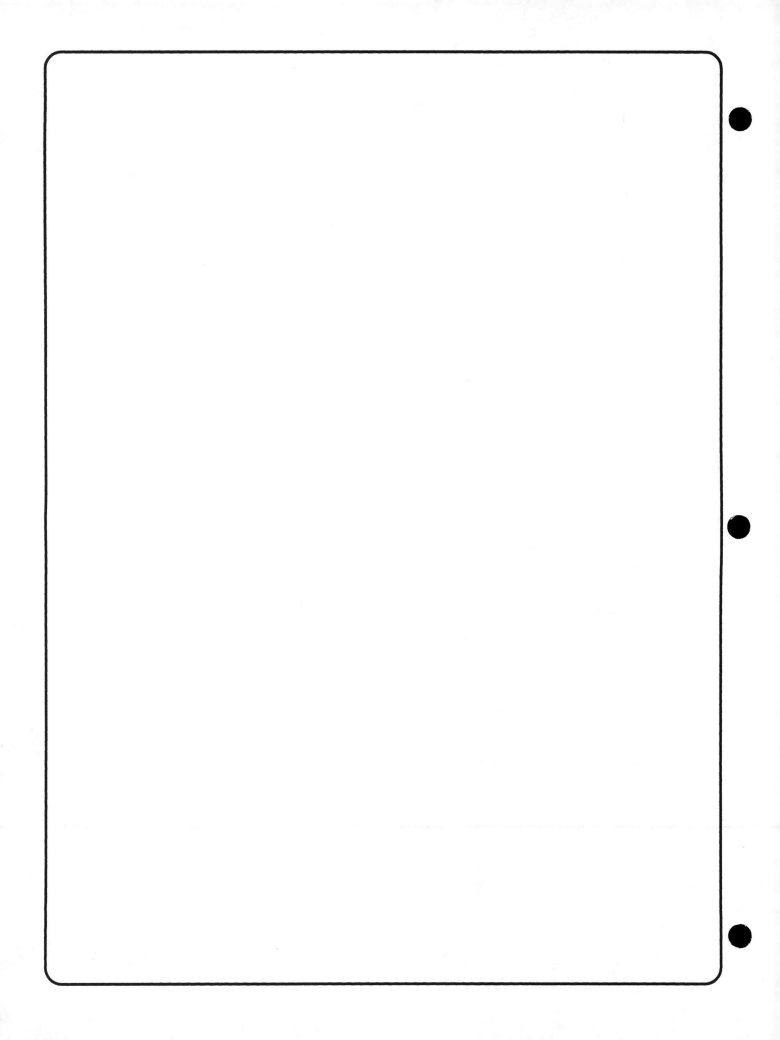

Excuses, Excuses

Space Requirements: Classroom or activity room

Equipment/Resource Requirements: Accompanying form, pencils

Group Size: Small group

Program Goals:
1. To increase participants' ability to identify personal leisure barriers.
2. To increase participants' leisure awareness.
3. To increase participants' personal understanding of leisure.

Program Description:

Preparation:
Copy Excuses, Excuses form, one for each participant.

Introduction:
Emphasize to individuals the goals of this exercise—to promote introspection and honesty with self. Discuss how personal attitudes and perceptions affect leisure choices and involvement.

Activity Description:
Hand out forms and pencils to each individual. Participants are instructed to think about what excuses they use to not participate fully in leisure. They are to place a check mark by those excuses they use most often. Allow about 10 minutes for completion.

Discussion centers on what excuses are used most frequently by the participants, to not participate fully in leisure (or life!). Focus on how to overcome these perceived barriers and how to make purposeful decisions.

Debriefing Questions/Closure:
Discussion may focus on (a) how internal barriers affect their personal lifestyles, (b) development of healthy attitudes toward leisure, and (c) how to empower individuals to change current leisure lifestyles.

1. Which excuse do you use the most?
2. In what ways are your answers similar to or different from the other participants?
3. Which are honest reasons and which are just excuses or "self-created" barriers?
4. What would you need to change or eliminate this barrier?
5. Where would you start? What actions could you take?
6. What effect would eliminating this excuse have on your leisure?

Leadership Considerations:
1. Prior to completing Excuses, Excuses form, a discussion may be held to increase understanding of barriers.

Variations:

1. This form may be used for a variety of situations and individuals. The focus is primarily on the decisions one makes, either consciously or unconsciously, and how this affects what he or she does in leisure and life.
2. This may be the first activity in a series about self-awareness and leisure attitudes.

Creator: Angela Rice, CTRS, St. Peters, Missouri, and Janine Roe, CTRS, Granite City, Illinois.

Excuses, Excuses

Directions: Place a check mark beside each excuse you have used.

1. I don't have enough time.   _____

2. I need a baby-sitter.   _____

3. I don't have enough money.   _____

4. I don't know where to go.   _____

5. I don't know what to do.   _____

6. I don't have anyone to go with me.   _____

7. The weather is bad.   _____

8. I'm not athletic.   _____

9. I don't have any energy.   _____

10. I don't know how to play.   _____

11. I don't want to look foolish.   _____

12. I'm not creative.   _____

13. I don't have the equipment.   _____

14. I don't have transportation.   _____

15. I can't . . .   _____

Other Excuses

16. _____   _____

17. _____   _____

18. _____   _____

19. _____   _____

20. _____   _____

21. _____   _____

22. _____   _____

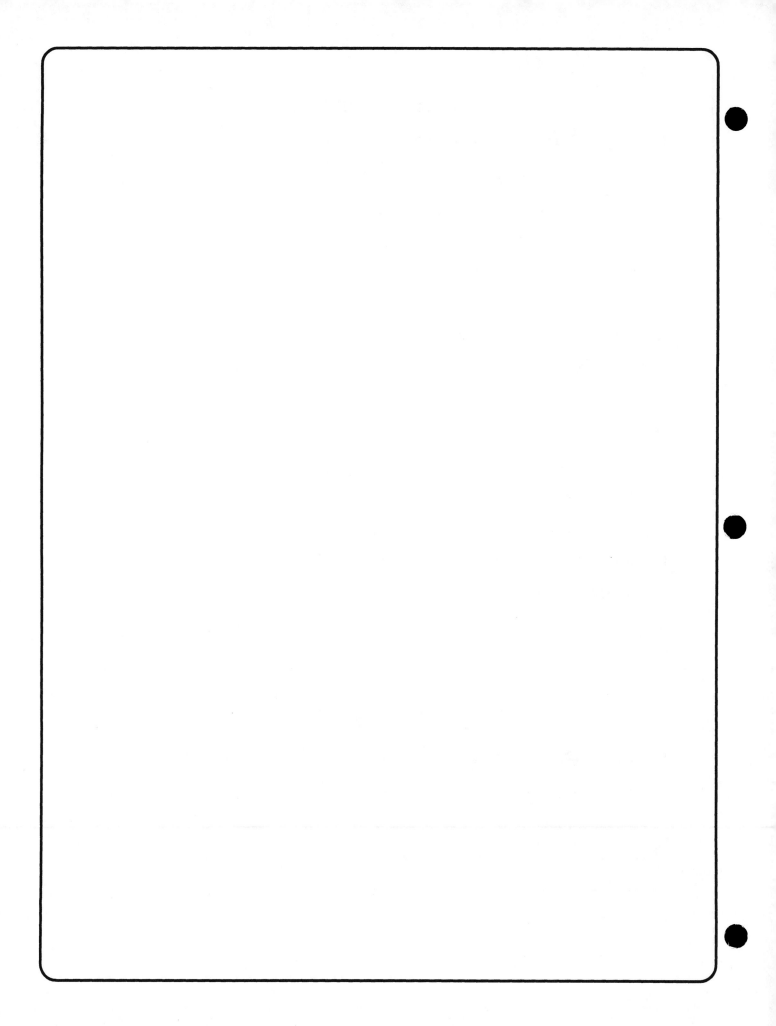

Luck of the Draw

Space Requirements: Classroom or activity room

Equipment/Resource Requirements: Tag board (cut into three-by-five-inch squares), flip chart or chalkboard, assorted bills or play money

Group Size: Small group

Program Goals:
1. To improve participants' awareness of leisure barriers related to participation in community leisure activities.
2. To identify strategies for overcoming personal leisure barriers to participation in community leisure activities.

Program Description:

Preparation:

Before activity, prepare the Luck of the Draw leisure barrier cards (see examples).

Cut poster board into three-by-five-inch rectangles—cut enough so that you have at least one card for each person in the group.

Type or write on each card one leisure barrier that could happen before or during participation in a community leisure activity, that is appropriate to the population with which you are working. For example, "You find out that you have no transportation to the activity you were going to participate in" or "You find out that the price of admission or fee to the leisure activity that you want to participate in is $2 more than you have."

Write a variety of community activities and their respective costs on the chalkboard or flip chart.

Introduction:

Introduce the idea of barriers to leisure by explaining what a barrier is (for example, a barrier is something that stops you or holds you back from doing a leisure activity). Ask each participant to identify two barriers to leisure participation in a specific leisure activity. Barriers may fall into the categories of money, transportation, social situations, or time constraints. For example:

> You want to go to a movie. You look in the newspaper and find out that the movie you want to see is at Timberlyne Theater at 1:20. The matinee costs $3.50. Your friend Jennifer says that she will go with you. However, your parents cannot take you.

In this example transportation is the leisure barrier. The purpose of this activity is to increase participants' awareness of barriers to leisure that they may face, and to develop strategies or alternatives for dealing with those barriers as they arise.

Activity Description:

Give each participant a predetermined amount of play money.

Ask each participant to choose a leisure activity from the chalkboard or flip chart in which he or she would like to participate. The specialist is the money manager. Ask the participants to pay the cost of their chosen activity with their play money, to demonstrate monetary costs of the activity.

One at a time, ask them to come to the front of the room and draw a Luck of the Draw card. Have the participant read the card aloud and verbally explain what implications the barrier has on the leisure activity choice that he or she has made. Does it affect him or her financially, socially, or transportation wise.

Discuss with the participant alternatives to, or strategies for overcoming his or her leisure barrier. Are there other options from which to choose? Can an alternative plan be created? Is there a way to get around this leisure barrier?

Close with a discussion of the purpose and goals of this activity, including the following debriefing questions.

Debriefing Questions/Closure:
1. Do you have leisure barriers in your life similar to the ones discussed?
2. How do you usually handle a leisure barrier?
3. How do you feel when a leisure barrier stops you from doing the leisure activity that you have chosen?
4. What are some positive ways to overcome leisure barriers?

Leadership Considerations:
1. Model or talk through a leisure barrier card before the participants do it so that they know the process. Have an example prepared ahead of time.
2. Give suggestions of alternatives and strategies to use to overcome or deal with leisure barriers.

Variations:
1. Ask the participants to come up with a list of their own leisure interest activities and respective barriers from which to choose.

Creator: Jennifer Laughrun, University of North Carolina at Chapel Hill, Chapel Hill, North Carolina.

Luck of the Draw

You find out that you have no transportation to your activity.	Your friend gets sick and cannot go with you.
You lose money on the way to the activity.	What you have chosen to do for leisure is at the same time as your dentist appointment.
It is a holiday and the place you are going to is closed.	The price of admission or fee to play is $2 more than you have.
Your activity starts at 7:00. It is 6:45 now and your parent said that you cannot go until your homework is finished. You have 25 minutes worth of homework left.	You cannot find anyone who wants to go with you to the activity you have chosen.

Luck of the Draw

You are not sure exactly where the place is that you need to go to do the activity you have chosen.

Your best friend calls and wants you to do something else.

The activity that you are going to lasts until 10:00. Your parents say that you have to be home before 9:30.

You get into trouble and find out that you can't go to the activity that you have chosen.

You forgot what time you are supposed to be there and what you need.

Diamond in the Rough

Space Requirements: Classroom or activity room

Equipment/Resource Requirements: Accompanying form, scissors, pens or pencils

Group Size: Individual or small group

Program Goals:
1. To help participants improve the occurrence of positive thoughts about themselves and their leisure.
2. To help participants decrease negative feelings related to leisure.

Program Description:

Preparation:

Make copies of Diamond in the Rough form, one for each participant.

Introduction:

Discuss with the clients how often it might be easy to focus on the negative instead of the positive. Review the purpose and goals of the activity.

Activity Description:

Give each participant the Diamond in the Rough diagram. Tell the participants that the diamond has rough, jagged edges, just like some people do. In each jagged piece (sections on the outside of the diamond), have the clients write negative things related to their leisure (e.g., negative attitude, lack of motivation, lack of skills). Encourage the participants to think of at least three negative aspects of their leisure (but they all must be true).

After the clients have written their items down, discuss how these negative aspects can be changed into positive behaviors. Focus on solutions and turning negatives into positives.

As positive aspects or solutions are discussed, have each client "cut off" each negative behavior to reach the diamond in the middle.

Close with a discussion of turning negative aspects into positive aspects. Review the purpose and goals of the activity. Use the following debriefing questions.

Debriefing Questions/Closure:
1. Why are the negative things a part of our lives?
2. How can the negative aspects be changed for the positive?
3. In general, what can you do to make your leisure more positive?
4. What is one specific action you are willing to take to make your leisure more positive?
5. In what ways do these negative aspects become barriers to your leisure?

Leadership Considerations:
1. Have work sheets copied ahead of time, and prepare samples of negatives turned into positives.
2. Give examples about the relationship between the uniqueness of each diamond and the individuality of each person.

Variations:
1. Have participants write barriers in the rough edges.
2. The activity and discussion can be directly related to substance abuse.
3. Have participants write down positive behaviors in the middle of the diamond.

Creator: Becky Klein, Illinois State University, Normal, Illinois.

Diamond in the Rough

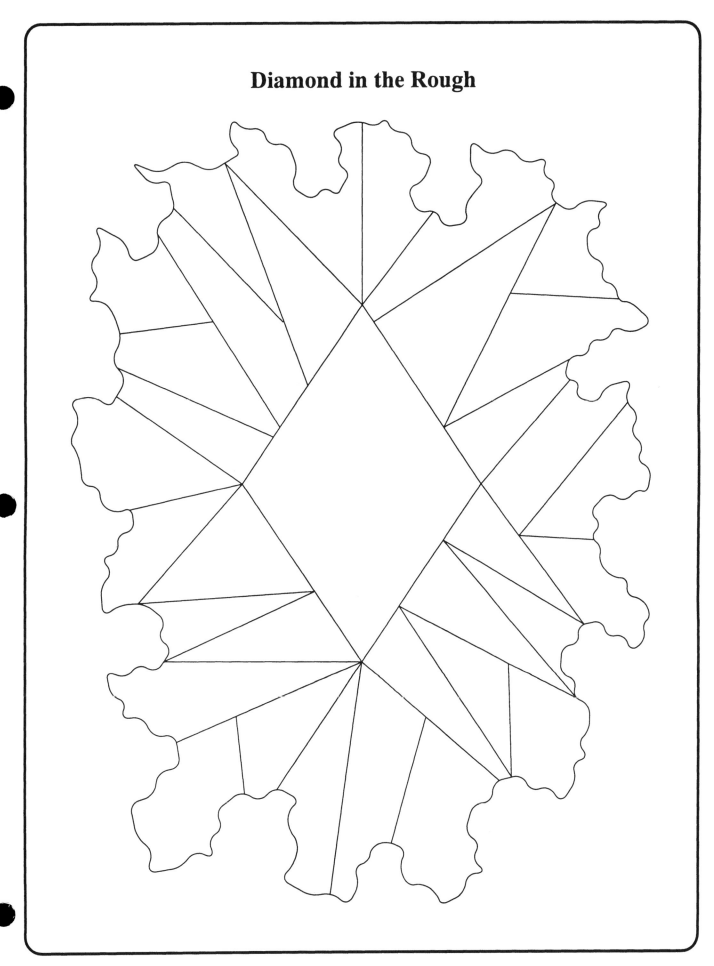

Leisure Benefits Box

Space Requirements: Classroom or activity room

Equipment/Resource Requirements: Shoebox with lid (one for each participant), construction paper, magazines, markers, scissors, glue, several blank slips of paper

Group Size: Small group

Program Goals:
1. To increase participants' ability to follow directions.
2. To increase participants' ability to identify leisure activities that are enjoyable to the participant.
3. To increase participants' ability to identify and describe benefits of activities that are enjoyable to the participant.

Program Description:

Preparation:
Cut several blank slips of paper. Prepare leader's box as example. Prepare boxes and materials for participants.

Introduction:
The tables in the room should be prearranged with the materials in the center of each table. The participants should be asked not to touch the materials on the table until directed to do so. The specialist should have a sample box to show to the group prior to the start of the activity.

Activity Description:
Each participant will be asked to choose a shoebox. The participants are then to use the construction paper to cover the outside of the box so that any writing cannot be seen. The inside of the box should remain open. The lid to the box should then be covered, using the same material, so that any writing cannot be seen. The lid should still fit over the top of the box.

The participants then cut a hole in the center of the lid of the box. The hole should be approximately one-half-inch wide by four-inches long. (The specialist may show the sample box as an example). Holes can also be cut prior to the activity to save some time.

Once the hole has been cut, the participants are asked to spend the next 20 minutes looking through magazines to find images of leisure activities that they enjoy, would like to try, would like to learn, that they like to do with others or by themselves. Once these images are found, the participants may cut the photos out of the magazine. If an image or printed words are not found, the participants may write the activity on the outside of the box.

Once the images have been cut out, the participants may glue the images to the outside of their boxes. After about 20 minutes, the participants need to take a blank slip of paper for each image or word pasted on the outside of the box (15 images = 15 blank slips).

For each of the activities pasted on the outside of the box, the participants must list three benefits of the activity chosen. When the blank slips have been completed, they are placed inside of the box. (If time runs out, participants may complete their blank slips at a later time.)

At the end of the session, the participants are asked to clean their work area, leaving behind the magazines, scissors, glue and construction paper. The participants are asked to bring their boxes to the next group session.

At the next group session participants are asked to choose three activities pasted on the outside of the box. Each participant will read his or her slips of paper to the group, for each of the three activities chosen. When all of the participants have had the opportunity to share, the group will have a discussion about the activity and leisure benefits.

Debriefing Questions/Closure:
1. What types of leisure activities are shown on the outside of your box?
2. What are some benefits of participating in leisure activities?
3. What are some benefits, of the activities you chose, of which you were not aware?
4. How often do you consider the benefits of an activity before deciding to participate?

Leadership Considerations:
1. Leader should have a sample box available while describing the activity.
2. Leader may want to precut the holes in the lids to avoid any potential injuries from working with the scissors.
3. Leader should check with participants frequently during the activity to ensure that the directions are being followed and to answer any questions.
4. Plan on spending two group sessions to complete this activity.

Variations:
1. Participants could create a mural of activities and work as a group to list the benefits of those activities drawn or pasted on the mural.
2. Positive Messages Box—photos of activities enjoyed on outside and positive messages from other group members on inside.
3. Chemical Dependency Box—box divided into two sides, one for barriers to leisure when using and one for benefits of leisure when sober; photos on outside, slips of paper on the inside.

Creator: Theresa M. Connolly, CTRS, Illinois State University, Normal, Illinois.

How Does My Family Play?

Space Requirements: Classroom or activity room

Equipment/Resource Requirements: Accompanying form and pencils or pens

Group Size: Individual or small group

Program Goals:
1. To increase participants' ability to identify past and present leisure activities done with the family.
2. To increase participants' awareness of the benefits of "family play."
3. To increase participants' knowledge of alternative or new leisure activities in which the family may participate in the future.

Program Description:

Preparation:

Make copies of accompanying form, one for each family.

Introduction:

The purpose of this activity is to get the client to interact with his or her family to discuss past and present leisure involvements and potentially new leisure involvements in which the entire family may participate.

Activity Description:

The first step is for the family to discuss and reminisce about past family leisure (e.g., past vacations, family gatherings, family outings). Help families focus on positive experiences. The family should then list three to five benefits of the activities discussed.

The same process is carried out for the present leisure activities of the family, again focusing on the positive and listing three to five benefits of the activities discussed.

At this point, the family must look at the activities named and the benefits listed, and look for a common theme in the leisure activities and the benefits (examples of activity themes: focus on aquatic activities, participate in team sports as a family, enjoy traveling; examples of benefits: learned more about each other, increased fitness, had fun, learned about another part of the country).

Once common themes in leisure activities and benefits have been identified, the family should discuss new methods and activities in which to participate that carry the same themes.

The last step of this activity is to encourage the family to continue to discuss new alternatives for leisure, as a family, and to explore new resources to carry out any type of family leisure planning.

Debriefing Questions/Closure:
1. How did this activity assist in identifying past and present leisure activities of the family?
2. How did this activity help to increase your awareness of the importance of family play?
3. What benefits did you find in your family's leisure?
4. How did this activity increase your knowledge of alternative leisure activities?

Leadership Considerations:
1. Families may sometimes learn from negative experiences, but monitor the family interactions so they remain positive in identifying activities and benefits.
2. Be prepared with suggestions for alternative activities and methods for the family to consider.
3. It may be beneficial for the family to write down past and present activities so the common theme may be more easily found.

Variations:
1. This activity could be done with siblings, following the same idea.
2. Each family member could write down what he or she feels the common leisure theme might be and then compare notes and see if the family agrees on the common leisure theme. If there is disagreement, ask the family to discuss the differing opinions.
3. The family may reminisce by using family photo albums or souvenirs. This approach may also make the common leisure theme more evident.

Creator: Theresa M. Connolly, CTRS, Illinois State University, Normal, Illinois.

How Does My Family Play?

1. What were some leisure activities or events in which your family participated in the past?

_____

_____

2. What were some of the benefits? What were the good things about participating as a family?

_____

_____

3. What are some leisure activities or events in which your family currently participates together?

_____

_____

4. What are some of the benefits? What are the good things about participating as a family?

_____

_____

5. What are some common themes among the family's past and current activities?

_____

_____

6. What are some common benefits from participating in past and current activities?

_____

_____

7. How can you get these same benefits from other activities?

_____

_____

8. What plans do you need to make in the near future for your family's leisure?

_____

_____

I'll Be There

Space Requirements: Classroom or activity room

Equipment/Resource Requirements: Marker, poster-size paper divided into 16 squares. Each square will contain a picture of a leisure activity, such as fishing, dancing, cooking, or riding in a boat.

Group Size: Small group

Program Goals:
1. To increase participants' awareness of making choices among activities.
2. To increase participants' awareness of others participants' similar or dissimilar interests.
3. To increase participants' awareness of the benefits of leisure participation.

Program Description:
Preparation:
Prepare poster board with either drawn pictures or those cut from magazines.

Introduction:
Explain to the group that the pictures drawn on the board are activities to do and places to go. Each person will be asked to look at the pictures and decide in which activity he or she would most like to participate.

Activity Description:
Begin by asking one participant, "In which of these activities would you most like to participate?" He or she then chooses a picture, thereby indicating a preferred activity and/or location. Write this participant's name in the square so the choice is recorded.

Ask the participant why he or she chose that picture to explore the benefits of participating (e.g., fun, relaxation). (The specialist may choose to write benefits on the poster board below each activity picture.)

The next participant repeats this process of selecting an activity, and naming the benefits of participation.

Different participants may choose the same picture as someone else on subsequent turns (as this will encourage discussions about similarities and differences among the participants), but each individual must choose a new activity on each round of play.

The activity continues as such with each participant getting an equal number of turns in the time allotted.

Debriefing Questions/Closure:
1. Why did you choose one activity over another?
2. What can you gain by discovering something in common with someone else?
3. Is it OK if you and your friends like to do different things?
4. Why might you want to try some different things once in a while?
5. Why is it good to have some favorite activities?
6. What were common benefits of leisure participation named by the group?

Leadership Considerations:
1. The specialist may wish to save time at the end of the activity to briefly review the participants' choices, e.g., similarities, differences, pictures that were not chosen.
2. Be sure to explain that there are obviously many more things to do than those in the drawn pictures, but for this activity, these will be the only ones used.
3. The specialist may wish to explain the pictures and activities to the group members to make sure they know what they represent. However, if not specifically explained, a picture may be left open to different interpretations which could prove interesting.

Variations:
1. Instead of choosing among separate and different pictures, create one large picture scene in which there are different areas and activities.
2. Discuss the positive aspects of doing the activities both independently and with others.
3. Examine the availability of the activities, i.e., how often the participants get to do them.

Creator: Tim Leer, West Central Human Service Center, Bismarck, North Dakota.

Leaves of Change

Space Requirements: Classroom or activity room

Equipment/Resource Requirements: Construction paper, scissors, markers, masking tape, relaxation music, tape player, accompanying form

Group Size: Small group

Program Goals:
1. To increase participants' awareness of personal change.
2. To help participants explore healthy coping skills through leisure activity.
3. To increase participants' self-awareness.

Program Description:

Preparation:
Cut leaves out of yellow*, orange*, red*, and green† construction paper. Make enough leaves for the whole group: average five green leaves per client. Cut a large tree, about five feet tall, with bare branches, from the brown construction paper. Tape the tree to the wall. Copy off the accompanying Leaves of Change form.

Introduction:
Discuss the positive aspects of personal change, the resistance to change, and the ability to adapt. Encourage the group members to begin examining their need for personal change to enhance their well-being. Review the purpose and goals of the activity.

Activity Description:
Hand each client the Leaves of Change form.

Read through the page together. When the group gets to the part where it says "Let's view ourselves as a tree beginning to change" have the clients assume a comfortable position and close their eyes. Turn on some relaxing music and use this part as a guided imagery exercise. Have them visualize their changes.

After completion have them open their eyes and encourage them at this time to list at least three changes they need to make at the present time. Hand each client five yellow, orange or red leaves and five green leaves. Write each personal change on a yellow, orange or red leaf. When that is complete, have the clients tape their leaves on the wall as if they were falling off the tree.

For each of the changes, have clients think of a healthy way or alternative to help deal with the change. (There could be more than one healthy alternative for each personal change, e.g., Personal Change: I want to lose weight; Healthy Alternatives: eat better, exercise, increase my activity level.) Write each healthy alternative on a green leaf.

Tape the green leaves on the branches near the appropriate personal change leaves (e.g., tape the green leaves that say eat better, exercise, and increase activity level by the leaf that states I need to lose weight).

Each client then proceeds to explain his or her leaves of change and alternatives.

---

*The multicolored leaves represent the change (as they fall off the tree).
†The green leaves represent growth (sprouting new healthy habits to overcome the personal change).

155

Debriefing Questions/Closure:
1. Are the changes you have identified realistic?
2. What did you learn from this activity?
3. Could you relate to the Leaves of Change story?
4. Is change hard for you?
5. Are you flexible and adaptable?
6. How can this leisure activity help when it comes to overcoming personal change?

Leadership Considerations:
1. Focus on healthy leisure time outlets throughout the activity to help clients become more aware of the therapeutic value of leisure.
2. Give examples of personal change to initiate activity, if needed.
3. Participants may need assistance. If they do, a buddy system may be helpful.

Creator: Shelley A. Vaughan, CTRS, St. John's Hospital, Springfield, Illinois.

Leaves of Change

As I look out the window . . . I see the leaves on the trees beginning to change. Change is all around us . . . at all times. It's not always noticeable but it is there.

The leaves changing colors paint a pretty picture. As they change colors, the trees shed their beauty one by one. Providing a blanket of beauty all around.

The trees will eventually be bare and will begin to accept the change of season. Winter is around the corner and the trees are ready. They've learned to survive and adapt to the changes.

But have you ever noticed there's always that one leaf that the tree wants to hold on to? The tree doesn't seem to want to let it go. Maybe it's not ready for the change. However, in the end, the tree gains the courage to let go. The tree was not afraid—it just had to take time to think about the changes ahead. It had to be sure . . . that it was the right time. The change was going to happen whether the tree let go or not . . . and the tree realized this. Sometimes there is not much control over changes. It just happens.

Trees go through changes every year. It becomes routine to them. They survive the changes and accept them. It's part of their life. They know in the spring they will sprout new leaves.

It's a new beginning . . . they'll continue to grow.

We face changes throughout our lives. We grow from the changes and the changes make us stronger. We're able to survive . . . and grow.

When we face changes there are reasons. We cannot always predict when these changes will occur. As with the trees . . . they change with the seasons. With us, we face changes almost on a daily basis. Some changes are easier to accept and deal with compared to others. Major life changes become more complicated.

Let's view ourselves as a tree beginning to change. . . .

It's time for us to face some changes within our lives. Our leaves begin to change colors. We let each leaf go one by one. They scatter themselves around us. We notice the beauty (or lack of beauty) that has been a part of our lives. There are some changes we need to make in order to maintain or restore the beauty. We may feel bare without the security of our leaves . . . but we need to find the strength to get through these changes. We may hesitate to let go of that last leaf. However, we'll take our time to think about our future. We'll build up our courage to go on with the changes. During the hesitation we'll explore our alternatives that will enable us to adjust and make the changes in our lives.

We finally let go . . . knowing we'll grow. We're looking forward to restoring (or maintaining) the beauty and harmony in our lives. We'll face the hard winter . . . and wait for the spring. As we accept our changes and use our alternatives—we'll sprout new leaves.

A new beginning. . . . Time to grow once more.

When it's time to face change once again . . . we'll shed our leaves . . . adjust and explore . . . and continue to grow. It will become our routine in life.

If we choose to ignore the changes that need to be made in our lives . . . we will not grow. Our leaves will fall off and we'll remain bare. We'll see the pieces of our lives scattered around us. We will not sprout a new set of leaves . . . until we welcome and accept the changes . . . and seek out the alternatives to help us through to make these changes.

Questions to Think About:
1. What changes do you need to make in your life? Make a list of them.
2. List alternatives to explore. How will these alternatives enable you to deal with these changes? List alternatives for each change you want to make.

Leaves of Change

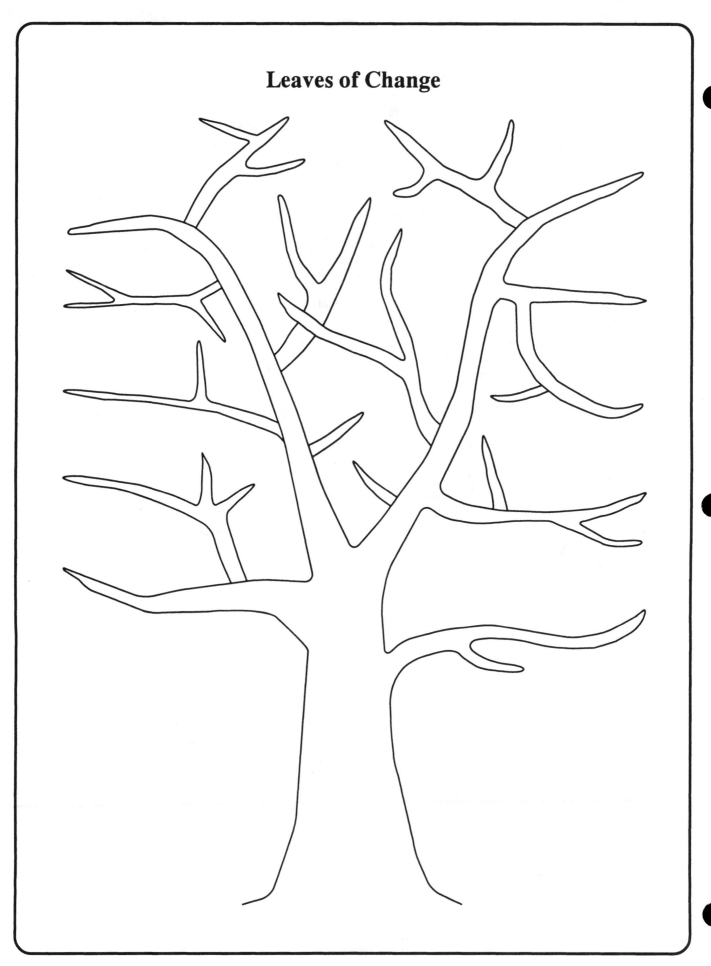

Calendar Day

Space Requirements: Classroom or activity room (with large table or floor area)

Equipment/Resource Requirements: Large paper (wall size), markers or paint, tape, open wall space or bulletin board

Group Size: Small group

Program Goals:
1. To increase participants' awareness of personal leisure schedule.
2. To increase participants' awareness of the leisure schedules of others in the group.
3. To encourage support within a group in terms of leisure activity.

Program Description:

Preparation:
See activity description below.

Introduction:
This activity is designed to provide a means in which participants can identify a personal leisure schedule as well as an awareness of leisure activities participated in by others. Participants are to work together to construct the actual calendar and contribute individually to the content of the calendar. Prior to the beginning of the activity, participants should be made aware of the purpose and goals of the activity.

Activity Description:
At the beginning of each month, group participants should jointly prepare the outline of a large calendar. The calendar should contain days, dates (numbers), and the month name. Individuals should be asked to work as a team to complete this portion of the activity.

When the first section of the activity is complete, the group is asked to participate in a discussion to identify activities in which to participate during the following week. The activity facilitator records the activities submitted by the participants. These activities can be active or passive activities, can relate to their treatment or personal goals, and can apply to either inside or outside the facility, depending on the program or group. This discussion allows individuals to become familiar with their own leisure schedule and with the schedule of others.

Following the discussion, the individuals are asked to write the dates important to them on the calendar. The activity facilitator can assist in reminding participants of activities mentioned during the discussion. After all group members have written on the calendar, a second discussion closes the activity.

Debriefing Questions/Closure:
1. What kinds of events were important enough to put on the calendar? Why are these events important?
2. How do things important to you differ from those that others identified?
3. How can group members support other members knowing these schedules?
4. How can you be held responsible for the items that you submitted to the calendar?
5. How can others assist you in attaining those things that you identified as important?
6. What new things did you learn about yourself through this activity?
7. How can individuals be recognized for accomplishing the items on the calendar?
8. How well did we meet the goals for this activity?

Leadership Considerations:
1. It is suggested that participants write activities on the calendar one at a time. The calendar is large, but participants may be more aware of others if they do not participate all at one time.
2. Participants may want to write their names by their activities. This makes it easier for individuals to identify their own important activities as well as to support the activities of others. In addition, participants are held more responsible for important items that are identified by their names.
3. Be sure to always include new participants on the calendar, as soon as they enter the group. The point of the activity is to provide the participants with group support, so all participants in the group need to be included.

Variations:
1. Activities for an entire month may be difficult for participants to remember or be aware of all at one time. If this is the case, the calendar outline can be made at the beginning of the month, and activities added weekly by the group.
2. As participants attain activities or goals on the calendar, a "ceremony" of achievement can be conducted at the beginning of each group session. This reminds participants of the goals that they have, and also provides recognition from the group for those individuals who have attained their goals.

Creator: Nikki Colba Harder, CTRS, Illinois State University, Normal, Illinois.

Stress Buster Ball

Space Requirements: Classroom or activity room

Equipment/Resource Requirements: A medium-soft cushioned ball (foam ball), small strips of paper, soft foam or padded bat, small container, masking tape, paper, pencils, markers, $8\frac{1}{2}$-by-14-inch sheets of paper

Group Size: Small group

Program Goals:
1. To increase participants' understanding of how physical activity can help relieve stress.
2. To help patients identify personal stressors and recognize leisure activity as a healthy outlet.
3. To promote fun and enjoyment through leisure participation and activity.

Program Description:

Preparation:
Make a home plate (using the masking tape to make an outline for the home plate) at one end of a hallway or open space. Approximately 15 to 20 feet from the home plate, use the masking tape to place a horizontal line across the hallway or open space to serve as the point line. Tape a white sheet of paper on a wall and write "Stress Busters" on the left side of the paper. On the right side of the paper, write "Stress Booster." These are the scoring sheets. The participants will play on the Stress Busters team and the group leader is the Stress Booster team.

Introduction:
Begin the group activity by discussing stress, both its detrimental effects and its benefits. Focus on how negative stress causes difficulty or impedes a person's level of functioning if not relieved in an effective manner.

Activity Description:
After the introduction and discussion, explain the rules of the game. Distribute five slips of paper to each participant. Have each participant write down five personal stressors that are causing him or her difficulty—one per piece of paper.

Fold the slips of paper in half and place them in the container. All of the participants are on the Stress Busters team. The group leader is the only player on the Stress Booster team.

Select one slip of paper from the container and read the stressor out loud. The participant who wrote that particular stressor is the batter. Have that participant go to home plate.

Encourage the participant who is the batter to visualize the ball as his or her stressor and focus on the feeling it represents rather than the stressor itself.

The goal for the batter is to hit the ball (stressor) over the point line. The group leader pitches the ball to the batter. If the ball (stressor) goes over the line, the Stress Busters get a point. If not, the Stress Booster gets the point.

The batter has three tries to hit the ball (stressor). Use the "three strikes you're out" rule. Repeat the procedure until time allowed is up or until all stressors have been used. Allow 45 to 60 minutes for completion of activity.

Close with group discussion, including the following debriefing questions.

Debriefing Questions/Closure:
1. Name at least three therapeutic benefits of this activity.
2. How much was the physical aspect of this activity beneficial to you?
3. How did it feel to "hit" your stressors away, even temporarily?
4. How important is physical release to stress management?
5. What are positive ways (versus negative ways) to relieve stress?

Leadership Considerations:
1. During the introduction and closing discussions, give examples of physical activities.
2. Give suggestions about where to go for these activities.

Variations:
1. Use tennis balls to knock down targets. The targets represent the stressors.

Creator: Shelley A. Vaughan, CTRS, St. John's Hospital, Springfield, Illinois.

Family Leisure Go Fish

Space Requirements: Classroom or activity room

Equipment/Resource Requirements: Pencils or markers, three-by-five-inch index cards (at least 10 for each participant)

Group Size: Small group

Program Goals:
1. To increase participants' ability to identify family, individual, and shared leisure activity skills.
2. To increase participants' awareness of the importance of family involvement.
3. To encourage leisure activity skill participation within the family.

Program Description:
Preparation:
Gather necessary materials.

Introduction:
This activity provides a means in which both the client and family can identify leisure activity skills that they can participate in together. It provides insight for both the client and the family as to needs and wishes of both parties. Prior to the beginning of the activity, it is important that the facilitator explain the differences between traditional and nontraditional leisure skill activities. Traditional activities are those such as baseball, volleyball, and checkers, and nontraditional activities are those such as reading the newspaper, watching television, and listening to the radio.

Activity Description:
Each family member who is present in the group, including the client, is given at least 10 index cards. On the index cards, the family members are to write an activity (either traditional or nontraditional) in which they participate. All index cards are placed into a deck and shuffled. The cards are redealt to participants.

The game is played similarly to the game "Go Fish"—one participant says "Do you have a 'Read The Newspaper' card?" to the participant on his or her right. If the participant asked has a match, that activity is set aside.

If the participant does not have a match, the card is open to other participants until the match is found (if there is one). If no match is found, that player sets that card aside and no longer plays with it.

The game continues in this fashion until at least three matches are found. When the three matches have been found, the family decides which of the three activities to participate in at the close of the game. This activity should be one that at least one family member plus the client matched on.

Debriefing Questions/Closure:
1. Did you realize that you had these activities in common with your family members?
2. Were you aware of the different leisure activity choices you had available to you?
3. What did you learn new about your family members through this activity?
4. What new leisure skills did you learn about?
5. During the course of the game, did you become aware of new leisure skills that you would like to begin participating in?
6. How can this activity improve your family involvement in leisure activities?

Leadership Considerations:
1. Have suggestions prepared in case none of the cards match between family members. If this does happen, suggest that the members decide on one activity out of the ones that are written down. Chances are there is something in that list that the participant and the family can enjoy together, even if they were not initially identified.
2. It is very important that the participants know the differences between traditional and nontraditional leisure activity skills. Before the activity begins, it may be helpful to provide examples and have the participants provide examples as well. Remind them that activity skills do not necessarily mean baseball and bowling, they can mean everyday leisure activities.
3. When the participants choose an activity to participate in at the close of the session, suggest that it be a nontraditional activity that can be carried out in the facility or with facility resources. Again, baseball or bowling may be a difficult on-the-spot activity, although it can be planned for a later date. The important thing is that an activity does actually get carried out.

Variations:
1. Instead of leisure activity skills, the cards could be made for leisure resources or related activities or items needed for that activity.
2. This could be an activity used for planning outings, or for decision-making skill improvement or assistance. In a group setting, individuals could discover what activities they have in common, assisting in the making of a group decision.

Creator: Nikki Colba Harder, CTRS, Illinois State University, Normal, Illinois.

Social Skills Activities

How I Feel

Space Requirements: Classroom or activity room

Equipment/Materials: Accompanying form, pens or pencils

Size of Group: Small group

Program Goals:
1. To increase participants' ability to identify how they feel in different social situations.
2. To provide a framework in which participants can discuss differences in social comfortability.

Program Description:
Preparation:
Make copies of How I Feel form, one for each participant.

Introduction:
The purpose of this activity is to provide a structure so that participants can discuss when they feel comfortable and uncomfortable; and identify those skills they may wish to work on. Begin with a discussion of how individuals differ in their comfort level in various social situations. Have participants identify situations in which they do and do not feel comfortable.

Activity Description:
Give each individual a copy of the How I Feel form and a pencil. Instruct the group members that they are to complete the form honestly and that they can share whatever answers they feel comfortable sharing with the group.

Allow five minutes for completion.

Discuss the group's answers, either one question at a time, or within the categories. Help individuals note differences and similarities between their answers.

Refocus the group on the purpose of the activity, and close with discussion and debriefing questions.

Discussion/Debriefing Questions:
1. In what areas were you least comfortable?
2. How did your answers differ from others in the group?
3. How does one go about learning to become more comfortable in some of these situations?
4. How are social skills learned?
5. What can you do to help increase your comfort level?

Leadership Considerations:
1. Know the survey well enough to be able to facilitate an in-depth discussion.
2. Have some examples ready to guide participants in the discussion.

Variations:
1. Print the survey on a large poster board and discuss each question one at a time.
2. Use the questions as discussion items, and do not have participants complete the written survey.
3. Use this activity as an introduction to a social skills instruction series. In the next session(s) teach participants the skills they need to be more comfortable in social situations.

Creator: Norma J. Stumbo, Ph.D., CTRS, Illinois State University, Normal, Illinois.

How I Feel

Directions: For each statement, rate your level of comfort. Circle the number which represents your reaction to each sentence.

        1 = I feel very uncomfortable   3 = I feel pretty comfortable

        2 = I feel pretty uncomfortable   4 = I feel very comfortable

When I: I feel:	Very Uncomfortable	Pretty Uncomfortable	Pretty Comfortable	Very Comfortable
1. Enter a group of people I know well	1	2	3	4
2. Approach a group of people I don't know well	1	2	3	4
3. Am approached by a stranger	1	2	3	4
4. Say I am glad to meet someone	1	2	3	4
5. Introduce two people to each other	1	2	3	4
6. Agree with what someone in the group is saying	1	2	3	4
7. Disagree with what someone in the group is saying	1	2	3	4
8. Ask someone in the group his or her opinion	1	2	3	4
9. Ask someone in the group to explain what he or she just said	1	2	3	4
10. Ask someone in the group to talk about himself or herself	1	2	3	4
11. Am asked to talk about myself	1	2	3	4
12. Make suggestions about things to do	1	2	3	4
13. Express my own opinion	1	2	3	4
14. Summarize what someone in the group has said	1	2	3	4
15. Try to settle an argument between two people	1	2	3	4
16. Express constructive criticism to someone in a group	1	2	3	4
17. Hear constructive criticism from someone else	1	2	3	4
18. Am being teased by someone in a group	1	2	3	4
19. Try to express my thoughts to a group	1	2	3	4
20. Try to express my feelings to a group	1	2	3	4
21. Share a personal experience with a group	1	2	3	4
22. Tell a funny story or joke	1	2	3	4

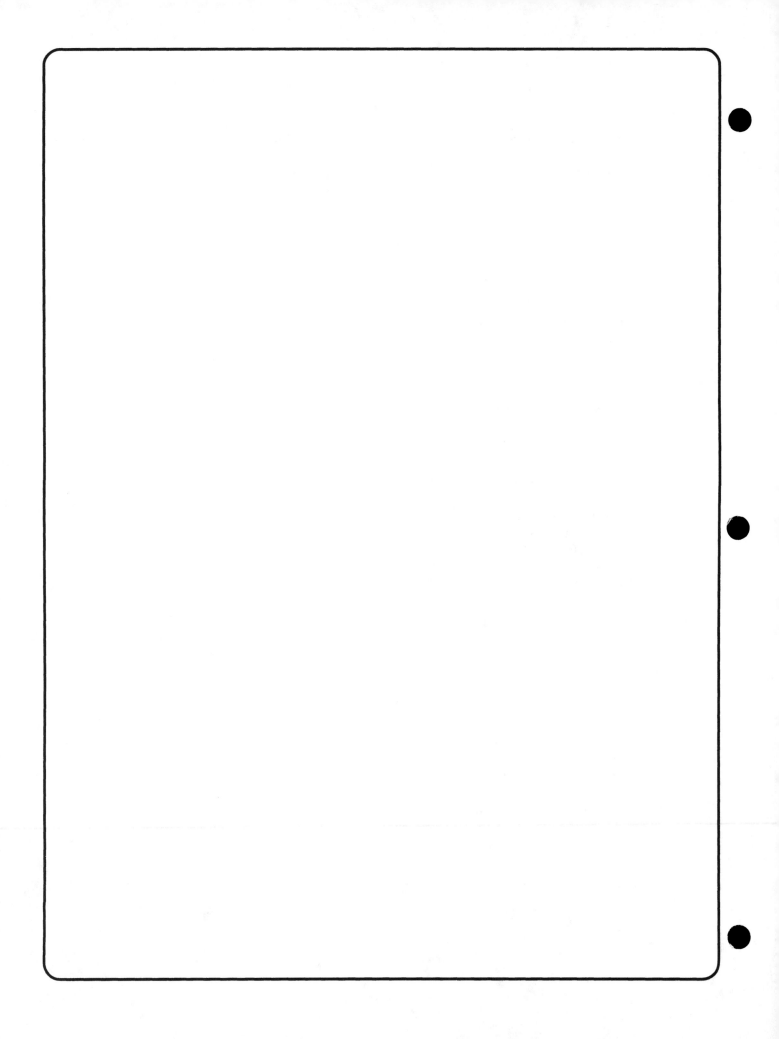

The Look of Emotions

Space Requirements: Classroom or activity room

Equipment/Resource Requirements: Drawing paper, markers, words of emotion, accompanying form

Group Size: Small group

Program Goals:
1. To increase participants' ability to recognize words of emotion.
2. To increase participants' ability to transfer an emotion into a drawing.
3. To increase participants' ability to identify various methods of coping with emotions.

Program Description:
Preparation:
Prepare cards with emotions written on them (see accompanying list). Gather materials.

Introduction:
The purpose of this activity is to teach participants to identify how varying emotions may look and to discuss ways to cope with those emotions. Review this purpose and the goals with the participants before starting the activity.

Activity Description:
Participants will be seated in a circle. The specialist will distribute drawing paper and markers to each participant. The specialist will display a word such as "anger" and ask the participants to draw a picture of how anger looks. A list of emotions is provided on the accompanying form.

Following the completion of each drawing, each participant will explain what he or she has drawn. This process is repeated three times, each time with a new word.

Ask participants to identify similarities and differences between participants' drawings. Are colors, strokes, faces, images the same or different?

Following the completion of the activity, the specialist may ask the participants to name other emotions. For each emotion, ask participants how they cope with that emotion, either positively or negatively. What are better ways which participants can use to cope with strong emotions—especially those that are negative? What ways work best for the participants?

Review the purpose and goals of the activity with participants. Use the following debriefing questions for closure. (Participants may need a more definitive follow-up activity on distinct methods—such as deep breathing, counting to 10, thinking positive thoughts—to cope with strong emotions.)

Debriefing Questions/Closure:
1. What are some strong positive emotions?
2. What are some strong negative emotions?
3. What are physical signs that you are experiencing a strong emotion?
4. How do you currently react or cope with strong emotions?
5. What are some alternative methods that may be more positive when coping with emotions?
6. How can you use what you have learned in this activity in the future?

Leadership Considerations:
1. Use a variety of positive and negative emotions.
2. Allow enough time for each participant to complete his or her drawing before beginning the discussion of each emotion.
3. Allow for questions and be prepared to define some of the emotions depending on the population.

Variations:
1. Using a chalkboard or mural paper, have participants draw on the same surface, step back and discuss the images drawn by everyone.
2. Play the activity following the idea of "Win, Lose or Draw." The participants are placed on teams and the teammates must guess the emotion being drawn on the board.
3. The participants can take turns facilitating the activity and creating own list of emotional words.

Creator: Theresa M. Connolly, CTRS, Illinois State University, Normal, Illinois.

The Look of Emotions

Joy	Hate	Grouchy
Frustration	Love	Puzzled
Sadness	Satisfaction	Pride
Confusion	Grief	Compassion
Happiness	Elation	Amused
Anger	Giddiness	Betrayed
Loneliness	Shyness	Enjoyment
Fear	Boredom	Mistrust

How Do You Feel?

Space Requirements: Classroom or activity room

Equipment/Resource Requirements: Accompanying form cut into slips and put into box

Group Size: Small group

Program Goals:
1. To increase participants' awareness of emotions.
2. To increase participants' ability to identify behaviors related to emotions.
3. To increase participants' ability to identify their own behaviors they would like to change.

Program Description:
Preparation:
Prepare slips of paper from How Do You Feel form, and put into a box or a hat.

Introduction:
Explain to the participants that the purpose of this activity is to help them develop an awareness of their own emotions, and what behaviors they might be exhibiting when they feel a certain way. Discuss how emotions influence our behaviors. Explain the rules of the activity—similar to charades.

Activity Description:
Starting with one participant, each person will draw a slip of paper from the box, and then be given two minutes to act it out in front of the group. The group is to guess what emotion or situation the person is portraying. In this particular version, there are no teams and no points are kept.

As one person acts out the emotion or situation, the other participants are to guess by saying their guess out loud. The leader will decide if the guesses are correct.

As each emotion or situation is guessed, ask the actor how his or her portrayal is different or similar to how he or she would react regularly to this emotion or situation (when not in front of a crowd). Would noticing a difference change the way he or she acts in real life?

Encourage participants to ask questions and be supportive. End with discussion questions and review the goals of the program.

Debriefing Questions/Closure:
1. How did your acting compare to how you act in real life?
2. What did you learn about your emotions?
3. What did you learn about your behaviors?
4. What would you want to change about your behaviors or reactions to emotions?
5. What could you do to change these?
6. How will you use this information in the future?

Leadership Considerations:
1. The leader might need to demonstrate how to act out an emotion.
2. Make sure that the group remains supportive and discusses emotions openly.

Variations:
    1. Change the emotions or situations to relate specifically to the group.
    2. Could be used in one-to-one, if participant was videotaped and the leader played back the tape for the participant to analyze himself or herself.

Creator: Norma J. Stumbo, Ph.D., CTRS, Illinois State University, Normal, Illinois.

How Do You Feel?

You win the game	You feel inadequate
You feel healthy	You are nervous
You lose the game	Someone disagrees with you
You feel tired	You are wrong about some fact
You are involved in leisure	You are recognized for your talents
You feel alone	You help a friend in need
You feel bored	Someone insults you
You withdraw from a crowd	You are trusted with a secret
You feel frustrated	You find out great news
You feel special	You will not admit you are wrong
You feel sad	You feel on top of the world
You feel like crying	You are surprised by a friend
You feel out of control	You feel like everyone is watching
You feel in control	You are embarrassed
You have done something wrong	You feel ashamed
You feel confident	Someone takes credit for your job
You feel controlled by others	You feel explosive
You feel anxious	You feel like no one cares
You receive an unexpected gift	You feel happy
You need to apologize	You feel needed
You are mean to a friend	You feel like a winner
You are late in arriving somewhere	You cannot solve a personal problem
You get great news	You are making good choices
Things do not go your way	You feel capable
You are using	You feel lovable
You argue with a loved one	You feel competent
You are sober	You feel like a success

Emotional Expressions

Space Requirements: Classroom or activity room

Equipment/Resource Requirements: Large pieces of paper (as tall as each participant's body), crayons or markers, tape

Group Size: Small group

Program Goals:
1. To increase participants' ability to identify personal emotions.
2. To increase participants' self-awareness in relation to emotions.
3. To promote appropriate adult interactions.

Program Description:

Preparation:
Gather materials. Place paper on the wall with tape.

Introduction:
The purpose of this activity is to encourage self-awareness through the identification of normal emotions. During this activity, individuals will create themselves using physical and emotional aspects.

Activity Description:
Each participant, at the beginning of the activity, should be paired with an adult staff member. These pairs can be chosen by the participants or may be assigned. Each child then is to choose a paper, already hung on a wall. The children are asked to wiggle at that station until the adult partner verbally stops the action.

When the child is still, the adult partner outlines the child with crayon or marker. After all children have completed the activity to this point, specific directions are given to color *only* the body of the figure, *not* the face. The participants should be given a specific amount of time for this part of the activity, as decided by the program leader.

The remainder of the activity is more specific to the emotional aspect of the individual. Each child is asked to finish the sentence "Most of the time I feel. . . ." The answer to this sentence is the expression to be drawn on the face of the outlined figure. The child also will have a specific amount of time to complete this task.

Upon completion, each participant will be asked to explain the emotion that he or she drew. If the emotion is negative (anger, sadness), the child also should be encouraged to verbalize how this emotion can be made more positive.

This activity helps to identify, for the child and for the specialist, what emotions the individual is familiar with and what emotions are prevalent in the personality of the child. If the individual can identify the negative emotions, then those emotions can be dealt with and transferred to positive ones. This activity can also promote positive interaction between a child and an adult, creating trust and encouragement between the two. Use the following debriefing questions.

Debriefing Questions/Closure:
1. What is the emotion on your face?
2. Is that a positive emotion or a negative one?
3. What makes you feel that way?
4. How can you change that?
5. How can you change the way you react to that?
6. What emotion would you like to see on your face most of the time?
7. What can you do to see that that happens?

Leadership Considerations:
1. During the drawing portion of the activity, the adult partner must be very aware of the child's personal space. If necessary, omit the lines infringing personal space until the child has moved away from the paper.
2. It is sometimes difficult to pinpoint what causes emotions. Gently encourage sharing, keeping in mind that the feelings of children are fragile.
3. This activity works best if the staff to participant ratio is one-to-one.
4. Be careful to use markers that do not stain or color clothing.

Variations:
1. This activity can be done through the eyes of another person. After the participant has been outlined, have another person draw the face, as that person sees the emotion of the individual that he or she is drawing. This can often be a rude awakening for the individual being drawn.
2. This activity can also be completed using comparisons of the original activity and variation 1. This gives a comparison between how the individual sees himself or herself and how others see him or her.
3. In settings dealing with substance abuse, the faces compared could be a "using" face and a "clean" face. This variation can be compared with only that individual or can be viewed through the eyes of others.

Creator: Nikki Colba Harder, CTRS, Illinois State University, Normal, Illinois.

A Little Character

Space Requirements: Classroom or activity room

Equipment/Resources Needed: "Emotions Poster" [sold commercially], chalkboard, chalk, die

Group Size: Small group

Program Goals:
1. To increase participants' awareness of different feelings and what causes them to happen.
2. To increase participants' ability to explore their own feelings in a nonthreatening way.
3. To encourage participants to accept themselves and each other as they are.

Program Description:

Preparation:
Prior to the start of the activity, purchase the "Emotions Poster," and hang on a wall at the front of the room.

Introduction:
Explain that each participant will have a character whose face the leader will draw on the board and that the participant will name. Explain that the "Emotions Poster" will be used to give feelings to each of the characters.

Activity Description:
Select one participant to begin. That participant rolls the die for a number between one and six. The leader starts at the top left of the emotions poster and counts off that number on the chart. The emotion "landed on" is written under the face of the person's character on the chalkboard.

Ask the participant why the character may be experiencing that feeling, e.g., "Why is Dan (the character) feeling angry (the emotion landed on)?" or "What makes Dan feel angry?"

Encourage responses in reference to the character. Also ask what the character could do about that emotion, e.g., "What actions should Dan take when he is angry?"

The activity continues as such with the next participant rolling the die. A new emotion is "landed on" and can be explored. Remind participants to respond in reference to the character, not themselves necessarily.

Close with a discussion that focuses on the goals of the activity, through the use of the following debriefing questions.

Debriefing Questions/Closure:
1. What emotions or feelings have been covered within this group?
2. How many of these emotions have you felt within the last week?
3. Where do these feelings come from?
4. What are some ways we can handle strong emotions?
5. What are the benefits of having emotions?
6. Why is it OK to have emotions and feelings?
7. What did you learn about actions you can take when experiencing an emotion?

Leadership Considerations:
1. Start subsequent turns from the square the first participant reached, so that each feeling is not repeated as often.
2. Refer to each participant's character's name regularly to keep the focus there and to keep the feeling exploration nonthreatening.
3. The character name chosen should not be one that belongs to someone the participant knows.
4. Be prepared for the participant to attribute his or her own feelings and experiences to the character. This provides the opportunity to explore one's own feelings in a nonthreatening manner.
5. Be sure to emphasize through discussion that a person's feelings are OK because they are a part of the person, but that they need to be handled appropriately. Also, each of us should accept ourselves for who we are and accept each other as well.

Variations:
1. Do not use character names. When a feeling is landed on, ask questions like, "Why might someone feel this way?"
2. For groups more comfortable talking about feelings, relate feelings specifically to each participant, e.g., "What might make *you* feel this way?"

Creator: Deland DeCoteau, West Central Human Service Center, Bismarck, North Dakota.

Emotions Charades

Space Requirements: Classroom or activity room

Equipment/Resource Requirements: Accompanying form or cards

Group Size: Small group

Program Goals:
1. To increase participants' understanding of the importance of nonverbal behaviors.
2. To increase participants' ability to express and read nonverbal behaviors of others.

Program Description:
Preparation:
Prepare emotions cards using the Emotion Charades form.

Introduction:
The purpose of this activity is to help participants identify the nonverbal behavior associated with certain feelings and emotions. Begin with a discussion of the importance of expressing emotions and reading the emotions of other people. Discuss the differences between verbal and nonverbal behaviors.

Activity Description:
Ask for two volunteers to get up in front of the group. They are handed a stack of five cards with one emotion written on each one. They are to act out the nonverbal behaviors associated with each emotion, one at a time. They are not allowed to speak. The rest of the group, who are observing, guess what emotion the pair is demonstrating. The pair demonstrates each emotion written on each card until the group guesses the emotions correctly.

Other pairs can volunteer until the stack of emotions cards are finished or time is up.

Discussion focuses on the importance of nonverbal expression of emotions—both expressing and reading these emotions. Suggested discussion questions follow.

Discussion/Debriefing Questions:
1. How difficult was it for the pairs to act out emotions?
2. Which emotions were difficult or easy to act out or to guess?
3. What nonverbal behavior is associated with sad emotions? happy emotions?
4. In what instances is it important to read nonverbal messages of another person?
5. Is it important to make sure verbal and nonverbal messages match?
6. How important is eye contact? posture? arm or leg motions?
7. Describe a recent situation in which you knew someone was angry, pleased, or afraid.

Leadership Considerations:
1. The specialist may group emotions together, such as sad emotions or excited emotions, or have them randomly placed throughout the deck.

Variations:
1. Like charades, a score can be kept.

Creator: Norma J. Stumbo, Ph.D., CTRS, Illinois State University, Normal, Illinois.

Emotions Charades

Anger	Enthusiasm	Fright
Happiness	Disappointment	Loneliness
Sadness	Apprehension	Contentment
Grief	Being Hurt	Respectfulness
Fear	Boredom	Affection
Trust	Dependency	Joy
Rejection	Anxiety	Self-Confidence
Embarrassment	Shame	Elation
Surprise	Nervousness	Kindness
Aggression		Excitement

Anger Envelopes

Space Requirements: Classroom or activity room

Equipment/Materials: Large pieces of construction paper, markers, magazines, glue, tape, scissors

Group Size: Individual or small group

Program Goals:
1. To increase participants' ability to identify situations in which they have become angered.
2. To increase participants' ability to identify negative ways with which they handle anger.
3. To increase participants' ability to identify positive ways with which they could handle anger in the future.

Program Description:

Preparation:
Gather materials needed for activity.

Introduction:
Begin with discussion of anger, when it happens, how participants handle it, and how frequently they experience it. Introduce the activity as one that will help participants identify more positive ways to handle anger than they might have in the past. Review the goals of the activity with the participants before beginning.

Activity Description:
Hand each participant one large piece of construction paper. By folding the paper in half and taping the sides shut, they will make an anger envelope.

Participants will be asked to go through magazines and find words or pictures that depict how they have handled anger in the past. They will cut these out and place them inside the envelope. They also will be asked to identify words or pictures that represent more positive ways to handle anger and these will be pasted or taped on the outside of the envelope.

Allow about 15 to 20 minutes for participants to find both sets of words or pictures.

Ask each participant to discuss his or her envelope, both what is in the inside and on the outside. Ask each participant if he or she has any insights to share about the differences between the contents of the inside and outside.

Allow 10 to 20 minutes for discussion, highlighting any significant changes or new alternatives to anger.

Review the goals of the activity and use the following debriefing questions for closure.

Debriefing Questions/Closure:
1. What did the inside of your envelope contain?
2. How was the outside different from the inside?
3. How many of the alternatives on the outside can you use on a daily basis?
4. Describe one situation that may come up today or tomorrow in which you can use one of the positive alternatives.
5. How can you remember to use the positive alternatives?
6. How many positive alternatives can you name?

Leadership Considerations:
1. Have several negative and positive examples on hand to get the participants started (examples of negatives: break things, hurt people, yell, kick and scream at others; examples of positives: relax, deep breath, take a fast walk, get plenty of sleep, eat well, talk to a friend).
2. Only have participants share as much as they are willing.
3. Be able to draw connections and facilitate the group to think of new alternatives and support one another.

Variations:
1. Can be changed to any content of opposites, such as barriers and how to overcome them; lack of leisure skills and where to learn them.
2. Have participants draw pictures of unmanaged anger to put on the inside and pictures of better anger management to put on the outside.
3. Give half sheets of paper to participants. Have them place words and pictures on one side of how they handled anger in the past, and on the other side, how they would like to handle anger in the future. They can post these on their wall with the positive side in view to remind them of better ways to handle anger.

Drawing Together

Space Requirements: Classroom or activity room

Equipment/Resource Requirements: Accompanying form, pencils or markers

Group Size: Small group

Program Goals:
1. To increase participants' awareness of nonverbal communication skills.
2. To increase participants' awareness of the need for cooperation.
3. To engage participants in a cooperative task.

Program Description:

Preparation:
Make copies of Drawing Together form, one for each pair of participants.

Introduction:
The purpose of this activity is to help participants develop and read nonverbal cooperation messages, as well as to cooperate. Begin with a discussion of nonverbal skills and cooperation. Nonverbal communication involves all the ways we communicate with one another without speaking. Cooperation is essential to get a common task completed. Ask the group for examples of nonverbal communication to get the message of cooperation across to the other person.

Activity Description:
Divide the group into pairs. Each pair gets a copy of the Drawing Together form and a pencil or marker. As a cooperating unit, the pair both holds the pencil and, without speaking, draws a leisure activity in the first section. One person in each pair moves on to form another pair with someone else. The paper stays with the person who remains seated.

Again, as a unit and without speaking, the new couple draws a piece of leisure equipment (e.g., tennis racket, basketball, hockey stick, in-line skates, book, pet). The person moves again to form a third pair, and the same procedure is used to draw a scene in a park. The last couple that is formed fills in the fourth square with anything they like (related to leisure).

After completion, the drawings are presented to the entire group. Discussion questions may include:

- What was it like to work with different partners?
- How much did the partners agree on what was being drawn?
- How much did each partner group cooperate in creating the drawing?
- How did partners express a message of cooperation?
- What were the expectations of the partners?
- How did it feel when the partners cooperated?
- How did it feel when they did not cooperate?

Refocus the group on the purpose of the activity and discuss the following questions. The drawings may be posted, as a reminder of nonverbal communication and cooperation.

Discussion/Debriefing Questions:
1. What do you think was the purpose of this activity?
2. How important are nonverbal messages to other people?
3. What are some nonverbal signals that communicate cooperation?
4. What are ways to get your message across without speaking?
5. How did you as pairs decide what to draw?
6. Did each partner contribute equally?
7. When is cooperation important?
8. How will you use these ideas and skills in the future?

Leadership Considerations:
1. Emphasize that drawing talent or skill is not an important part of this activity.

Variations:
1. The content of the four squares may be changed depending on the group and the purpose of the activity.

Creator: Norma J. Stumbo, Ph.D., CTRS, Illinois State University, Normal, Illinois.

Drawing Together

Part 1 Leisure Activity	Part 2 Leisure Equipment
Part 3 Scene in a Park	Part 4 Your Choice

Positive and Negative Statements

Space Requirements: Classroom or activity room

Equipment/Materials: Accompanying form, pens or pencils

Group Size: Individual or small group

Program Goals:
1. To increase participants' ability to identify between positive and negative statements toward others.
2. To increase participants' ability to identify which type of statement they most often use.
3. To increase participants' ability to identify three situations where they can use positive statements.

Program Description:

Preparation:
Make copies of Positive and Negative Statements form, one for each participant.

Introduction:
The purpose of this activity is to help participants identify their own statements and whether they are positive or negative. Begin with a discussion about positive and negative statements in conversations. Sometimes people can tend to be negative and not realize that they are. Ask participants if they know someone who is usually negative (not in the group!) and give an example of something they might say. Discuss how people react to consistently negative comments from someone. What reactions do people have? How do they treat the negative person? The group may discuss the different types of positive and negatives statements that people might make.

Activity Description:
Hand out the Positive and Negative Statements form and a pencil to each participant. Have participants give at least two additional examples of statements under each category. Allow 10 to 15 minutes for this part of the activity.

Next, ask participants to identify whether they typically make positive statements or negative statements toward others. If the group members know each other well, ask them to give each other feedback about whether they are correct.

Third, ask participants to complete the last part of the form asking them to identify three situations that will occur in the next three days, where they can plan to make positive statements. For individuals who tend to make negative statements, some thought and practice using positive statements will be helpful.

Review the tasks and purpose of the activity. Help participants meet the activity goals through asking the debriefing questions.

Debriefing Questions/Closure:
1. What is easy or difficult about identifying positive and negative statements?
2. What are different categories of positive and negative statements?
3. Which do you most often use when talking to others?
4. Describe the situation that will be happening in the next three days where you can use positive statements.
5. How comfortable will you feel doing this?
6. How will you be accountable for this?
7. How can what you have learned in this activity help you interact with people?

Leadership Considerations:
1. Try to make sure the group remains on a positive note and strives toward self-improvement.

Variations:
1. Ask individuals to give feedback to others directly about their positive and negative statements.
2. Focus more on the consequences of being positive or negative.

Creator: Norma J. Stumbo, Ph.D., CTRS, Illinois State University, Normal, Illinois.

Positive and Negative Statements

Positive Statements:

Thank Yous:
"Thanks for taking me to the movies."
"Thanks for coming to see me."

_____

_____

Compliments:
"You look great!"
"You finished that task in record time!"

_____

_____

Encouragements:
"You can do it!"
"I'll bet you can make the team."

_____

_____

Optimistic Outlooks:
"Things will be better tomorrow."
"Every day you'll get a little healthier."

_____

_____

Negative Statements:

Refusal to Acknowledge:
"Why make such a big deal of it?"
"I can't see what all the fuss is about."

_____

_____

Put-Downs:
"I can't believe how stupid you are."
"Are you a goofball or what?"

_____

_____

Discouragements:
"There is no way you can do that."
"There is no use, it just won't work."

_____

_____

Negative Outlooks:
"It'll probably only get worse."
"Looks like tomorrow will be worse."

_____

_____

Which type of statement, positive or negative, do you use most often?

_____

Name three situations that will occur in the next three days where you will have the opportunity to use positive statements. For example, someone coming to visit you, going out for the weekend, interacting with a staff member, or talking to your family.

_____

_____

_____

How Do I (Should I) Respond?

Space Requirements: Classroom or activity room

Equipment/Resources Needed: Accompanying form, pens or pencils

Group Size: Small group

Program Goals:
1. To increase participants' awareness of appropriate verbal responses.
2. To increase participants' usage of appropriate verbal responses.
3. To provide participants instances in which appropriate verbal responses may be necessary.

Program Description:

Preparation:
Make copies of How Do I Respond form, two for each participant.

Introduction:
Individuals who have experienced a stroke or other disabling condition very often lose the skills that enable them to interact appropriately with others. This activity supplies example scenarios in which appropriate verbal responses are necessary. These scenarios are very basic, but oftentimes they are a good place to start further discussion. Begin with a discussion about how we respond and react to other people, sometimes positively and sometimes negatively. Often we respond and react quickly, without taking time to think through what we are saying and how it might be taken by the other person(s). Discuss the goals of the activity.

Activity Description:
Begin activity by giving participants a copy of the accompanying form and asking them to fill out a response to as many questions as they can in a five-minute time period.

After participants have responded to the questions in a manner they feel appropriate, pair participants and have them discuss their answers. After five minutes, ask participants to share their answers with the larger group. Ask some questions to aid discussion:

- How appropriate was that response or reaction to that situation?
- How would you feel if someone responded that way to you?
- What are some alternative response options?
- How appropriate are those responses?
- When would you use a different response?
- How did your responses differ from others in the group? Why do you think that is?

Following this large group discussion, the participants are given a second copy of the work sheet and asked to respond to the situations again. A second round of discussion then follows.

Ask participants how their answers may have changed from the first time to the second time. Discuss what responses and reactions are appropriate and how each person may try to respond or react in the future. Close with discussion questions.

Debriefing Questions/Closure:
1. How are your answers the second time similar or different from the first round?
2. If they are different, what did you change and why?
3. How comfortable are you handling situations with these responses? Why or why not?
4. How would you feel if someone responded to you in the way you responded to the first set? the second set?
5. How can you most effectively apply this activity to everyday life?

Leadership Considerations:
1. The activity leader should prepare answers to the questions prior to the activity and be ready to share and explain why those responses are appropriate for that situation.
2. Prepare twice the amount of question sheets as there are participants expected—it may be helpful to use a variation on the spot, that has questions specific to the population.
3. Be ready to elaborate on the situations given for participants who require more detail in order to respond.

Variations:
1. The questions could be expanded to include items that would explore self-awareness and leisure awareness, or the questions could be used as the basis for a decision-making oriented session as opposed to an appropriate response session.
2. For individuals with disabilities in fine motor coordination, a buddy system may be a helpful approach. In this manner also, they can work together to form appropriate responses.
3. For individuals with severe disabilities in social skills, it may be necessary to only discuss and address one question at a time. If this variation is used, the success rate of the individual remembering and using that response may be greater.

Creator: Nikki Colba Harder, CTRS, Illinois State University, Normal, Illinois.

How Do I (Should I) Respond?

Write a response that you feel is appropriate to each of the following situations.

1. Someone thanks you for information that you have given him. How do you respond?

   _____

2. Someone has complimented you on your hairstyle. How do you respond?

   _____

3. Visitors have arrived at your door. How do you greet them?

   _____

4. You'd like some cookies for dessert. How do you ask for them?

   _____

5. Your telephone is ringing. How do you answer it?

   _____

6. Someone offers you some help, but you don't need it. How do you respond?

   _____

7. Someone is standing in your way. How do you ask to get by?

   _____

8. You've hurt someone's feelings. How do you react?

   _____

9. Someone accidentally kicks your foot on the bus. He apologizes. What is your response?

   _____

10. Someone has asked you a question that requires you to think before you speak. How do you let her know you're thinking?

    _____

11. Someone has asked you to do something that you'd be glad to do. How do you respond?

    _____

12. Someone has asked you to participate in something you'd rather not. What is your reaction?

    _____

13. A friend is leaving after a visit. What is the appropriate thing to say?

    _____

14. Someone has insulted you and not offered an apology. How do you respond?

    _____

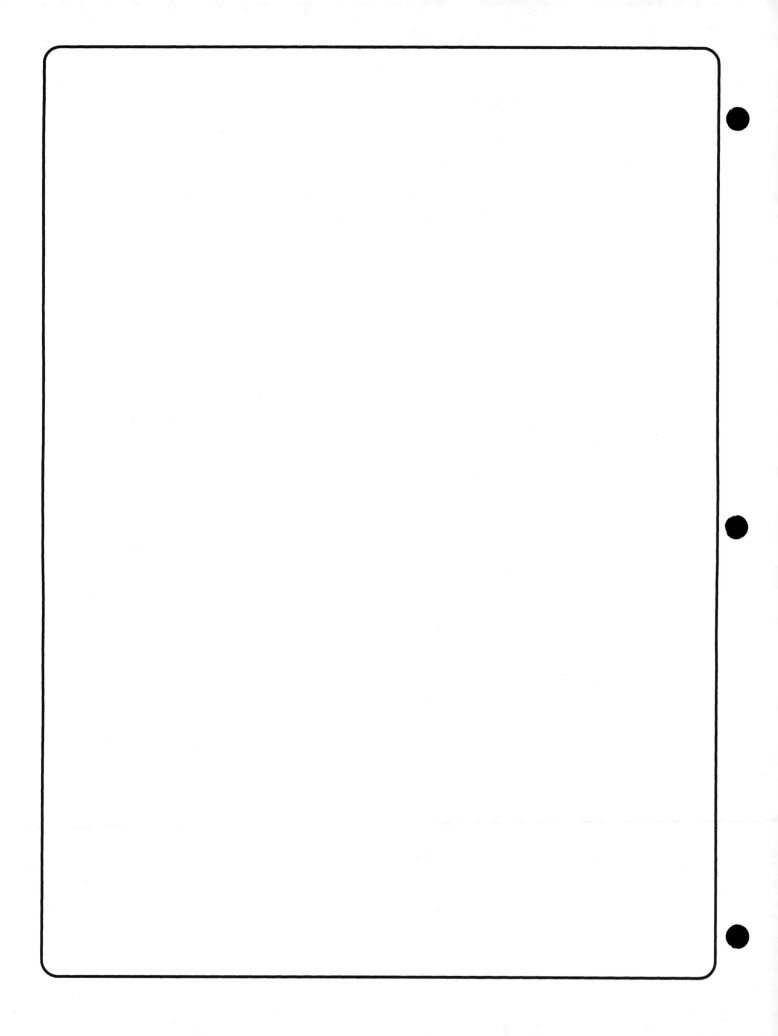

Listening and Interrupting Skills

Space Requirements: Classroom or activity room

Equipment/Resource Requirements: Accompanying form

Group Size: Small group

Program Goals:
1. To increase participants' understanding of the consequences of interrupting someone else in a conversation.
2. To increase participants' understanding of the types of verbalizations that are typical of interruptions within a conversation.

Program Description:

Preparation:
Make one copy of accompanying form for leader, or one for each participant.

Introduction:
The purpose of this activity is to help participants understand and practice listening skills, and to identify problems with interrupting. Begin with a discussion of listening skills and how interrupting a speaker probably means that the other person is not listening well. Ask participants to give examples of when they have interrupted a speaker or been interrupted by someone else. Discuss the circumstances of these conversations.

Activity Description:
Ask for two volunteers to role play in front of the group. One is to speak on a topic of his or her choice. The other is to show he or she is not listening, using verbal or nonverbal ways of demonstrating this. Have them switch roles. Ask the two volunteers how they felt in their two roles. Ask the other participants how this relates to the incidents that they have experienced.

The second part focuses on interrupting. Have participants sit in a semicircle. One person sits at the opening of the circle. This person begins a story. The other participants are to interrupt him or her as much as possible to change the story or topic line. (The leader may prepare the remarks on the Listening and Interrupting Skills form on cards ahead of time to give participants ideas on how to interrupt.)

The story or topic will be different at the end than what was intended at the beginning.

After five minutes, stop the activity and have participants discuss how they felt about being interrupted and interrupting. Discuss how this relates to listening skills and maintaining conversations.

Close with debriefing questions, and emphasize the goals of the activity.

Discussion/Debriefing Questions:
1. How did it feel to be interrupted?
2. How did it feel to interrupt?
3. What effect does interrupting have on conversations?
4. What are the instances when interruptions are appropriate?
5. How often do the participants use the given remarks to interrupt others' conversations?
6. What other comments are often used to interrupt?
7. How will you use what you have learned in this activity in your future conversations?

Leadership Considerations:
1. Be able to control the interruptions to some extent, because often this can get out of hand.

Variations:
1. Have the participants generate their own list of typical interruptions.

Creator: Norma J. Stumbo, Ph.D., CTRS, Illinois State University, Normal, Illinois.

Listening and Interrupting Skills

Typical Interrupting Remarks:

That reminds me . . .

I don't happen to agree with that . . .

It's good that you mentioned that because . . .

Let me tell you about what happened when . . .

Do you remember when . . .

Well, according to my experience . . .

That's just like . . .

That's almost identical to what happened to a relative of mine . . .

Did I ever tell you about . . .

That's nothing, let me tell you . . .

Who cares about that? I think . . .

Did you hear what happened to . . .

What Are You Saying?

Space Requirements: Classroom or activity room

Equipment/Materials: Several pictures with distinct features and shapes drawn on small pieces of paper, chalkboard or flip chart, chalk or marker

Group Size: Individual or small group

Program Goals:
1. To increase participants' ability to give clear, specific directions.
2. To increase participants' awareness of the need for clear communication.
3. To increase participants' ability to ask questions for clarification.

Program Description:

Preparation:
Draw several pictures on pieces of paper.

Introduction:
Review goals and purpose of activity. Distribute one picture to each participant. Ask each participant not to share his or her picture with other group members. Explain that each participant will be taking a turn describing to the leader how to draw his or her picture on the chalkboard.

Activity Description:
One participant begins by describing to the leader how to draw his or her picture, e.g., shapes, size, features, orientation to the paper. The leader will follow the directions, but will be following the directions exactly as they are presented, that is probably unclearly or very generally.

When the incorrect picture has been drawn, the leader explains that he or she did not ask for clear directions and did not clarify what the participant said. And, as a result, the picture was not drawn correctly.

The process is redone with the same participant redescribing the same picture, and with the leader asking for clear directions, thereby getting it right.

Review by comparing the two pictures, emphasizing the differences which were the result of either unclear directions or not asking for clarification.

The activity continues, with each participant having a chance to describe a picture to the leader. Have extra pictures prepared if there is time to do more than one picture per person.

If there is time, reverse roles and have the leader describe pictures to the participants, one time with general and vague terms, and one time more clearly.

Discuss with participants how clear communication can affect everyday life. Why do people need to communicate clearly? What happens when they do not? When is it appropriate to ask for clarification? Review purpose and goals of activity. Close with debriefing questions.

Debriefing Questions/Closure:
1. Why is it important to make sure directions are clear?
2. What are some situations where it is especially important to have clear communication?
3. What are situations in which it is really easy to get confused?
4. What can you do to better understand what someone tells you?
5. Whose responsibility is it to see that directions are clear and understood?

Leadership Considerations:
1. You may want to give some thought to how a picture will likely be described so that you can be prepared to respond only to those directions.
2. Encourage the participants not to show you the picture and not tell you what it is. Even if they do one or both of these, their descriptions may still be unclear.
3. As you are in the process of drawing the incorrect picture, the participant(s) may try to correct you at the time of the mix-up. Don't change it, however. Simply encourage further directions, and if it happens to be in regard to the mix-up, try to mix it up even further.

Variations:
1. Reverse positions, with you describing the picture to the participant, but with unclear directions.
2. Have one participant describing and another participant drawing.
3. Pass the picture around the table, with one participant giving the first direction, the next participant giving another direction, and so on.

Creator: Deland DeCoteau, West Central Human Service Center, Bismarck, North Dakota.

I Hear You

Space Requirements: Classroom or activity room

Equipment/Resource Requirements: Flip chart or chalkboard (optional)

Group Size: Small group

Program Goals:
1. To increase participants' awareness of the need to listen to others.
2. To increase participants' ability to listen to others.

Program Description:
Preparation:
Obtain flip chart or chalkboard and marker or chalk, if needed.

Introduction:
Begin with discussion of listening skills, what it means to listen to another person, and how it feels when someone is listening to you. The purpose of this activity is to increase the participants' awareness and use of listening skills.

Activity Description:
Explain activity and divide participants into pairs. One person in the pair talks about a topic of his or her choice for two to three minutes, while the other partner listens. When the speaker finishes, the other person is to repeat what was said in his or her own words. The speaker judges whether the listener came close in listening and repeating what was originally said.

Switch roles of speaker and listener, and allow another two to three minutes.

Have each pair decide if the other person did an excellent, good, or poor job of listening and repeating back the original topic. Bring the group back together and have the whole group discuss what characterized excellent, good or poor listening skills. The specialist may want to list these on a flip chart or chalkboard.

Refocus the group on the purpose of the activity and discuss the following questions.

Discussion/Debriefing Questions:
1. What characterizes excellent, good, and poor listening skills?
2. How did the speakers know when they were being listened to?
3. What are the advantages or benefits of being an excellent or good listener?
4. How can you improve your listening skills?
5. In what situations do you need excellent listening skills?
6. How do listening skills help social relationships?

Leadership Considerations:
1. The specialist may have a list of characteristics and benefits of listening prepared, in case the group has a difficult time in creating a list.

Variations:
1. The specialist may give topics to the speakers, such as part-time jobs, summer vacations, up-coming weekend plans, favorite tourist spot, or favorite leisure activity.

Creator: Norma J. Stumbo, Ph.D., CTRS, Illinois State University, Normal, Illinois.

Self-Disclosing Cards

Space Requirements: Classroom or activity room

Equipment/Resources Needed: Regular deck of playing cards (including the jokers)

Group Size: Small group

Program Goals:
1. To increase participants' comfort when self-disclosing in a group setting.
2. To increase participants' socialization skills with peers through participation in a structured group.

Program Description:

Preparation:
Prepare questions (see examples). Gather deck of playing cards.

Introduction:
The participants will be asked to be seated in a circle. The specialist should relate to the participants that the activity will be about self-disclosure—telling the group about favorite experiences or desires.

Activity Description:
Shuffle a regular deck of playing cards, including the jokers. Deal each participant one card per round. Each card (number value) represents a question which the participant must answer.

Examples:
- Ace: What is your favorite leisure activity? Why?
- 2:   What is your favorite car? Why?
- 3:   What is your favorite season? Why?
- 4:   What would you do if you won a million dollars?
- 5:   Name your favorite vacation place (one you have visited before or one you want to visit some day).
- 6 to King: (Questions are to be determined for each.)
- Joker: Tell your favorite joke.

Ask one participant to start, share his or her card, and answer the topic or question. Help the participant to expand on his or her answers. Proceed to the next person, and continue this until all persons in the group have answered a question. Collect all "used" cards and set aside.

Begin round two by dealing each person another card. If a person gets the same card as he or she did in the last round, give the participant a new card.

Repeat procedure above, with each person sharing, either by asking the same questions or new ones. Continue until time ends or all participants have been able to self-disclose.

Close with discussion about self-disclosure. Review goals and purpose of the activity.

Debriefing Questions/Closure:
1. How did you feel sharing personal information with the group?
2. How easy or difficult do you find sharing personal information without the structure of an activity like this?
3. What makes some people hesitate to self-disclose?
4. What are topics that are easier to disclose than others (leisure, weather, vacation plans)?
5. What are topics that are more difficult to self-disclose (salary, personal problems)?
6. What are appropriate topics to disclose to strangers?
7. What are appropriate topics to disclose to close friends and intimates?

Leadership Considerations:
1. Have questions prepared prior to group.
2. Try to use open-ended, instead of closed-ended, questions when possible.

Variations:
1. Use leisure resource questions, instead of self-disclosure questions. For example:

   - Name a place to see a professional sport game.
   - Name a place to see a concert.
   - Where do you find out what is going on in town?

Creator: Cathy Pacetta and Julie Beck, Elgin Mental Health Center, Elgin, Illinois.

One Step Ahead

Space Requirements: Classroom or activity room

Equipment/Resources Needed: Accompanying form, chalkboard, chalk

Group Size: Individual or small group

Program Goals:
1. To improve participants' ability to accept no as an answer.
2. To increase participants' attention and observation skills.
3. To increase participants' awareness of the need for patience in communication.

Program Description:

Preparation:
Make copies of One Step Ahead form, one for specialist and one for each participant. Gather other materials.

Introduction:
Begin this activity with a discussion about the need for clear communication and what may happen when communication is not clear. Also as a part of this discussion, talk about how it feels when someone tells you that you are incorrect. Explain the purpose, goals and rules of this activity.

Activity Description:
Provide each participant with a copy of the One Step Ahead form. The page has pictures of similar items. Explain that the specialist will be drawing pictures on the board one at a time, and the participants will take turns, one at a time, to guess what each picture is. Encourage them to keep trying to figure out what the pictures are even if they guess incorrectly.

One person is selected to be the guesser. The drawer chooses a "category" (or row of pictures) and begins to draw slowly one item from the category. The participant makes a guess. If it is incorrect, the participant is told he or she is incorrect and that item is crossed off. If the guess is correct, the participant is told the guess is correct and play continues.

Begin the process again with a new drawing from the same or from a different group, with a different participant as the guesser. Repeat procedure until all participants have had a chance to guess a picture.

Review the purpose and goals of the activity and use the following debriefing questions for closure.

Debriefing Questions/Closure:
1. How did it feel to be told you were incorrect—"no, you are not correct"?
2. How did it feel to be told you were correct—"yes, you are correct"?
3. What can we learn from being told no?
4. How did you benefit from paying close attention to what was being drawn?
5. What did you learn about the need not to jump to quick conclusions?

Leadership Considerations:
1. Be sure to draw gradually and only have one person guessing at a time so that the pictures are not hurried through.
2. Reinforce each incorrect guess with "Good guess!" or "It looks like it, but that's not right" to keep the enthusiasm and the guesses coming.

Variations:
1. Vary the order the pictures are done, e.g., one picture from one group of similarly designed pictures then one from the next group.
2. Periodically allow someone to be right early in the drawing to vary the no responses.

Creator: Deland DeCoteau, West Central Human Service Center, Bismarck, North Dakota.

One Step Ahead

Rabbit	Cat	Dog	Pizza
Cherry Pie	Bicycle Wheel	Raccoon	Elephant
Balloons	Eggs and Nest	Baseball	Basketball
Orange Slice	Pumpkin	TV Show	Painting
Window	Door	Beachball	Clock

M.Y.O. Business Cards

Space Requirements: Classroom or activity room

Equipment/Resources Needed: Two sets of M.Y.O. Business Cards
(Both sets of cards are made of construction paper, about the size of business cards. Have the one set of M.Y.O. Business Cards be a bright color, like red or orange, with "M.Y.O.B." printed on one side. On the other set of cards, have questions printed, which will be used by the specialist. Each question will ask for a participant's opinion, yet will have numerous potential responses.)

Group Size: Individual or small group

Program Goals:
1. To increase participants' awareness of the importance of minding their own business.
2. To increase participants' ability to not answer questions asked of someone else.

Program Description:
Preparation:
Prepare M.Y.O. Business Cards as described.

Introduction:
Explain to the group members that this activity will involve everyone practicing minding their own business, and encourage the participants to do so. Explain that the specialist will be asking questions to one person at a time while everyone else should "M.Y.O.B." or they will get an M.Y.O. Business Card.

Activity Description:
Ask one participant a question from the set of cards. Try to ask it in such a way that it not only attempts to get his or her opinion, but also makes it very tempting for everyone else to answer. For example, "In your opinion, what is the best tasting soda pop? What soda pop do you think we should like the best?"

If another participant does not mind his or her own business, he or she is given an M.Y.O. Business Card along with the lighthearted reminder about what he or she did.

Briefly discuss the participant's answer to the question, both to learn about what he or she thinks, and to give the group a little time to be tempted to answer and resist the urge to do so.

If a participant gets four M.Y.O. Business Cards, he or she will be out of the game. This rule may be amended if necessary (if your group members are particularly unskilled at minding their own business, for instance).

Close the activity with a discussion of appropriate social skills. Focus on the importance of not interrupting and of minding one's own business. Close with the following debriefing questions.

Debriefing Questions/Closure:
1. Why is it important to mind our own business?
2. How does it feel when someone interrupts you?
3. What can a person do instead of interrupting someone?
4. What happens if you have something really important to say?
5. How difficult is it not to interrupt sometimes? Why?

Leadership Considerations:
1. Be aware of participants' mood and tolerance level.
2. Keep the atmosphere lighthearted rather than punitive.
3. Emphasize that a participant gets an M.Y.O. Business Card as a reminder to use appropriate social skills, not as a penalty for what he or she did.
4. It is possible that a participant will try to get cards, either because it is fun or attention getting. Encourage him or her not to and emphasize how few others have.

Variations:
1. Develop cards which will target other problem behaviors (e.g., repeating, being aggressive).
2. Develop cards to reinforce appropriate skills (a "way to go" card).
3. Incorporate the use of cards into day-to-day activities and groups as reminders for appropriate behaviors.

Creator: Deland DeCoteau, West Central Human Service Center, Bismarck, North Dakota.

What Did You Say?

Space Requirements: Classroom or activity room

Equipment/Materials: Pads of paper, pencils, black marker, index cards

Group Size: Small group

Program Goals:
1. To improve participants' awareness of the need for good communication skills.
2. To increase participants' understanding of the barriers to good communication.

Program Description:
Preparation:
Prior to the start of the activity, prepare index cards. On each card, draw a design or diagram, with a black marker. Do not make the design or diagram too complex. No more than seven to 10 lines or markings. Unfamiliar designs make the activity more complex.

Introduction:
Review the goals and purpose of the activity. Discuss with the group what "good" communication means. Ask each participant to identify one benefit of good communication and also one barrier to good communication.

Activity Description:
Have the group pair off into sets of Partner A and B. Each Partner A should sit in a line, next to other Partner As, with his or her back to the back of his or her Partner B (partners sitting back to back in a line next to each other).

Distribute index cards to one row of the partners (Partner As). (Each person on the Partner A side should have a different drawing on his or her card.) Explain to the other partners (Partner Bs) not to look over their shoulders to see their partner's card. Distribute pads of paper and pencils to the Partner Bs who did not receive index cards.

Explain to the group that the Partner A with the card, will be describing his or her design to his or her Partner B. Partner B is to draw the design as best he or she can.

Explain that this is not a race. Set the rule of not turning around or peeking over each other's shoulders. Add the final rule that the participants (Partner Bs) with the paper and pencil may not speak or ask questions.

Tell the Partner As to begin their descriptions and their Partner Bs to begin drawing. Give the group approximately 30 seconds to one minute. Have the two partners compare their drawings.

Have the partners switch roles. Be sure to switch cards so that each partnership has a new card.

Close with a discussion about the need for clear communication skills, as well as some barriers to communication. Review the purpose of the activity. Use the following debriefing questions to wrap up discussion.

Debriefing Questions/Closure:
1. What barriers or problems did each of you encounter?
2. Which was easier: listening or describing? Why?
3. What are the benefits of facing each other when communicating?
4. Why are eye contact and nonverbal gestures important to communication?
5. What are some reasons for miscommunication? What are some barriers?

Leadership Considerations:
1. Show an example card and how you would describe it.
2. Monitor the silent partners, as they may be tempted to speak.
3. Have the group sit in a line, back to back, and be sure one side of the line has the cards, while the other has the paper.

Variations:
1. Have the describers use only geometrical descriptions, instead of characteristics of the diagram.
2. Allow the drawing partners to ask yes or no questions of the partners who are describing.

Creator: Amy Payne-Johnson, CTRS, Orchard Place Child Guidance Center, Des Moines, Iowa.

I'm Listening

Space Requirements: Classroom or activity room

Equipment/Resource Requirements: None

Group Size: Small group

Program Goals:
1. To improve participants' awareness of the importance of listening.
2. To improve participants' ability to recognize nonverbal messages.
3. To improve participants' ability to listen to others.
4. To improve participants' ability to critique others in a constructive manner.

Program Description:
Preparation:
None needed.

Introduction:
The purpose of this activity is to help participants to understand and practice listening skills. Begin with discussion of listening skills and the importance of listening to communication between people.

Activity Description:
The specialist asks for three volunteers to participate in a conversation. Person A speaks first for two minutes. Person B listens first, and at the end of the two minutes must summarize what Person A said. Person C summarizes the action, and helps to make sure Person B does not distort, interpret, add to, or leave out important information from Person A. Person C is also responsible for observing and reporting the nonverbal behavior of Person A and Person B.

Roles may be switched, depending on time and size of group. End with discussion, including the following questions.

Debriefing Questions/Closure:
1. How did you feel about your role?
2. What difficulties were experienced in this role?
3. What nonverbal behaviors were expressed and how did they match the topic being discussed?
4. How is it possible to express attention nonverbally?
5. How do we prefer others listen to us?
6. How much does the amount of attention paid by other people and the way they pay attention to us affect our own readiness to listen to them?
7. What are ways we can improve our listening abilities?
8. How is it possible to make sure others will listen to us?

Leadership Considerations:
1. The specialist may want to prepare a few topics ahead of time, if participants will have a difficult time developing their own.

Variations:
1. Person A can either choose a topic or can use one supplied by the specialist, such as vacation plans, a favorite recreation facility, what leisure and recreation means, the importance of leisure to a balanced lifestyle, or a favorite hobby.

Creator: Norma J. Stumbo, Ph.D., CTRS, Illinois State University, Normal, Illinois.

Welcoming Newcomers

Space Requirements: Classroom or activity room

Equipment/Resource Requirements: Accompanying form made into situation cards

Group Size: Small group

Program Goals:
1. To increase participants' awareness of different responses to newcomers' attempts to join a group.
2. To increase participants' understanding of what it feels like to be a newcomer.
3. To increase participants' understanding of what it feels like to be part of a group that either accepts or rejects a newcomer.

Program Description:

Preparation:
Make one copy of the Welcoming Newcomers form for the leader and situation cards for each participant.

Introduction:
Begin discussion with any situations in which the participants have been outsiders to a group they wanted to join. Ask participants to describe the situation, including how each was treated by the group they wanted to join. Focus on the feelings associated with different reactions from the group they wanted to join.

Activity Description:
Explain the activity and ask for three volunteers to leave the room. Divide the other participants into three groups. Hand each group a situation card about how they are to react when a person returns to the room and wants to enter their group.

Group 1:
Have one person return to the room and ask him or her to proceed to Group 1. The members of Group 1 will be discussing a topic of their choice. They are to follow the instruction card (to ignore the newcomer) as the person tries to enter into their conversation. Continue for three to four minutes before stopping action.

Group 2:
Have a second person return to the room and ask him or her to proceed to Group 2. The members of Group 2 will be discussing a topic of their choice. They are to follow the instruction card (to be rude to the newcomer) as the person tries to enter their conversation. Continue for three to four minutes before stopping action.

Group 3:

Have the third person return to the room and ask him or her to proceed to Group 3. The members of Group 3 will be discussing a topic of their choice. They are to follow the instruction card (to accept the newcomer and help him or her take part in the conversation) as the newcomer tries to enter their conversation. Continue for three to four minutes before stopping action.

Reconvene the whole group and discuss what happened in the three scenarios.

Debriefing Questions/Closure:
1. How did the newcomers feel, depending on which group they tried to enter?
2. What actions did each group take to represent their instruction card?
3. How did the group members feel, depending on which group they belonged to?
4. How does this relate to other situations which participants have experienced?
5. How will participants treat newcomers in other situations in the future?
6. What actions can newcomers take to be better equipped to join groups?

Leadership Considerations:
1. Make sure the people leaving the room know that the purpose of the activity is to see poor ways of welcoming newcomers, and then to practice and learn the right way (the third scenario) to welcome newcomers.

Variations:
1. Many variations exist depending on the size of the group. For example, only one person may be sent out of the room, but this happens three times; or the same group gives all three reactions.

Creator: Norma J. Stumbo, Ph.D., CTRS, Illinois State University, Normal, Illinois.

Welcoming Newcomers

Group 1:

A newcomer wants to join your group.

You are to ignore the newcomer and not let
him or her enter the group.

Group 2:

A newcomer wants to join your group.

You are to be rude to the newcomer and not
let him or her join the group.

Group 3:

A newcomer wants to join your group.

You are to accept the newcomer and help
him or her take part in the conversation.

Friendship Pizza

Space Requirements: Classroom or activity room

Equipment/Materials: Several pieces of poster board in red and off-white for "crust" and "sauce," small pieces of orange or yellow paper for "cheese," magazines, glue, scissors

Group Size: Small group

Program Goals:
1. To improve participants' awareness of the characteristics of a friend.
2. To improve participants' understanding of their own ability to be a friend.

Program Description:

Preparation:
Prior to the start of the activity, cut large circles of the off-white poster board for the crust of the pizza. Cut slightly smaller circles from the red poster board for the sauce. Cut small pieces of the orange or yellow paper to represent the cheese topping. Glue the red circle (sauce) on top of the larger off-white circle (crust). Glue pieces of orange or yellow paper randomly on top of the sauce to appear like cheese topping.

Introduction:
Begin the activity by discussing what it takes to be a good friend. What are the ingredients of being and having a good friend? Review the purpose and goals of the activity with the participants. Explain the activity to the group.

Activity Description:
Hand each participant a pizza crust with sauce and cheese. Put several magazines, the glue and scissors in the middle of the table. Instruct participants to look through the magazines and cut out any word or picture that represents some aspect (ingredient) of friendship to them (e.g., secret, trust, fun, smart).

Allow 10 to 15 minutes for participants to locate and cut out items in the magazines.

One at a time, ask the participants to put their ingredients on top of their pizza. As they put on each ingredient, have them explain why that particular ingredient represents friendship. The specialist should facilitate the participants becoming aware of the similarities and differences in their answers.

Close with discussion about the ingredients of friendship and whether the participants think they make a good friend. Use the following debriefing questions.

Debriefing Questions/Closure:
1. What were common ingredients for friendship, mentioned by several participants?
2. What were some of the unique ingredients mentioned?
3. Which of these characteristics do you have already?
4. Which of these characteristics do you need to work on?
5. How is friendship important to our lives?
6. What are some of the benefits of friendship?

Leadership Considerations:
1. Have materials prepared ahead of time.
2. The idea of using a pizza may be more helpful to children and adolescents.

Variations:
1. The theme could be almost anything: ingredients for a sober lifestyle, ingredients for being able to solve a problem, barriers to leisure.
2. Create a family pizza with the important ingredients for a family.
3. Add new ingredients when you want to add another goal area (for example, adding brown paper "sausage" for how many good friends they have).

Creator: Becky Klein, Illinois State University, Normal, Illinois.

Friendship Mobile

Space Requirements: Classroom or activity room with tables and chairs

Equipment/Resource Requirements: Magazines or construction paper, paste or glue sticks, scissors, markers, straws, heavy string, paper clips

Size of Group: Small group

Program Goals:
1. To increase participants' ability to identify their friendship networks.
2. To increase participants' ability to identify reasons for building and maintaining a strong friendship network.

Program Description:
  Preparation:
  Gather materials.

  Introduction:
  The purpose of this activity is to help individuals identify who is in their friendship networks and the "balance" that these individuals may bring to their lives. Begin with discussion of friendship and the importance of building and maintaining a friendship network. Explain the procedures of the activity to the participants.

  Activity Description:
  Participants are to each make a hanging mobile of their friendship networks. Either have prepared "faces" cut out of construction paper or allow participants to cut faces or profiles out of magazines. Each person also is to draw or find a figure that represents himself or herself. Make a small hole in the center top of each figure and tie a four- to six-inch string to it.

  Starting at the top of the mobile, place the participant's representation of himself or herself in the middle. In pyramid fashion under their own figures, individuals should place figures hanging from strings attached to the straws. To properly balance the pyramid so it hangs well, paper clips may be placed as weights on some of the pictures.

  The leader may note that the placement of the friendship network is important. Best friends are to be placed closer to the top of the pyramid. The descending order represents the network from closest friends to more distant friends.

  Allow 15 to 20 minutes for the participants to find, cut out and construct their pyramid mobile.

  Ask each individual to discuss who is in his or her friendship network, and how balanced the network is or is not. Refocus on the purpose of the activity and close with a wrap-up discussion.

  Participants may take the mobiles and hang them in their rooms, or they can be hung in the activity room.

Discussion/Debriefing Questions:
1. How important are friends to each of the participants?
2. How did you develop your friendship network?
3. What actions do you take to maintain your friendship network?
4. How can you build a friendship network or keep a friendship network growing?
5. What are the characteristics of individuals in your friendship networks?

Leadership Considerations:
1. Make sure magazines are appropriate to the group of participants.
2. Family members may be included if the participants feel they are also friends.

Variations:
1. The mobile can represent leisure activities, pieces of leisure equipment, or leisure resources.

Creator: Norma J. Stumbo, Ph.D., CTRS, Illinois State University, Normal, Illinois.

Role Models

Space Requirements: Classroom or activity room

Equipment/Materials: Accompanying form, pens

Group Size: Individual or small group

Program Goals:
1. To improve participants' ability to identify personal role models.
2. To improve participants' ability to develop personal definition of role model.
3. To improve participants' ability to identify consequences of choosing poor role models.

Program Description:
Preparation:
Make copies of Role Models form, one for each participant.

Introduction:
Introduce topic of role models by explaining that everyone has role models and that because of these role models, everyone develops certain values and models themselves accordingly. Review goals and purpose of activity.

Activity Description:
Have participants each create their own definition of a role model and share this with the group. Facilitator can use this definition:

> Role models are people whom we look up to as a good example. A role model is someone we would like to 'model' ourselves after, and it is someone who has influenced our life in a positive way.

Have each participant identify one of his or her role models (e.g., parent, teacher, neighbor, clergy member, athlete). Have each person describe his or her relationship with his or her role model.

Introduce the topic of peers as role models. Have the participants identify peers who are good role models using the Role Models form. Ask participants for other descriptors of their peer role models.

Discuss the similarities and differences among answers of the group members for each question. How familiar is each person with the role models presented by others? Close with discussion of the impact role models can have on everyone's life, include the following questions for debriefing.

Debriefing Questions/Closure:
1. How are role models chosen? How did you choose your role models?
2. How does it feel to be identified by another peer as a good role model?
3. For what characteristics might you be chosen as someone's role model?
4. Why is choosing good role models so important?
5. What are the drawbacks of choosing poor role models?
6. What are the characteristics of poor role models?

Leadership Considerations:
1. Keep the participants focused on the positive traits of peers, avoid having them bring up negatives.

Variations:
1. Change the activity sheet so participants can choose models outside their peer group.

Creator: Penny J. Hogberg, CTRS, Anoka-Metro Regional Treatment Center, Anoka, Minnesota.

Role Models

Directions: Identify peers who are good role models. Fill in the blanks below with individual participants' names.

1. _____ always appears neat and well-groomed.

2. _____ is eager to greet me and gives me a warm welcome on a daily basis.

3. _____ is so polite and considerate of others.

4. _____ makes me laugh like no one else can.

5. _____ has a very special talent of _____.

6. _____ has one of the nicest smiles.

7. _____ has so many interesting stories to tell.

8. _____ is so good about sharing with others.

9. _____ is a very good athlete.

10. _____ is friends with everyone.

11. _____ is always trustworthy.

12. _____ is considerate of others' feelings.

13. _____ brings out the best in other people.

14. _____ takes pride in his or her work.

15. _____ is able to make good decisions about his or her life.

16. _____ is able to keep it together, even in tough times.

17. _____ always keeps a promise.

18. _____ does his or her share of the work.

19. _____ keeps a friend's secret.

20. _____ continually tries to improve himself or herself.

21. _____ treats others with respect.

22. _____ talks well of other people.

23. _____ has a positive influence on those around him or her.

Conflicts Between Friends

Space Requirements: Classroom or activity room with tables

Equipment/Resource Requirements: Accompanying form, pens or pencils

Group Size: Small group

Program Goals:
1. To increase participants' ability to identify conflicts that may happen in friendships.
2. To increase participants' understanding of what may precede conflicts between friends.

Description/Procedure:

Preparation:
Make copies of Conflicts Between Friends form, one for each participant.

Introduction:
Begin with a discussion of friendships. While sometimes it is easy to get along with one another, sometimes it is difficult. Discuss various conflicts within friendships, such as revealing secrets, gossip, jealousy, and untrustworthiness. The purpose of this activity is to help group members identify what types of situations they think create the most conflicts.

Activity Description:
Hand each participant a copy of the accompanying form and a pencil. Have each participant rate the statements on whether they are bothered a lot, somewhat, or very little. There are additional spaces to allow participants to identify additional conflicts.

Allow five to 10 minutes for participants to complete the rating.

Discuss which conflicts the participants felt were most troublesome and least troublesome. Discuss how participants' ratings differed, and what led them to their ratings. Reemphasize the purpose of the activity.

Discussion/Debriefing Questions:
1. How did your ratings look alike or different from others in the group?
2. How did you select your ratings?
3. Give an example of a situation you've experienced where there has been conflict in a friendship.
4. Describe the worst friendship conflict you have ever experienced.
5. What do your ratings tell you about what you value in friendships?
6. How can you reduce the conflicts in your relationships?

Leadership Considerations:
1. Be aware of participants' relationships with one another.

Variations:
1. Allow participants to develop their own list of things that create conflict within a friendship.
2. Adapt the Conflicts Between Friends form to discuss conflicts within the participants' families.

Creator: Norma J. Stumbo, Ph.D., CTRS, Illinois State University, Normal, Illinois.

Conflicts Between Friends

Directions: Below is a list of situations that may cause conflicts between friends. Rate each situation according to whether it bothers you a lot (1), somewhat (2), or very little (3).

Conflict: This bothers me:	A Lot	Somewhat	Very Little
1. Tattling	1	2	3
2. Gossip	1	2	3
3. Disloyalty	1	2	3
4. Telling secrets	1	2	3
5. Oversensitivity	1	2	3
6. Insults or name calling	1	2	3
7. Wanting to make friends with a third person	1	2	3
8. Competitiveness	1	2	3
9. Jealousy	1	2	3
10. Moodiness	1	2	3
11. Poor sportsmanship	1	2	3
12. Teasing	1	2	3
13. Not listening to my problems	1	2	3
14. Not being able to control anger	1	2	3
15. Showing off	1	2	3
16. Ignoring me	1	2	3
17. Getting into trouble	1	2	3
18. Poor hygiene	1	2	3
19. Not being kind	1	2	3
20. Cheating in school	1	2	3

Handling Conflicts

Space Requirements: Classroom or activity room with tables

Equipment/Resource Requirements: Accompanying form, pens or pencils

Group Size: Small group

Program Goals:
1. To increase participants' ability to identify responses to conflicts in friendships.
2. To increase participants' ability to identify win-win solutions to conflicts.

Description/Procedure:
Preparation:
Make copies of Handling Conflicts form, one for each participant.

Introduction:
The purpose of this activity is to help group members identify situations that may cause conflicts in friendships, and ways to deal with these conflicts. Begin with a discussion of friendships. Sometimes it is easy to get along with one another, sometimes it is more difficult. Discuss various conflicts within friendships, such as revealing secrets, jealousy, and unequal contributions.

Activity Description:
Hand each participant a copy of the Handling Conflicts form and a pencil. Have each participant explain his or her feelings and actions on paper. Allow five to 10 minutes for completion.

Then discuss the scenarios as a group, either after every scenario or after all four. Ask participants to answer the questions after each scenario.

Discuss the responses given by the participants. Focus on the problem-solving aspects of the situations and win-win resolutions. Refocus on the purpose of the activity.

Discussion/Debriefing Questions:
1. What is the central problem raised by each scenario?
2. What coping strategies were suggested for each scenario?
3. What is common among these solutions?
4. How do we go about looking for win-win solutions?
5. How are these similar to what participants have dealt with, and how did they handle it?
6. What are broad themes or actions to take when handling conflicts?

Leadership Considerations:
1. Be prepared with some probable win-win solutions.

Variations:
1. Instead of handing out the Handling Conflicts form, place information on poster board for the participants to discuss as a group.
2. Change the scenarios to meet the needs and interests of the participants.

Creator: Norma J. Stumbo, Ph.D., CTRS, Illinois State University, Normal, Illinois.

Handling Conflicts

Situation 1:

My friend, Tanisha, usually comes to meetings without having completed her projects, and asks me to do them. One day I did not get all my work done before the big meeting, and I asked her to help me complete it. Tanisha refused.

1. What did Tanisha say? _____

2. How did I feel? _____

3. What do I intend to do or say? _____

Situation 2:

Gary asked me to do some work for him. Usually I don't mind doing something like that, but if I give in to his request, I won't be able to finish my work. I don't want him to think that I don't want to help him.

1. What do I say to Gary? _____

2. How do you think Gary will respond? _____

3. How will I react to his response? _____

Situation 3:

Rose is the most popular woman in the group. Rachel told Rose a secret about her best friend Leslie so that Rose would become friends with Rachel.

1. Why is it important to Rachel to be friends with Rose? _____

2. How will Leslie react when she finds out about what Rachel has done? _____

3. What will Rachel say to Leslie if Leslie confronts her? _____

Situation 4:

Ron says, "Don, did you hear? There's going to be a big party Saturday night at Rick's. Are you coming?" Don says, "No, I wasn't invited."

1. How does Ron feel? _____

2. How does Don feel? _____

3. What will Ron say next? _____

1 + 1 + 1 = 3

Space Requirements: Classroom or activity room with tables

Equipment/Resource Requirements: Accompanying form, pens or pencils

Group Size: Small group

Program Goals:
1. To increase participants' understanding of the possible effects of a third person on an existing two-person friendship.
2. To increase participants' ability to problem-solve solutions to these friendship situations.

Description/Procedure:
Preparation:
Make copies of 1 + 1 + 1 = 3 form, one for each participant.

Introduction:
The purpose of this activity is to help participants explore the effects of a third person on a two-person relationship. Begin with a discussion about what happens to a close friendship when a third person appears in the friendship. How does the third person affect the relationship between the two individuals?

Activity Description:
Hand each individual a copy of the 1 + 1 + 1 = 3 form and a pencil. Ask each participant to complete the form, with information he or she is willing to share with the group.

Allow five to 10 minutes for completion of the form.

Discuss the responses given by the participants. Either discuss them one at a time, or allow participants to complete all three and then discuss.

Discuss the responses given by the participants. Focus on the solutions given by the group. Refocus on the purpose of the activity.

Discussion/Debriefing Questions:
1. What would you do in these situations?
2. Have you ever encountered a situation similar to any of those described on the 1 + 1 + 1 = 3 form?
3. Identify some ways to resolve this conflict.
4. Which are good solutions and which are problematic?
5. How have you dealt with these situations in the past?
6. What are alternative ways to deal with these in the future?
7. How can you make new friends without abandoning current friends?

Leadership Considerations:
1. Be prepared with examples of solutions to these situations.

Variations:
1. Put the information on the 1 + 1 + 1 = 3 form on a poster board and discuss the situations as a group.

Creator: Norma J. Stumbo, Ph.D., CTRS, Illinois State University, Normal, Illinois.

1 + 1 + 1 = 3

Situation 1:
Debby and Maria are good friends. In the past, they have helped each other, they understand one another, and spent a lot of time together. Lately, Debby has been going around with Lena. Sometimes she asks Maria to join them, but most of the time, Maria says no.

1. Maria feels that: _____

2. Debby feels that: _____

3. Maria would like to do (or say): _____

4. How would Maria behave in Debby's place? _____

Situation 2:
Ian and Brian are good friends who spend a lot of time together. Recently Ian met Susan and they have started going out together. As a result, Ian has not been able to spend as much time with Brian as before.

1. How does Brian feel? _____

2. How does Ian feel? _____

3. What would Brian do if he were in Ian's place? _____

Situation 3:
Sally and Beverly live around the corner from each other. Last month a new girl, Cheryl, moved to Sally's block. Sally has been spending a lot of time getting to know Cheryl.

1. How does Beverly feel? _____

2. How does Sally feel? _____

3. How does Cheryl feel? _____

4. What might Beverly say to Sally? _____

Comfort Level

Space Requirements: Classroom or activity room

Equipment/Resources Needed: Accompanying form, pens or pencils

Group Size: Small group

Program Goals:
1. To increase participants' ability to identify when events have made them uncomfortable.
2. To increase participants' ability to identify actions they can take to make someone else feel more comfortable in a social situation.

Program Description:

Preparation:
Make copies of Comfort Level form, one for each participant.

Introduction:
Introduce the topic by discussing feelings of being accepted and rejected by peers. Everybody has experienced being left out or unwelcome at some time in his or her life. It is not a good feeling but an important one to experience so that we can try and avoid making others feel that way. What are actions that others may take that cause us to feel unwelcome? What are actions that others may take that allow us to feel welcome to be in the group? Identify the difference between these actions.

Activity Description:
Distribute Comfort Level form and pens to each group member. Ask the participants to complete the form. Let the participants know they will be sharing the information within the group. Allow five to 10 minutes for the participants to complete their work sheet.

Ask a participant to volunteer one time, situation, or event in which he or she felt uncomfortable or unwelcome. Ask clarifying questions about the specific actions members of the group took that made the participant uncomfortable. Ask the participant about his or her reactions to those. Focus on the behaviors and language of the situation, not the personalities.

Ask a second participant about his or her uncomfortable situations. Also ask about behaviors and language. After several participants have had a chance to respond, summarize what they have said. Bring out similarities and differences in their answers.

Ask for a second round of volunteers to talk about situations or events in which they felt very comfortable. Similar to above, ask about specific behavior and language.

After several participants have had a chance to respond, summarize what they have said. Again, bring out similarities and difference in their answers. Ask how they might make peers or people they have just met more comfortable in social situations.

As a group, compare the answers from the first question of being comfortable to the second one about being uncomfortable.

Close the session with a discussion about the following questions.

Debriefing Questions/Closure:
1. What were the behaviors and language of making someone more comfortable?
2. What were the behaviors and language of making someone less comfortable?
3. What actions could you take in a social situation to make someone else more comfortable?
4. When will you next have a chance to display behaviors that help someone become more comfortable?
5. How does this apply to new participants or their families?

Leadership Considerations:
1. Encourage members to listen to others, and be willing to share thoughts and feelings with group members.

Variations:
1. For additional opportunity for sharing without embarrassment, participants may benefit from partner work.

Creator: Penny J. Hogberg, CTRS, Anoka-Metro Regional Treatment Center, Anoka, Minnesota.

Comfort Level

Everybody has experienced being left out or unwelcome at some time in his or her life. It is not a good feeling but an important one to experience so that we can try and avoid making others feel that way.

List three social events or situations in which you have felt unwelcome.

1.

2.

3.

What three actions can you take to help a peer feel welcome and comfortable around you?

1.

2.

3.

My Group Comfort Level

Space Requirements: Classroom or activity room

Equipment/Materials: Accompanying form, pencils or markers

Size of Group: Small group

Program Goals:
1. To increase participants' ability to evaluate their comfort level in a continuing group.
2. To increase participants' ability to evaluate their own progress in the group.
3. To increase participants' ability to identify their similarities and differences with other members of the group.

Program Description:

Preparation:
This activity is appropriate only for groups that have worked together for some time and are familiar with one another. Make copies of My Group Comfort Level form, one for each participant.

Introduction:
The purpose of this activity is to help individuals evaluate their own comfort level with the group. Begin with a review of the group's previous activities. The specialist may ask the participants to comment on what they have learned, how the group has developed, their individual contributions to the group. This may come at the end of treatment, or at an appropriate interim point.

Activity Description:
Distribute the My Group Comfort Level form and pencils, and ask each participant to complete the form as honestly as possible. Depending on the group, participants may be told they are expected to share their answers or only share whichever answers they feel comfortable sharing.

Allow five to 10 minutes for completion of the form.

After the participants have completed the evaluation, the specialist is to facilitate a discussion about their answers. Refocus on the purpose and use the following questions for discussion.

Discussion/Debriefing Questions:
1. What answers do you have that are similar to other people?
2. What answers do you have that are different from others?
3. Do you remember how you felt and behaved at the beginning of this group?
4. How have you changed since the beginning of this group?
5. What are examples of how the group has developed or progressed?
6. In what areas do you still feel uncomfortable?
7. How can you improve on these things?
8. What have you learned about yourself?

Leadership Considerations:
1. Alter the questions, depending on the level of the group.

Variations:
   1. Discuss the questions as a group rather than complete the form individually.

Creator: Norma J. Stumbo, Ph.D., CTRS, Illinois State University, Normal, Illinois.

My Group Comfort Level

	I feel very comfortable	I feel somewhat comfortable	I feel somewhat uncomfortable	I feel very uncomfortable
1. Saying I am glad to meet someone	1	2	3	4
2. Agreeing with the opinions and feelings of one of the group members	1	2	3	4
3. Encouraging one of the group members to finish telling about an idea	1	2	3	4
4. Asking one of the group members to explain what he or she just said	1	2	3	4
5. Asking one of the group members to express an opinion about different things	1	2	3	4
6. Asking one of the group members to talk about himself or herself	1	2	3	4
7. Suggesting things to the group	1	2	3	4
8. Expressing my personal opinion	1	2	3	4
9. Summarizing what someone else in the group has said	1	2	3	4
10. Saying I disagree with something someone in the group has said	1	2	3	4
11. Expressing justified criticism of someone in the group	1	2	3	4
12. Disagreeing with the leader	1	2	3	4
13. Talking about my feelings in front of the group	1	2	3	4
14. Sharing a personal experience with the group	1	2	3	4

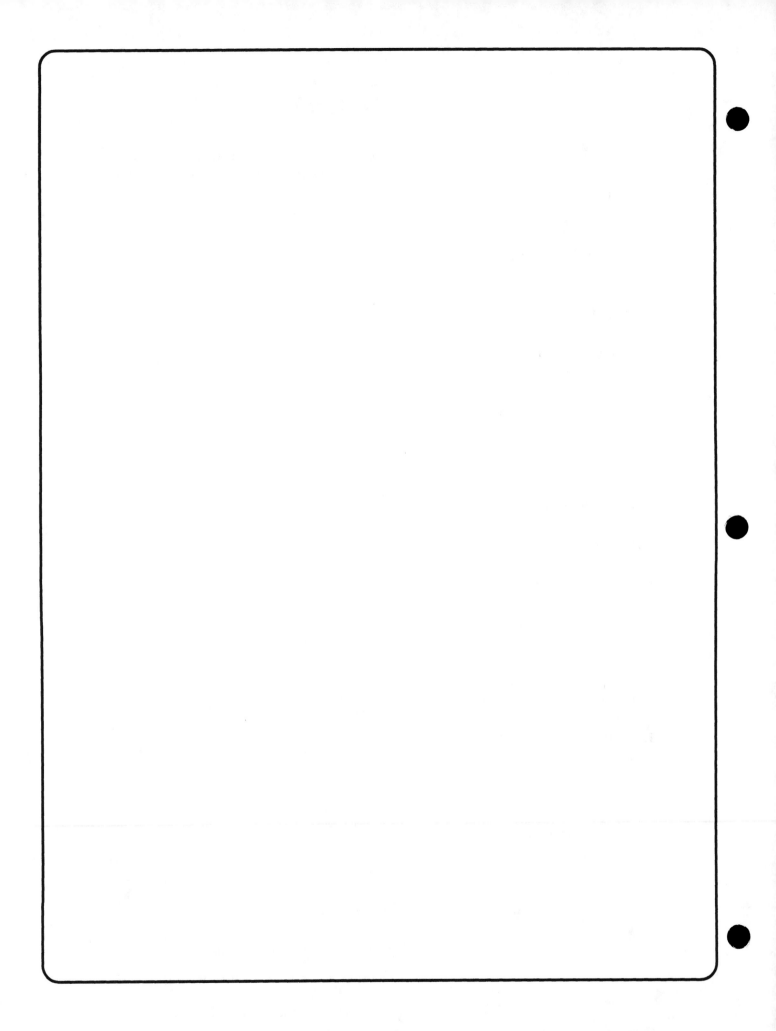

The ABC'S of Compliment

Space Requirements: Classroom or activity room

Equipment/Resources Needed: Two different color balls (any size), music (to be turned on and off), alphabet cards, backup prompts

Group Size: Small group

Program Goals:
1. To increase the participants' awareness of the importance of giving and receiving compliments.
2. To increase participants' comfort level with giving and receiving compliments.
3. To increase participants' group dyad interaction skills within a small group.

Program Description:

Preparation:
Prior to the activity, the specialist should prepare: (1) the alphabet cards with the letters *A* to *Z*, one each per index card; (2) extra compliment "prompts" in case participants have difficulty coming up with them on their own (such as physical feature, behavior, character, treatment of others); and (3) music with player.

Introduction:
This activity focuses on the giving and receiving of compliments. Individuals with social skill deficits, low self-esteem, or difficulties with interaction skills could greatly benefit from this activity.

Participants should sit in a circle, either on the floor or in chairs, with the alphabet cards in the middle. Participants should be aware of the goals and rules of this activity before it begins.

Activity Description:
Two participants are given the two balls (one red and the other yellow, for example), and asked to pass them around the circle in any direction. The specialist begins playing the music. The participants continue to toss the balls while the music plays.

When the music stops, the leader selects one alphabet letter from the pile. The individual holding the red ball must compliment the individual with the yellow ball. The compliment must start with the letter of the alphabet chosen.

The person with the yellow ball must appropriately (as directed by the facilitator) respond to the compliment. This means not minimizing the compliment, but accepting it. The individual with the yellow ball must continue to try to acknowledge the compliment until the response is acceptable to the facilitator and to the group.

If one individual has both balls in hand when the music stops, he or she must compliment himself or herself, also using a letter from the collection. The individual, though, does not respond to his or her own compliment. The process is repeated until all participants have participated in either the giving or receiving of a complement, or both.

Close with a discussion that focuses on the purpose and goals of the activity. Use the following debriefing questions.

Debriefing Questions/Closure:
1. How comfortable were you giving a compliment to someone else?
2. What was difficult about giving a compliment to someone else?
3. How comfortable were you receiving a compliment from someone else?
4. What was difficult about receiving a compliment from someone else?
5. Why are compliments important—both giving and receiving?
6. How often do you receive compliments? How do you usually respond?
7. How often do you give compliments?
8. Did you already know how to appropriately respond to a compliment given to you?
9. What have you learned from this activity? How well was the activity goal reached?

Leadership Considerations:
1. Be prepared to provide examples of giving and receiving compliments to the group. It may be helpful to let them try first, give examples, then resume the activity.
2. It is important that everyone be given an opportunity to participate in the activity. The balls can be passed off pretty quickly, so keep a close eye on who really had it when the music stopped.
3. It may be helpful to remove each letter as it gets used. This way, the same words cannot be used by more than one individual participating.

Variations:
1. This activity can also be used as a leisure awareness or leisure resource activity. As the letters are pulled from the collection, individuals can name one activity they participate in or one resource they utilize beginning with that letter. One ball could mean an activity and one ball could mean a resource.
2. This activity could be used to strengthen other areas of the social skill spectrum as well. The individual with the red ball could say, "Thank you," and the individual with the yellow ball would be expected to respond with, "You're welcome." This variation may be a bit limited, but if examples are provided instead of letters, there would be greater success.
3. If participating individuals are lacking teamwork skills, a variation could include the same activity using the two different balls to determine teams. Together, these individuals must decide who to compliment, what to say, and how to say it.

Creator: Nikki Colba Harder, CTRS, Illinois State University, Normal, Illinois.

Compliment Web

Space Requirements: Classroom or activity room

Equipment/Materials: One large ball of yarn

Group Size: Small group

Program Goals:
1. To improve participants' ability to compliment a peer within a small group.
2. To improve participants' ability to politely receive a compliment from a peer within a small group.

Program Description:
Preparation:
Obtain a ball of yarn.

Introduction:
Begin by discussing the importance of being able to give and receive compliments. What role can compliments play in a friendship? Why are compliments important? Discuss how to give a compliment, how compliments must be genuine, and how compliments should be given frequently. Have participants practice giving and receiving compliments, if they do not possess these skills. Explain the rules of the activity.

Activity Description:
Ask participants to sit in a circle, either on the floor or in chairs. One person starts with the ball of yarn and pulls about a three-foot length from the ball. (The yarn stays attached to the ball as it is thrown and will form a web.) This person will say the name of another person in the group, and give that person a compliment. The ball of yarn is then tossed to that person.

The second person must respond appropriately by saying, "Thank you." This person then pulls about a three-foot length from the ball of yarn. The person continues by saying the name of another person in the group, giving that person a compliment, and tossing the ball of yarn.

That person responds to the compliment, and the game continues until all individuals have been given and have received compliments. At the end of the activity, all participants should be connected with the yarn.

Close with a discussion about giving compliments. Ask how easy or difficult it is for participants to give and receive compliments. The specialist may choose to lead a skill session specifically addressing skills needed to give and receive compliments, if participants lack these skills. (Often people have the skills but little motivation.)

Use the debriefing questions that follow to end the activity session.

Debriefing Questions/Closure:
1. How easy or difficult was it for you to give compliments?
2. How easy or difficult was it for you to receive compliments?
3. How do compliments make you feel?
4. Why do compliments have to be genuine?
5. How often do you give compliments to those around you?
6. How would people be affected if you gave more compliments?
7. How will you use what you have learned in this activity in the future?

Leadership Considerations:
1. Have examples of compliments ready (e.g., physical features, helpfulness, attitude, interactions, appearance, clothing, skills).
2. Give participants time during the activity to take in and enjoy the compliments they are given.
3. Use lots of positive reinforcement throughout the activity.

Variations:
1. Other content can be used instead of compliments, such as leisure skills they have in common or places they have been.

Express Ways

Space Requirements: Classroom or activity room

Equipment/Materials: Assorted construction paper squares on each of which is written a different means of expressing affection for someone, reflecting the closeness of a relationship, e.g., talking, gift giving, handshake, hug, kiss (prepare five squares for each of these means of affection); markers; list of relationships written on chalkboard, e.g., parents, siblings, roommates, friends, peers, teachers, counselors, strangers; chalkboard; chalk.

Group Size: Small group

Program Goals:
1. To increase participants' ability to express feelings of affection for others.
2. To enhance participants' ability to identify and express affection appropriately.
3. To increase participants' awareness of the various ways to show affection.

Program Description:

Preparation:
Prior to the start of the activity, prepare construction paper squares by writing one way to express affection on each, making five copies of each expression (for example, make five squares with the word *hug* on them). Examples include kiss, handshake, wave, give a gift, pat on the arm, talking, and being intimate. Tape the squares face down on the board, and number the back sides randomly. Write the list of relationships (parents, siblings, teacher, counselor) down one side of the chalkboard, to be used as a prompt.

Introduction:
The purpose of this activity is to help participants learn different ways to express affection to someone. Briefly explain what is meant by affection and emphasize that, depending on the closeness of a relationship, there are many different ways to express affection. Ask the participants to come up with two examples of how to express affection.

Activity Description:
One person is chosen to start, and selects a colored square from the board, by calling out the number. That person is to tell to whom, on the list of relationships, he or she would display that means of affection. The specialist can prompt the participant by saying, "To whom would you give a hug?"

Responses will vary with each participant, depending on how comfortable he or she is with expressing affection, and how close he or she is to his or her family. However, responses will need to reflect appropriate behavior. If a response seems inappropriate, either by excessive expression or lack of closeness, ask the participant to explain further.

Repeat the process with the next participant. That participant chooses a new square from the board.

The same answer cannot be given for a means of expressing affection when it is picked again, however, it can be given for other means, as this will allow for difference among the participants.

Close with discussion of affection, relationships and appropriate displays of affection. The following debriefing questions may be helpful in closing discussion.

Debriefing Questions/Closure:
1. Why do we want to express affection for others?
2. Who must be comfortable when expressing affection?
3. Is it OK that people display affection differently from one another? Why?
4. What if you are comfortable giving a friend a hug and he or she is not?
5. How can you tell when someone is comfortable or uncomfortable with your display of affection?

Leadership Considerations:
1. The possibility exists that a participant has experienced family problems and may be guarded when discussing closeness or relationships.
2. Emphasize that there are similarities and differences in how people express affection, and that they are based on personal choice.
3. Be prepared to discuss the ramifications and consequences which would result from expressing affection inappropriately.

Variations:
1. Participants may specify particular people rather than give a generic description, e.g., "My friend Bob Smith" rather than a "friend."
2. Explore particular feelings one may have towards a significant other.
3. Participants respond in a reverse manner, i.e., rather than responding to "Who would you give a hug to?" participants would be asked "From whom would you be comfortable getting a hug?"
4. Have participants prepare a list of consequences about the inappropriate expression of affection and use this list as a topic of discussion.

Creator: Deland DeCoteau, West Central Human Service Center, Bismarck, North Dakota.

Dear Abby, Dear Abby I

Space Requirements: Classroom or activity room with tables

Equipment/Resource Requirements: Paper, pens or pencils, accompanying form

Group Size: Small group

Program Goals:
1. To increase participants' ability to generate solutions to social problems.
2. To increase participants' ability to recognize that several solutions may exist to solving problems.

Program Description:
Preparation:
Make copies of Dear Abby, Dear Abby I form, one for each participant.

Introduction:
The purpose of this activity is to have participants generate solutions to problem areas in typical social situations. Begin with a discussion of social situations that might require solving some sort of problem (e.g., what to say to an individual whom you have just met, how to say no to a friend, how to handle a refusal).

Activity Description:
Hand each individual a copy of the Dear Abby, Dear Abby I form and a pencil. Ask each individual to write back to the individual who is experiencing a problem.

Allow five minutes for participants to respond to each of the letters. Either discuss them one at a time, or allow participants to complete all three and then discuss.

Discuss the responses given by the participants. Focus on the problem-solving aspects of the situations. Reiterate that the purpose is to help generate solutions to social situations.

Discussion/Debriefing Questions:
1. How many of the solutions were similar? dissimilar?
2. How did you come up with a solution? What were alternatives you examined?
3. Have you experienced any of these problems in the past? What did you do?
4. Do you anticipate facing problems like these in the future?
5. How has hearing other participants' solutions helped you?
6. How will you use what you learned in this activity in the future?

Leadership Considerations:
1. Modify the situations to fit the group.
2. If participants have difficulty writing, use a chalkboard to record answers for the group.
3. If the group is not familiar with the advice columnist "Dear Abby," bring in a copy from the local newspaper.

Variations:
1. See Dear Abby, Dear Abby II.

Creator: Norma J. Stumbo, Ph.D., CTRS, Illinois State University, Normal, Illinois.

Dear Abby, Dear Abby I

Dear Abby,

I'm new in town and really shy. I find it difficult to make friends, but I want to be able to go places with people. What do you suggest that I do to make new friends?

Signed, New in Town

Dear New in Town:

_____

_____

_____

_____

_____

Dear Abby:

My best friend has begun to ignore me and go out with another set of friends. I want to ask what's wrong, but I'm afraid to. I feel really rejected and down. I'm not sure what to do. What do you think I should do?

Signed, Puzzled

Dear Puzzled:

_____

_____

_____

_____

_____

Dear Abby:

My best friend has started using drugs. All she wants to do is to hang out with other people who use drugs, and sit around. She used to be really active. I really like my friend but have a hard time with what she's doing. She seems to be headed toward trouble. What can I do?

Signed, Don't Do Drugs

Dear Don't Do Drugs:

_____

_____

_____

_____

_____

Dear Abby, Dear Abby II

Space Requirements: Classroom or activity room with tables

Equipment/Resource Requirements: Accompanying form, pens or pencils, paper

Group Size: Small group

Program Goals:
1. To increase participants' ability to identify problems they may have in social situations.
2. To increase participants' ability to generate possible solutions to problematic social situations.

Description/Procedure:

Preparation:
Make copies of Dear Abby, Dear Abby II form, one for each participant.

Introduction:
The purpose of this activity is to have participants identify problem areas and to have the group generate potential solutions. Begin with a discussion of social situations that might require solving some sort of problem (for example, what to say to an individual whom you have just met, how to say no to a friend, or how to handle a refusal).

Activity Description:
Hand each individual a copy of the Dear Abby, Dear Abby II form and a pencil. Ask each individual to write a letter to "Dear Abby" about a problematic social situation. These letters will need to be shared with the group.

Allow five to 10 minutes for participants to write their letters.

One by one, ask the participants to share their letters with the group. The group is to help generate possible solutions to each letter. The individual writing the letter is to evaluate each solution to see if he or she feels comfortable following the advice.

Discuss the responses given by the participants. Focus on the problem-solving aspects of the situations. Reiterate that the purpose of the activity is to help identify and generate solutions to social problems. Use the following debriefing questions to close the activity.

Discussion/Debriefing Questions:
1. How many of the solutions were similar? dissimilar?
2. How did you come up with solutions? What were alternatives that you examined?
3. Have you experienced any of these problems in the past? What did you do?
4. Do you anticipate facing problems like these in the future?
5. How has hearing other participants' solutions helped you?

Leadership Considerations:
1. If participants have difficulty writing, use a chalkboard to record answers for the group.
2. If the group is not familiar with the advice columnist "Dear Abby," bring in a copy from the local newspaper.

Variations:

    1. See Dear Abby, Dear Abby I.

Creator: Norma J. Stumbo, Ph.D., CTRS, Illinois State University, Normal, Illinois.

Dear Abby, Dear Abby II

Dear Abby:

_____

_____

_____

_____

_____

_____

Solutions Generated by the Group:

    1. _____

    2. _____

    3. _____

Dear Abby:

_____

_____

_____

_____

_____

_____

Solutions Generated by the Group:

    1. _____

    2. _____

    3. _____

Dear Abby:

_____

_____

_____

_____

_____

Solutions Generated by the Group:

    1. _____

    2. _____

    3. _____

What's a Good Option?

Space Requirements: Classroom or activity room

Equipment/Materials: Accompanying forms, chalkboard, chalk, envelopes, scissors

Group Size: Individual or small group

Program Goals:
1. To improve participants' ability to select appropriate responses to social situations.
2. To improve participants' ability to differentiate between positive and negative social responses.
3. To lay foundation for a later social skill building session.

Program Description:

Preparation:
Prior to the start of the activity, copy off as many What's a Good Option responses forms as there are participants. Cut each form into pieces and place into response envelopes. Each participant will also need one copy of the What's a Good Option questions form.

Introduction:
Begin with a discussion about how a lot of situations require that we have adequate social skills. Usually this means that we have to interpret the situation and respond with an appropriate social response. There are many social responses from which to choose, some positive and some negative. Discuss the consequences of both positive and negative social responses. Review the purpose and goals of the activity.

Activity Description:
Hand each participant a copy of the What's a Good Option questions form, and one envelope containing the slips of What's a Good Option responses. Ask participants to start with the first question and decide what would be an appropriate response from the options in the envelope. For example, the question is: "The people next to you are talking loudly. What do you do?" Ask participants to sort through the responses and select one or two that seem appropriate.

Ask them to share their answers with a partner. How similar are their responses? Ask for the partners to share with the larger group. Have the group come to a consensus, through discussion of positive and negative responses, before moving on.

Repeat procedure with several or all questions. Allow time for discussion and justification of answers.

Close with a review of the goals of the activity, asking the following questions.

Debriefing Questions/Closure:
1. What do the positive responses have in common?
2. What do the negative responses have in common?
3. Why is it important to respond positively to people?
4. What can you do to be more positive in your responses?
5. How can you help people be positive towards you?
6. Name one positive response you can use today.

Leadership Considerations:
1. Reduce the number of responses in the envelopes to accommodate the participants' abilities.

Variations:
1. Use the response sheet by itself to have participants divide responses between positive and negative.
2. Change the questions to suit the needs, ages and situations of the population.

Creator: Norma J. Stumbo, Ph.D., CTRS, Illinois State University, Normal, Illinois.

What's a Good Option?

What do you do questions:

The people next to you are talking loudly.

You want something from the person next to you.

You think you are being ignored by staff.

You accidentally kick someone as you walk by.

Someone says something hurtful to you.

A new person walks in the door.

Someone is talking to you.

Someone is trying to get your attention.

The person talking to you is making you nervous.

Someone is in your way.

Someone is giving you directions to a place you want to go.

You are eating a meal with friends.

You meet an old friend you haven't seen for a while.

A friend shares a secret with you.

You want to borrow a friend's book.

Someone hurts your feelings.

Someone says something nice about you.

Your best friend wins a neat award.

Someone accuses you of lying.

Someone asks how you're doing.

Someone eats the snack you were saving for after lunch.

Someone is being introduced to you.

Someone asks for your help.

You want to get someone's attention.

A friend breaks your radio.

A friend disagrees with something you've said.

Someone walks by and compliments the person next to you.

Someone says something mean to you.

Someone gives you a nice compliment.

You want to join in on a conversation.

You said something that hurt a friend's feelings.

What's a Good Option?

Responses:

Ask for what I want.	Compliment the person.
Do something silly to get attention.	Talk about myself for a really long time.
Get angry.	Ask the person for money.
Stomp away.	Hug the person.
Get mad and show I am mad.	Escort the person out the door.
Show an honest emotion.	Start an argument with an unkind statement.
Ask more questions to clarify.	Use my best manners and be polite.
Take a deep breath to calm myself.	Eat my food really quickly.
Walk away.	Complain about all that I have to do today.
Ignore what the other person says.	Say something really nasty about the person.
Act as if it doesn't matter when it really does.	Tell the person's secret behind his or her back.
Listen carefully.	Congratulate the person on winning the award.
Smile and say "Hi."	Eavesdrop on their conversation.
Shake hands with the person.	Mind my own business.
Ask the person to fight.	Say, "Hey, get out of my way!"
Show signs that I'm bored.	Say, "Give me that!"
Fidget and fuss with my clothing.	Let her borrow it until tomorrow.
Look away frequently.	Play the "victim" and look sad.
Look the person in the eyes.	Pay close attention to what the person is saying.
Tap the person on the shoulder.	Keep the person's secret to myself.
Say, "Please, can I. . . ?"	Act like I'm not afraid when I am.
Say, "Thanks for sharing!"	Help the person however I can.
Say, "Excuse me. . . ."	Smack the person hard to get his or her attention.
Repeat what the other person said.	
Say, "I'm sorry for what I said. . . ."	
Ask how the person is feeling.	

Beads in a Bottle

Space Requirements: Classroom or activity room

Equipment/Resource Requirements: Narrow-necked bottles, beads, string, floor padding

Size of Group: Small group

Program Goals:
1. To increase participants' ability to identify the benefits of cooperation in a group.
2. To increase participants' understanding of the need to put group goals over personal goals, in some situations.

Program Description:

Preparation:
Prepare bottles ahead of time.

Introduction:
Begin with a discussion about cooperation and how it is essential for a group to cooperate to complete common tasks. Ask the participants to describe a situation in which they cooperated with a group, and a situation in which they did not cooperate well. How did the two situations differ? In which situation did they succeed and feel better about their accomplishments? How can cooperation help a group get to its goal?

Activity Description:
Divide participants into groups of four to five individuals. On top of floor pad (e.g., carpet square, in case bottle falls over), place one bottle in the center of each group. In each bottle are placed the beads on individual strings. The group members are instructed to each hold a string and get their bead out of the bottle as quickly as possible. (The bottle needs to have a neck narrow enough so that only one bead may be pulled out at a time.) The first group to get its beads all out of the bottle first "wins." It will become obvious to the group members that they must communicate so that people take turns and the group succeeds. The point is giving up one's personal benefit for the good of the group.

The specialist may have the group reverse this action, and have each group place its beads back in the bottle, with the first group finishing "winning."

Refocus on the goals of the activity, and finish with a discussion about cooperation.

Discussion/Debriefing Questions:
1. What did you learn from this activity?
2. How did you feel when you needed to wait your turn in order for the group to win?
3. What were successful strategies? unsuccessful strategies?
4. What are the benefits of cooperating?
5. What are drawbacks of cooperating?
6. What did you learn that you can use in the future?
7. What are similar situations to this in everyday life?

Leadership Considerations:
1. Make sure that bottles are stable enough to not fall over and break.
2. Make sure the group does not get out of control.

Variations:
1. Have different sizes and colors of beads represent something, like special teams or team leader.

Creator: Norma J. Stumbo, Ph.D., CTRS, Illinois State University, Normal, Illinois.

Holiday Wall Mural

Space Requirements: Classroom or activity room

Equipment/Resources Needed: Large sheets of paper, pencils, crayons, markers, chalk, tape, small pieces of paper

Group Size: Individual or small group

Program Goals:
1. To improve participants' positive group peer interactions.
2. To improve participants' awareness of the need for teamwork or others' contributions.
3. To encourage individual and group creativity.

Program Description:

Preparation:
Gather listed materials.

Introduction:
The purpose of this activity is to encourage teamwork, and to show that a worthwhile project can result from many participants. At the beginning of the activity, the participants are told the purpose of the activity and challenged to work together during the activity.

Activity Description:
The activity begins with the participants being asked to name items or themes associated with a given holiday. The ideas are individually written on pieces of paper, which are then folded to cover the written word. Each participant then chooses a paper until all ideas have been distributed. The participants may be allowed to trade ideas, but only the number of times determined by the program leader.

Examples of ideas for Halloween items or themes include ghosts, trick or treating, haunted houses, witches, pumpkins, skeletons, candy, spider webs, monsters and goblins, costumes, masks, and cemeteries. The leader may have ideas ready for the specific holiday to prompt the participants.

The participants then move to the large paper, to be hung on the wall, to create the holiday mural. Each participant is to draw on the paper the themes or ideas that have been chosen by him or her on the given paper. Each participant has a different theme and a different idea as to how that theme should be represented.

When the paper is full and the participants are satisfied with the mural, it can be hung with pride for all to see. The leader then reviews the purpose and goals of the activity, focusing on the following debriefing questions.

Debriefing Questions/Closure:
1. Are you happy with how the final drawing looked?
2. How did teamwork benefit the project?
3. How did working with others affect your creativity?
4. What comment can you make on someone else's work?
5. Would it look the same if someone had been left out?
6. What did you learn from this activity?
7. Did anything get in your way?
8. How did you resolve that conflict?

There are many ways this activity can prove to be effective, depending on the group involved. In itself, the activity promotes teamwork, the respect of personal space and creativity, and has the potential for positive interaction between the participants. With the use of the variations, it also can be modified to fit or better serve a given population.

Leadership Considerations:
1. Throughout this activity, it is very important to remind the participants that they need to respect others' personal space and personal ideas. Each individual has a different idea about how the project could be completed.
2. If one of the variations is being used, it may be helpful to have the group "elect" a leader. This can be helpful to get the group together as a group instead of using individual minds and ideas.

Variations:
1. The activity can become a little more specific in that the participants may be asked to choose, or vote on, only one type of coloring material (crayons, markers, or chalk). This would demand the agreement on a decision between all of the participants before the project even begins.
2. The participants may be asked to create a specific scene as opposed to an abstract mural. This would allow them to plan where each individual item would be placed, the decision to include or reject specific items, and would create a teamwork atmosphere.

Creator: Nikki Colba Harder, CTRS, Illinois State University, Normal, Illinois.

First Impressions Bouquet

Space Requirements: Classroom or activity room

Equipment/Resources Needed: Variety of flowers and greenery (enough to create a bouquet of flowers), vases

Group Size: Individual or small group

Program Goals:
1. To increase participants' awareness of the difference between individuals.
2. To increase participants' ability to identify and verbalize differences in people.
3. To increase participants' awareness of the relationship between appearance and how people judge others on the first impression.

Program Description:

Preparation:
Obtain flowers, greenery and vases.

Introduction:
Discuss the impact of first impressions. Ask participants to recall an experience where they can remember the impression made by someone the first time they met. What was special about the impression that the participant remembers?

Activity Description:
Have flowers, greenery, and vases on a table. Hand each person a vase. Allow the participants to start creating a flower design in their vases. Encourage discussion as individuals complete their arrangements.

Discuss the differences in the flowers and their unique aspects. Relate the flowers' unique differences to unique differences in human beings. Talk about participants' first impressions of the flowers. Which are most appealing? Which are least appealing? What can you see when you look beyond just the surface? What characteristics do you find at a deeper level, when you take more time to look?

Relate their first impressions of the flowers to that of people. Discuss how first impressions are important, but how sometimes upon closer inspection, there is more to a flower or person than first meets the eye.

Discuss how to make a good first impression. What sorts of things impact on that first impression? What actions can participants take to make good first impressions? How can they help others take a second, deeper look if they do not make a good first impression?

Close with participants being able to list several ways to make a good first impression and being able to list ways to make a good second impression. Include the following discussion questions.

Debriefing Questions/Closure:
1. Why are first impressions important?
2. What are strategies to make a good first impression?
3. What are strategies to make a good second impression?
4. How do we help others make a good first impression?
5. Why is it important to look deeper into someone's character, than just rely on looks?

Leadership Considerations:
1. This activity is most successful with more than five people in attendance.
2. Try to generate discussion by providing your own input.

Variations:
1. Silk flowers or magazine pictures of flowers can be used instead of real flowers.

Creator: Lisa Scherer, CTRS, and David Griggs, CTRS, Choate Mental Health and Developmental Center, Anna, Illinois.

Body Image Awareness

Space Requirements: Classroom or activity room, with adequate open floor space

Equipment/Resource Requirements: Six feet of paper per person (as tall as the participant's body), drawing utensils

Group Size: Small group

Program Goals:
1. To increase participants' awareness of their body images.
2. To increase participants' ability to identify positive attributes of their bodies.

Program Description:

Preparation:
Prior to the start of the activity, cut paper in adequate lengths to match the height of the participants. For example, for smaller children, three to five feet of paper per person will be adequate; for adults, at least six feet per person may be needed.

Introduction:
Open activity with a discussion about personal body images. People feel differently about their bodies, some parts they may like, some parts they may not. The purpose of this activity is to help participants identify positive personal messages about their bodies.

Activity Description:
Hand each participant one large piece of paper and a marker. Have the participants find a partner. Ask one person to lay his or her paper on the floor, and to lie on top of it lengthwise. The other partner is to trace around the participant on the piece of paper. When the partner is finished tracing the first person, they switch and the other partner traces the participant. Allow five to 10 minutes for completion of body tracings.

After everyone is finished tracing each other, each person is to identify body parts he or she likes about himself or herself and write or draw those on his or her body outline. For example, a person might draw a pretty smile, a well-shaped ear, a strong arm, a dimpled knee, or a hairy chest. Allow 15 to 20 minutes for participants to think about and draw their positive messages. The specialist should check on each participant during this part of the activity, to help him or her identify positive messages.

When all participants are finished, the specialist asks the participants questions about the positive messages they drew or wrote about their bodies. For example:

- "Who had something positive to say about his or her hands?"
- "What were the good points of your legs?"
- "What positive messages did you have about your face?"

Close with debriefing questions and reiterate the purpose of the activity. Allow participants to keep their body posters and hang them in their rooms or take them home.

Debriefing Questions/Closure:
1. How many positive messages were you able to identify about your body?
2. How is your body similar or different from others in the group?
3. What messages were similar to one another between group members?
4. What messages were really different from one another?
5. Why is it important to have a positive body image?
6. What are the consequences of having a poor body image?

Leadership Considerations:
1. Participants must be wearing appropriate clothing.
2. Be aware of the comfort level of participants in being drawn and drawing around another person. The specialist may need to be the one who draws around participants.
3. If the above two are a problem, have predrawn generic body forms that participants may use.

Variations:
1. The specialist may ask the participants to offer positive body image messages to others in the group.

Creator: Jennifer Matkowich, Illinois State University, Normal, Illinois.

Healthy Selves

Space Requirements: Classroom or activity room

Equipment/Materials: Accompanying form, pens or pencils

Group Size: Individual or small group

Program Goals:
1. To increase participants' ability to self-determine if they have a healthy self-image.
2. To increase participants' positive perception of self.

Program Description:

Preparation:
Make copies of Healthy Selves form, one for each participant.

Introduction:
Ask participants to describe the concept of a self-image. What is the difference between a healthy self-image and a poor self-image? How can you tell which a person might have? What are factors that might influence someone's self-image? Review the goals of the activity and let participants know that they will be exploring their own self-image.

Activity Description:
Hand a copy of the Healthy Selves form and a pencil to each participant. Ask the participants to look at the pairings and put a check mark by the characteristic they most identify with.

(Do not tell them yet that in the left column are characteristics of healthier self-images and the characteristics in the right column are characteristics of poorer self-images.)

Ask the participants to identify which characteristics they think belong to someone with a healthy self-image. Ask them to identify characteristics they think belong to someone with a poor self-image. How can they tell the differences? Does everyone in the group agree?

If participants feel they can share, ask them on which side they made most of their check marks. Are there similarities within the group?

Reveal, if they have not guessed, that the left side is positive and the right side is less positive. Discuss the implications of a healthy and poor self-image. How can individuals with poorer self-images develop more positive ones? What actions can they take?

Close with the following debriefing questions.

Debriefing Questions/Closure:
1. How do people with positive self-images act?
2. Name a public person who has a positive self-image. How can you tell?
3. How do people with a poorer self-image act?
4. Name a public figure who has a poorer self-image. How can you tell?
5. How can people develop a more positive self-image without being egotistical?
6. What actions can you take to develop a better self-image?
7. What actions can you take to help friends develop a better self-image?

Leadership Considerations:
1. Be aware of the self-disclosure level of the participants.
2. While you want individuals to identify their own self-image, allow people the right to privacy.

Variations:
1. Replace some behaviors on the work sheet with behaviors displayed by members of the group.

Creator: Norma J. Stumbo, Ph.D., CTRS, Illinois State University, Normal, Illinois.

Healthy Selves

Make a check mark by which option best describes you.

I usually: **I usually:**

I usually:	I usually:
❏ Tell the truth	❏ Lie whenever I need to
❏ Display creativity	❏ Rely on someone else to come up with ideas
❏ Accept compliments and affection	❏ Steer away from compliments and affection
❏ Enjoy being by myself	❏ Hate being by myself
❏ Am able to memorize lists when I need to	❏ Have difficulty memorizing lists
❏ Feel optimistic that I can succeed	❏ Don't think I'm going to make it
❏ Manage my anger pretty well	❏ Get angry pretty quickly
❏ Am able to express joy and happiness	❏ Have trouble being happy
❏ Have enthusiasm for a project I'm working on	❏ Don't care too much about anything
❏ Am able to express my opinions	❏ Have a hard time getting my point across
❏ Am able to accept when people have a different opinion	❏ Dislike when people disagree with me
❏ Am assertive when I need to be	❏ Am either too aggressive or too passive
❏ Stand up for myself when I need to	❏ Prefer that others take care of me
❏ Am in control of what I do and say	❏ Lose control when I'm angry or tired
❏ Am able to empathize with others	❏ Have no pity for others
❏ Am sensitive to the feelings of others	❏ Focus mostly on how I feel
❏ Remain pretty positive	❏ Can get pretty negative
❏ Am able to concentrate	❏ Cannot concentrate, even when I need to
❏ Make and act on my own decisions	❏ Rely on others to make a decision

Cage Ball Dare

Space Requirements: Gym or outdoor area

Equipment/Resources Needed: Cage ball (or other soft, but large ball), dare cards

Group Size: Small group

Program Goals:
1. To increase participants' ability to take personal risks within a small group setting.
2. To increase participants' ability to distinguish between positive and negative risks.

Program Description:

Preparation:
Gather materials. Prepare dare cards, such as "Sing your favorite song," "Tell a clean joke," "Tell the group what is your favorite possession," "Tell about one of your aspirations."

Introduction:
Begin the activity with a discussion about personal risk taking. For some people, risk taking is easier than for others. Ask a few members in the group to describe a recent situation where they took a personal risk, or did not take a personal risk, but may have thought about it. Discuss the difference between positive risks, that help us grow, and negative risks, that jeopardize our health and well-being. Ask participants to give examples of each.

Activity Description:
Have the group form a circle sitting on the floor. Explain that the object of the game is to kick the ball, using only the sole of the foot, over another person's (opponent's) head.

Each time the ball is kicked out (leaves the circle), the person whose head it went over needs to stand up and perform a dare.

The dare is selected by the leader from the dare deck. The dare card stunts may range from simply stating a favorite food to singing a song to the group as comfort levels increase.

There is no set winner or loser. If there is a question of whom the ball went over, the leader should have both parties in question perform the dare. If an illegal kick is used or hands are used, the person must perform a dare.

Close with a discussion about personal risk taking, including the following debriefing questions.

Debriefing Questions/Closure:
1. How comfortable were you when called upon to perform a dare?
2. In what ways did the risks become easier?
3. How did or did not the group members support one another?
4. What cooperative relationships were formed?
5. How can you apply this to risk taking in the future?
6. What is a current situation in which you really need to take a personal risk?

Leadership Considerations:
1. Stand outside of the circle for the best view of activity.
2. Prepare the dare cards prior to activity implementation.
3. Depending on the population, it may be necessary to set ground rules to minimize embarrassment.

Variations:
1. Play the game in a team fashion instead of individually.
2. The person who hits the ball over another person's head decides the dare.
3. Players are asked to use only one foot.

Creators: Stacy McNerney, CTRS; Stacy Zawaski, and Sherby Philpot, Glen Oaks Medical Center, Glendale Heights, Illinois.

Short Story Writing

Space Requirements: Classroom or activity room

Equipment/Resources Needed: Paper, pencils (enough for each participant), typewriter, typing skills

Group Size: Small group

Program Goals:
1. To improve participants' awareness of leisure interests and their positive effects for peer relations.
2. To help participants improve team skills and social skills in a small group.
3. To help participants identify and clarify their values within a social context.

Program Description:

Preparation:
Gather materials necessary for activity.

Introduction:
Begin with a discussion of leisure interests. Ask participants to name some of their interests and find ones in common with other members of the group. Explain the purpose and goals of this activity. The participants will write a short story, developing three to five characters, with participants using their own leisure interests in bringing all the characters together in the plot. The purpose of creating the story is to increase participants' awareness of how leisure interests and activities can bring people together socially.

Activity Description:
Divide into groups of three to five participants. Ask the participants in each small group to determine the number of characters for the story, their gender and their age.

Assign character development among group members. Some participants may work in pairs, others independently on this portion of the activity. Participants need to include the following in developing their character(s):

- first name
- age
- gender
- occupation
- three or four different leisure interests or activities
- relationship status

Allow 10 to 15 minutes for the participants to develop their individual character(s).

When they are completed, ask the participants to review the identities of the characters, within the larger group. Ask them to individually begin plot development by using leisure interests of characters to start social interactions and relationships.

All participants write their own individual story endings, with the leader making sure that each plot development includes leisure interests and activities. Allow 10 to 15 minutes for plot development.

Ask the participants to share their different endings, with the group members discussing the possibilities and potential of each. Ask the group members to decide on which story ending they like the best. Type story parts from day to day. (This activity may take three to four sessions depending on the story length and participants.)

Close each session with appropriate discussion, using the following debriefing questions.

Debriefing Questions/Closure:
1. How did the characters differ from one another?
2. What behaviors of the characters did you like, not like, or feel neutral toward?
3. What were some of the leisure interests and activities of the characters?
4. How did the leisure interests and activities of the characters help them to interact with one another?
5. How can your own leisure interests and activities help you interact with other people?
6. How does your leisure affect your social interactions with others?

Leadership Considerations:
1. List the characters' demographic headings for each participant to assist with development.
2. Request volunteer(s) to type story prior to activity.

Variations:
1. Add one to two chapters if story plot allows.
2. If any participant has artistic interests or abilities, include pictures in the story.

Creator: Barb Sauer, CTRS, and Kristen Geissler, CTRS, Anoka-Metro Regional Treatment Center, Anoka, Minnesota.

Social Skills Game

Space Requirements: Classroom or activity room

Equipment/Resource Requirements: Game board, one die, prepared game cards, game pieces (e.g., paper clips, coins)

Group Size: Small group

Program Goals:
1. To increase participants' ability to identify and practice conversational skills.
2. To increase participants' ability to identify and practice manners and being polite.
3. To increase participants' ability to identify and practice being able to refuse a request.
4. To increase participants' ability to identify and practice asking for assistance.

Program Description:

Preparation:

Prior to the start of the activity, the specialist should prepare game cards. The questions to place on game cards are located on the Social Skills Game form. The specialist should make a copy of the game board and a set of cards per every four players.

Introduction:

At the start of the activity, the specialist should explain the idea of social skills. The four categories of this activity are conversational skills, manners and being polite, refusing a request, and asking for assistance. Ask participants to give some examples of each of the four kinds of social skills. Continue until all participants are familiar with the concepts and terms. Review the goals of the activity.

Activity Description:

Each group of four participants gets one complete game board set. Explain the rules of the game. Each person rolls the die once and the one with the highest number goes first. Play will continue to that person's left. Make sure all players understand the concepts of game play before beginning.

Have each person select a game piece and place it on the *start* square. The person who won the roll of the die begins and rolls the die again. He or she moves his or her game piece that number of spaces, and selects the top card that corresponds with the space on which he or she lands.

He or she picks up the card, reads it aloud to the other participants and either answers the question or completes the action required. When completed to the satisfaction of the other players and the specialist, play continues with the person to the left. He or she rolls the die, moves that number of spaces and responds to the card he or she picks up.

Play continues in this fashion, until time to quit, or someone crosses the finish line. The specialist should facilitate discussion throughout the game.

Close with a focus on the goals of the activity and the following debriefing questions.

Debriefing Questions/Closure:
1. What did you learn about conversational skills?
2. What did you learn about manners and being polite?
3. What did you learn about refusing a request?
4. What did you learn about asking for assistance?
5. Was any one skill more difficult than the others?
6. Which skill(s) do you need to practice?
7. How will knowing these skills help you in the future?

Leadership Considerations:
1. Encourage players to think about everyday situations that require these social skills.
2. Players should use examples appropriate to their ages and disability.
3. The specialist should help focus on discussion of topics, beyond just quick answers.

Variations:
1. Change content of cards according to what participants need to learn from the game.
2. Change the number of squares, adding more of one skill if desired.

Creator: Norma J. Stumbo, Ph.D., CTRS, Illinois State University, Normal, Illinois.

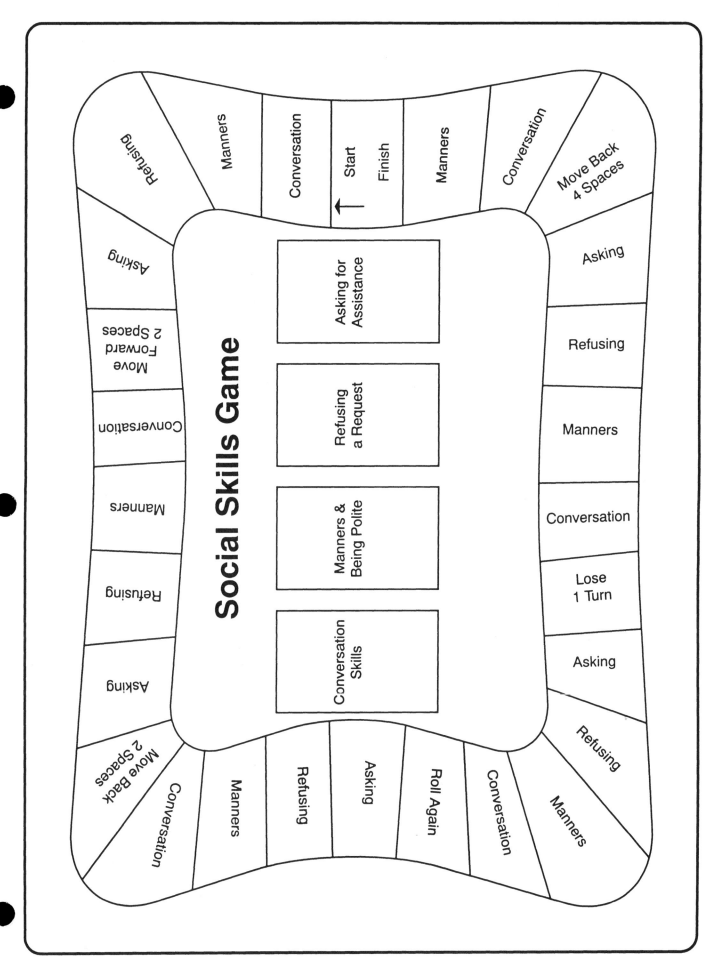

Social Skills Game

Social Skills Game

Ideas for conversational skills:

Show us how you would introduce your sister to a friend.

Name two topics of conversation that are safe with a stranger.

Show us how you would welcome someone into a group.

Ask the person to your left to show us a proper greeting.

Ask the person to your right how to end a conversation.

Ask the person across from you to show how to respond to, "How are you?"

Show us how to let someone know you are listening to what he or she is saying.

Show us how to greet a good friend.

Tell us how you respond when someone says, "I'm troubled."

Show us how you should answer the telephone.

Ideas for asking for assistance:

Show us how you would ask for help to reach something high on a shelf.

Show us how you would ask for help to solve a tough problem.

Show us how you would ask for help when you're running low on cash.

Ask the person to your right to ask for your immediate assistance with a problem.

Ask the person to your left to give an example of when he or she asked for help in the last week.

Show us how you react when someone asks for your help.

Show us how to wait patiently when someone cannot help you right away.

How do you know when you need to ask for assistance?

How do you know who to ask for assistance?

Who would you ask to help with a personal problem?

Ideas for manners and being polite:

Show us an example of sharing.

Show us an example of taking turns.

Show us an example of not interrupting a conversation.

How loud should your voice be when talking in a group?

Ask the person to your right to show how to chew their food.

Tell us why being polite is important.

Ask the person to your right what he or she thinks is the most important time to be polite.

Are manners to be used in public or private places or both?

How does respect for others relate to manners?

Show us how you say, "Thank you," to someone who has done you a favor.

Ideas for refusing a request:

Show us how you turn down a friend who asks to borrow your radio.

Show us how you refuse an offer to go to the movies.

Ask the person to your left to offer you money, and you refuse it.

Ask the person across from you to give two tips for refusing an unreasonable request.

Ask the person to your right to show you how to refuse an offer of unwanted help.

Show us how to refuse an offer of unsolicited advice.

Show us how to turn down a stranger who wants a ride in your car.

Show us how to turn down a request to help when you do not need the help.

Name one thing you would let someone borrow and one thing you would not.

Show us how you react when someone says no to your request to borrow a personal item.

Decision-Making Activities

Problem-Solving Skill Building

Space Requirements: Classroom or activity room

Equipment/Resource Requirements: Accompanying form, pens or pencils, prepared situation cards

Group Size: Individual or small group

Program Goals:
1. To increase participants' awareness of a logical decision-making and problem-solving model.
2. To increase participants' ability to solve problems using a sequence of decisions.

Program Description:
Preparation:
Prepare situation cards. Some suggestions are given on the accompanying form—custom design these cards to fit the needs of the participants.

Introduction:
Begin with a discussion of problem solving and decision making. Hundreds of times per day, we make decisions and solve problems. We decide whether to take a shower, what clothes to wear, what to eat for (or whether to eat) breakfast. Sometimes we make good decisions and sometimes we make bad decisions. Ask the participants to give examples of good decisions they have made recently and examples of poor decisions. Ask participants to give examples of problems they have solved recently or have been unable to solve. These may be large or small (e.g., not having enough money to do what you want to do on Saturday night; wanting to wear clothes that are dirty and there's no time left to wash them; not knowing how to confront a friend about money he owes you).

Emphasize that a large part of solving problems is being able to make decisions, and this usually requires a logical process for the problem to be solved in the long term.

Review the goals of the activity and state the expected outcomes.

Activity Description:
Explain to participants that there are four basic steps to solving a problem. (These might be made into a poster and put on the wall.) They are:

1. Recognizing that there is a problem,
2. Defining the problem,
3. Seeking and looking at alternative ways to solve the problem, and
4. Deciding which solution is the best way to solve the problem.

This activity will require the participants to use these four steps to problem solving in a variety of situations. Start with an example for the group to complete as a whole (e.g., someone borrows your clothes without asking you or telling you they did it). Have the group go through the four steps.

First, how do you know this is a problem?

Possible answers: You want to wear the clothes and they are missing.

The clothes are in the laundry.

You see the person wearing your clothes.

The clothes are returned damaged.

Second, what is the problem?

Possible answers: A person borrowed your possessions without asking.

A person did not respect your privacy or property.

Your clothes are not there when you want them.

Third, what are alternate ways to solve the problem (brainstorm, do not reject any answers)?

Possible answers: Be angry and hurt the person.

Lock your closet door.

Ask the person to request your permission before borrowing anything again.

Simmer, but say nothing to the person.

Fourth, which of the above alternate ways is the best solution? Go through each answer above and look at the consequences—also use "assertive behavior" (versus passive or aggressive) as the goal.

Possible answer: Ask the person to request your permission before borrowing.

If that doesn't work, lock the closet door.

Use the Problem-Solving Skill Building form to go through sample scenarios; first individually, then share as a group. Help participants look for assertive solutions and decisions that help solve the problem, not create a new one.

Close with discussion about this four-step process. Focus on using this in real life events.

Debriefing Questions/Closure:

1. How can you remember each of the four steps?
2. What is a situation you will probably face within the next couple of days that you can use these four steps?
3. What is the benefit of using these steps to help make a decision?
4. Why is assertive behavior (not aggressive or passive) beneficial to all parties?
5. How do you feel when you have been assertive?
6. How do you think the other person feels when you are assertive, and not aggressive or passive?

Leadership Considerations:

1. Help participants remember the four steps by consistent and repeated use.
2. Keep it positive and keep it assertive.

Variations:

1. Change scenarios to meet the needs of the participants.
2. In a previous session, have participants originate the scenarios.

Creator: Norma J. Stumbo, Ph.D., CTRS, Illinois State University, Normal, Illinois.

Problem-Solving Skill Building

Scenario A: Your best friend wants to stay inside and watch television all day and all night long. You would prefer to do something more active outdoors.

1. First, how do you know this is a problem?

   Possible answers: _____
   _____
   _____

2. Second, what is the problem?

   Possible answers: _____
   _____
   _____

3. Third, what are alternate ways to solve the problem (brainstorm, do not reject any answers)?

   Possible answers: _____
   _____
   _____

4. Fourth, which of the above alternate ways is the best solution?

   Possible answers: _____
   _____

Scenario B: You do not seem to have energy to do the things you enjoy any more. You really want to be more involved, but you are tired most of the time.

1. First, how do you know this is a problem?

   Possible answers: _____
   _____
   _____

2. Second, what is the problem?

   Possible answers: _____
   _____
   _____

3. Third, what are alternate ways to solve the problem (brainstorm, do not reject any answers)?

   Possible answers: _____
   _____
   _____

4. Fourth, which of the above alternate ways is the best solution?

   Possible answers: _____
   _____

Three Weeks

Space Requirements: Classroom or activity room

Equipment/Resource Requirements: Accompanying form, pens or pencils

Group Size: Small group

Program Goals:
1. To increase participants' awareness of leisure choices.
2. To increase participants' knowledge of the effects of decisions on leisure situations.
3. To improve participants' awareness of their leisure values.

Program Description:

Preparation:

Make copies of Three Weeks form, one for each participant.

Introduction:

Begin this activity with a discussion about choices people make in their leisure. Ask participants to describe the amount of freedom they have in their leisure. The participants should next name some things that limit them in their leisure.

Activity Description:

The participants are told that they have a full three weeks in which they are to do nothing but recreation. They have no worries, no important work to be done, no deadlines to meet, and no other annoyances. Allow the participants to think about this scenario for a few minutes.

Give each participant a copy of the accompanying form and a pencil. Ask the participants to think about the questions and write in their answers in the blanks provided.

Once every participant has completed the handout, have the participants share their responses. Close the session with the following debriefing questions.

Debriefing Questions/Closure:
1. How realistic is this scenario for you?
2. Would you like this scenario to be true?
3. Do you feel you want to increase your knowledge about leisure before this scenario were to become true so you could better appreciate this time or do you feel you could adequately appreciate the time if the scenario were to happen right now?
4. What kinds of choices or options did you consider before you decided what to do?
5. How easy or difficult was it for you to make decisions?
6. How did making one decision affect making decisions in other situations?
7. What values were you expressing by making the choices you did?
8. How do your values, as expressed by your choices, differ from other group members' values?

Leadership Considerations:
1. A discussion after each question has been answered might help participants to stay focused on the activity.
2. The leader should be prepared to assist the clients in understanding the scenario.
3. The leader may want to have an example prepared ahead of time.

Variations:
1. The participants could be paired up and asked to complete the activity with a partner.
2. The participants could first be asked to visualize three weeks without leisure and then to complete the activity with the scenario of three weeks of leisure.

Creator: Julie Keil, CTRS, Illinois State University, Normal, Illinois.

Three Weeks

Where would you go during these three weeks?

_____

_____

_____

What supplies would you want to have with you?

_____

_____

_____

Would you want to have everything provided for you or would you like to have to get your own supplies when necessary?

_____

_____

_____

Would you go to more than one place?

_____

_____

_____

What would you do during these three weeks?

_____

_____

_____

Would you want anyone to be with you, and if so, who?

_____

_____

_____

Why did you choose the place(s) you did and why did you choose the people you chose to be with you?

_____

_____

_____

_____

An Adventure in Leisure

Space Needed: Classroom or activity room

Equipment/Resources Needed: Accompanying form, pencils, envelopes, easel, large tablet, markers

Group Size: Small group

Program Goals:
1. To help participants develop creativity regarding their leisure.
2. To increase participants' awareness of and the need for leisure resources.
3. To increase participants' awareness of the need for leisure planning skills.

Program Description:

Preparation:
Prepare five envelopes: Places, Cost, Weather, Time, People. Cut An Adventure in Leisure form into pieces and place paper pieces into corresponding envelopes.

Introduction:
Discuss the idea of having a "sense of adventure." Include in the discussion the need we all have for leisure, and how leisure planning skills and knowledge of leisure resources helps us experience leisure. Tell individuals that they are about to encounter a leisure adventure . . . one that they may experience again and again.

Activity Description:
Pass around the five envelopes one at a time. Ask each individual to select one piece of paper, without looking, from each of the five envelopes. Allow five to 10 minutes for each individual to look at his or her paper slips and create his or her own leisure adventure. Encourage realistic creativity.

Ask individuals to share their leisure adventure in detail. Ask specific questions to help participants focus on decision making with regard to leisure planning skills and leisure resources. For example, the specialist may ask:

- How would you get there?
- What equipment will you need?
- What transportation will you need?
- What modifications are necessary for you to participate in this adventure?
- What activities could you participate in?
- How would you decide just who to take with you?

Focus on decision making, leisure planning skills, and utilization of leisure resources.

Close with a discussion about how the participants can make their own adventures in leisure. Use the following debriefing questions for closure.

Debriefing Questions/Closure:
1. How possible would this adventure be for you?
2. How did you make decisions regarding what you would do?
3. How much planning would this type of adventure require?
4. What types of leisure resources were necessary to participate, e.g., equipment, facilities, partners?
5. Who had the most well-thought-out plan for his or her adventure? What were the elements of this plan? How did they achieve that?

Leadership Considerations:
1. This activity works best with a small group—10 maximum.

Creator: Angela Rice, CTRS, St. Peters, Missouri, and Janine Roe, CTRS, Granite City, Illinois.

An Adventure in Leisure

Cut out the following items under each category and put in envelopes marked with the proper headings: Places, Weather, Time, Cost, and People.

Places:

In the country . . .

Close to an ocean . . .

In the city . . .

A private area . . .

A resort area . . .

Close to a lake . . .

A park . . .

A public area . . .

At your home . . .

Mountainous or hilly area . . .

Weather:

Warm, summer day . . .

Cool, sunny, fall day . . .

Snowy day . . .

Foggy day . . .

Icy day . . .

Cloudy, winter day . . .

Rainy spring day . . .

Windy, fall day . . .

After warm rainfall . . .

Thunderstorms . . .

Time:

Midnight

10:00 A.M.

Noon

2:00 P.M.

8:00 P.M.

7:00 A.M.

11:00 A.M.

1:00 P.M.

6:00 P.M.

9:00 P.M.

Cost:

$10.00

$30.00

$50.00

$70.00

$90.00

$20.00

$40.00

$60.00

$80.00

$100.00

People:

Alone . . .

With family . . .

With large group . . .

With special interest group . . .

With significant other or spouse . . .

With coworker . . .

With small group . . .

With strangers . . .

With pet . . .

With peer . . .

The Decision Tree

Space Needed: Classroom or activity room

Equipment/Resources Needed: Accompanying form, pencils

Group Size: Individual or small group

Program Goals:
1. To increase participants' awareness of the importance of prioritizing.
2. To assist participants in identifying the process of making a decision.
3. To increase participants' ability to understand and utilize a decision-making process.

Program Description:
Preparation:
Make copies of the Decision Tree form, one for each participant.

Introduction:
The purpose of this activity is for participants to identify positive and negative consequences to different alternatives when making a decision (for example, take a vacation). Going to an exotic place may be exciting (positive) but cost more than the participant can afford (negative). One of the aspects of making a decision is to weigh the positive effects versus the negative effects.

Activity Description:
Hand each participant one copy of the Decision Tree form. Each person is to select one decision that he or she will be making in the near future, and write this at the bottom of the tree trunk. The facilitator should help people keep focused on leisure-related decisions (for example, whether to drop out of the bridge club, whether to visit relatives over the upcoming holiday, how much to spend on that new piece of exercise equipment, or how to develop new friendships).

Each participant is told to begin the decision-making process by writing the alternative in question at the base of the tree trunk (for example, choosing the Bahamas over a more local vacation site). The participants then identify the good and the bad points about each alternative. These points are written on the tree, good on the left and bad on the right, climbing the tree.

Allow about five to 10 minutes for participants to generate alternatives and positive and negatives aspects. When participants are finished, begin discussion about decision making.

Most decisions have both good and bad aspects to them, with one outweighing the other. This can be seen by the participant as one aspect, good or bad, climbs higher and closer to the top of the tree. This activity is very helpful in identifying both good and bad aspects of a decision or choice. Often, individuals only consider the good points in the decision, making it difficult to find reason not to choose an activity that could have a negative outcome.

Close the activity with the following debriefing questions.

Debriefing Questions/Closure:
1. Was it easy or difficult to identify negative or bad points about the decision?
2. Was it easy or difficult to identify positive points about the decision?
3. What was the outcome of the decision? Did this surprise you?
4. Was it easier to see the outcome and reasons on the tree as opposed to just imagining them? How will this help you in the future?
5. Were the goals of this activity met?

Leadership Considerations:
1. It is very important for the leader in this activity to strongly encourage honesty on the part of the participants. If they are not honest, making a sound decision will become much more difficult.
2. It may be helpful to begin by giving a scenario in which the individual will have to make a decision. This not only gives practice in identifying the aspects of the decision, but it shows that decisions are made in everyday life.
3. It may be necessary for the facilitator to play devil's advocate in the identification of negative or bad aspects of a certain decision, particularly if the participant has difficulty with this part. Try to be positive, even in negativity.
4. This is an easy and uninvolved activity and can be used many times after being completed once.

Variations:
1. The decision tree can also be used to decide between two different activities or choices. In this case, the base of the trunk can hold two choices, with the branches holding only the positive aspects of each activity.
2. The two activities can also be completed in succession. In this variation, once an activity is found to be acceptable, it can be compared to others as well.
3. Instead of a tree use a ladder or stairs.
4. To make activity more active or group oriented, have tree drawn and taped on wall. Red apples equal positive decisions, rotten apples equal negative decisions.
5. Allow the group as a whole to decide instead of as individuals.

Creator: Nikki Colba Harder, CTRS, Illinois State University, Normal, Illinois.

The Decision Tree

Winner:_____!

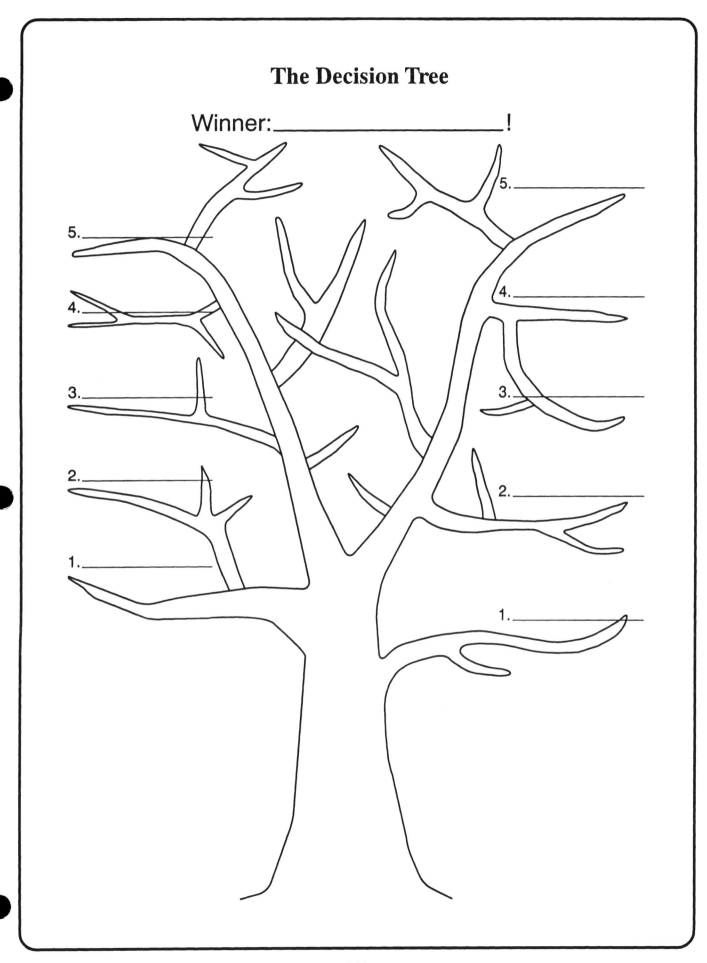

Problem-Solving Journal

Space Needed: Classroom or activity room

Equipment/Resources Needed: Journal for each person participating (see accompanying form), pen or pencil

Group Size: Small group

Program Goals:
1. To increase participants' ability to recognize and identify daily problems encountered.
2. To increase participants' awareness of appropriate ways to manage and cope with daily problems encountered.
3. To provide the opportunity for participants to document daily problems encountered and how those problems were managed and coped with.

Program Description:

Preparation:
Prepare journals for each participant. Copy off the number of pages needed (see Problem-Solving Journal form), and create journals by stapling pages together. Journals may have several pages and participants may add pages as needed.

Introduction:
Start the activity by discussing the types of typical problems encountered by the participants (for example, they keep forgetting where they lay down the book they are currently reading, they fight with a sibling over what program to watch on television, they have a best friend who does not take showers frequently enough, they lack enough energy by midafternoon to exercise). Discuss how these problems may be big or little, one time or enduring, extremely aggravating or merely annoying. Review the purpose and goals of the activity.

Activity Description:
Hand each participant his or her own copy of the problem-solving journal. The specialist explains that these journals are meant to be used on a daily basis to document "problems" encountered each day. Review the contents of the blank journal page, and what will be expected of the participants.

Review problems that may be encountered by the participants: arguing with another participant, losing a private possession, having a question about something, or getting into trouble during a group meeting. Ask each participant to identify one problem that he or she has experienced very recently.

The specialist then explains that once the problem has been identified, the participants are to document how they managed and coped with the situation. After participants have documented how they managed the situations encountered, they are to identify three alternative methods that are more appropriate ways of how to manage or cope with the stated problem.

The specialist may go through the procedure with the participants, using one of the example situations. The participants are then told that this activity is to be done on an individual basis and is their responsibility to complete.

Once per week, the group will meet to discuss the various problems encountered by the participants and offer suggestions on how similar situations may be managed more appropriately in the future. Journals are to be used for the entire length of stay.

Debriefing Questions/Closure:
1. What are some of the common problems being encountered by the group?
2. What are some of the negative ways that problems have been handled by group members?
3. What are some healthier, safer alternatives to solving those problems?
4. What are some key aspects of solving problems positively?
5. Name some problem-solving techniques that you learned and describe how they can be used in other situations encountered.
6. How can keeping a journal of problem-solving techniques be beneficial to your everyday life?

Leadership Considerations:
1. Keep the journal in a three-ring binder so additional pages can be added if needed.
2. As the length of stay progresses, participants may forget to keep entries in their journals, periodically remind participants to continue writing in their journals.
3. During discussion of journals each week, allow the participants to offer suggestions to one another.

Variations:
1. Keep a journal on chemical dependency—every time a participant feels the urge to use, the participant should list three alternative activities that could be done in place of using alcohol or drugs.
2. Keep a journal on behavior misconduct—every time a participant acts out, the participant should list three reasons why he or she acted out and three things that can be done next time rather than act out.
3. Keep a journal on positive verbal communication—every time a participant has a negative thought or says a negative comment to someone else, the participant should write down what was thought or said and list alternative methods for conveying message in a positive manner.

Creator: Theresa M. Connolly, CTRS, Illinois State University, Normal, Illinois.

Problem-Solving Journal

Date: _____

Time: _____

Identify the problem encountered (use just a few words):

Explain what you did to manage the problem encountered (be very specific, include all details):

List *three* alternative solutions that could be more appropriate for managing the problem encountered:

1.

2.

3.

So Much Leisure, So Little Time

Space Needed: Classroom or activity room

Equipment/Resources Needed: Accompanying form, pens or pencils, chalkboard, chalk

Group Size: Individual or small group

Program Goals:
1. To increase participants' awareness of daily time available for leisure.
2. To increase participants' ability to identify leisure interests.
3. To improve participants' ability to prioritize leisure interests.

Program Description:
Preparation:
Write on the chalkboard the same information as on the accompanying form.

Introduction:
The specialist introduces the activity to the group by asking a few questions to help participants begin to think about their time and leisure; for example:

- Who feels they have adequate time to fulfill their leisure needs on a daily basis?
- Who feels that there is not enough time in a day to include leisure in their schedule?
- Who feels that they have too many leisure interests and have a difficult time deciding what to do when time is available for leisure?

Allow adequate time for participants to discuss these questions. Introduce the purpose and goals of this activity.

Activity Description:
Hand each participant a copy of the So Much Leisure, So Little Time form. The specialist should ask the participants to complete each section of the work sheet. The chalkboard can be used as a guideline or example for the participants.

First, have the participants, using the work sheet, create a list of the things that they have to do today or tomorrow. The list should include the time of day each responsibility will be completed and the amount of time each responsibility will take to complete.

Second, after all participants have completed the first step, ask the participants to now make a list of time available for leisure.

Third, after all participants have completed the second step, ask participants to create a list of all the leisure activities in which each would like to participate. Once the list has been completed, the participants are to then prioritize the listed activities into most important to least important, including amount of time each activity may take and the estimated cost of each activity.

Fourth, after the first three stages have been completed, ask the participants to review their time available and list of prioritized leisure interests. The idea is to match up the time available and the leisure interest. Ask the participants to write down any activities that match the time available.

Last, if the participants have any matches, the last stage is to actually do the research and locate the resources to carry out the activity.

305

Close with discussion about the importance of leisure and how everyone has to plan in order to make sure they have some leisure in their day. The following debriefing questions will help wrap up the discussion.

Debriefing Questions/Closure:
1. How did this activity assist you in increasing your awareness of daily time available for leisure?
2. How did this activity assist you in increasing your ability to identify your leisure interests?
3. How did this activity improve your ability to prioritize your leisure interests?

Leadership Considerations:
1. Allow enough time for each participant to finish each stage before moving to the next.
2. Allow for questions and discussion following the completion of each stage.
3. The specialist may want to do the activity with the participants rather than stand in silence waiting for the group to finish.

Variations:
1. This activity can be completed on an individual basis rather than a group setting, the participants may want to look at a whole month rather than just one day or week.
2. The participants may have common interests and time available, allow the participants to work in groups to make plans to carry out one of the chosen activities.
3. This activity can be done by the group as a whole rather than individually, and with the supervision of the specialist, the group can plan a large group activity if time and resources are available.

Creator: Theresa M. Connolly, CTRS, Illinois State University, Normal, Illinois.

So Much Leisure, So Little Time

List of things to do today (include time of day each activity will be done and amount of time needed to complete each activity):

_____   _____

_____   _____

_____   _____

_____   _____

_____   _____

_____   _____

List time available for leisure:

_____   _____

_____   _____

_____   _____

_____   _____

Create a list of activities in which you would like to participate (include amount of time to be spent on each activity and the approximate cost of each activity):

_____   _____

_____   _____

_____   _____

_____   _____

_____   _____

_____   _____

Do you have a match? Write down any activities that match the amount of time you have available for leisure.

Now, go find the resources so you can participate in the activities listed!!!

Things to Do List

Space Requirements: Classroom or activity room

Equipment/Resource Requirements: Accompanying form, pens or pencils, colored markers

Group Size: Small group

Program Goals:
1. To increase participants' ability to create a list of tasks to accomplish.
2. To increase participants' ability to prioritize the importance of individual tasks in relation to other tasks.
3. To assist participants in identifying time for leisure within their daily schedule.

Program Description:
Preparation:
Make copies of Things to Do List form, one for each participant.

Introduction:
Begin activity by introducing topic of time management and being able to complete tasks in a timely manner. Ask participants how well they are able to meet the demands placed upon them daily, and how often they accomplish everything they wanted to get done during a day. Review the importance of time management, being able to prioritize tasks for completion, and fitting leisure into their schedules.

Activity Description:
Hand each participant the Things to Do List form and pens and pencils. Have blue, yellow, pink, and green markers or crayons available for the group to share.

Ask participants to complete the top of the form for tasks they need to accomplish within the next few days. These may be regarding any personal or professional task they need to accomplish. It does not matter how "small" the task is, as long as it is important to the participant.

Allow five to 10 minutes for participants to complete the Things to Do List. Have pairs of participants share their Things to Do Lists with one another.

Next, participants are to color-code their Things to Do Lists, using the following colors of markers:

- pink: any type of task that needs to be completed within the next 24 hours;
- yellow: work-related task that needs to be completed within the next few days;
- blue: family task that needs to be completed within the next few days; and
- green: leisure activity that will take place in the next few days.

Then, they use the bottom half of the page to decide within which day and which time frame, the task will be completed. Each participant should be able to have a Things to Do List for tasks he or she needs to accomplish within the next week.

Explain how a Things to Do List can be helpful in keeping up with obligations and can help manage time better so more time might be available for leisure. Close with following debriefing questions.

Debriefing Questions/Closure:
1. How were you able to fit in all your tasks that you needed to accomplish?
2. Which activities did you label as immediate, professional, family, or leisure tasks?
3. Which did you make sure were placed first in the weekly schedule?
4. How does a Things to Do List help with time management?
5. How does your leisure time benefit from a Things to Do List?
6. How will you be able to make sure you take some time for leisure every day?
7. How was your list of things to do similar or different from others in the group?

Leadership Considerations:
1. Consider the population and how familiar or unfamiliar they might be with a Things To Do List before introducing the activity.
2. Encourage people to prioritize tasks as they put them on their schedule.

Variations:
1. This format may be used for home therapy schedules.

Creators: Samantha Rudolph, Illinois State University, Normal, Illinois, and Norma J. Stumbo, Ph.D., CTRS, Illinois State University, Normal, Illinois.

Things to Do List

Write down tasks you need to accomplish within the next few days. These may be regarding any personal or professional task you need to accomplish. It does not matter how "small" the task is, as long as it is important to you.

1.

2.

3.

4.

5.

6.

7.

8.

9.

10.

After color-coding the above tasks, list each task under the day you need to accomplish that task.

Monday	Tuesday	Wednesday	Thursday	Friday	Saturday	Sunday
___	___	___	___	___	___	___
___	___	___	___	___	___	___
___	___	___	___	___	___	___
___	___	___	___	___	___	___
___	___	___	___	___	___	___
___	___	___	___	___	___	___
___	___	___	___	___	___	___

House on Fire

Space Requirements: Classroom or activity room

Equipment/Resource Requirements: Blank paper, pens or pencils

Group Size: Small group

Program Goals:
1. To help participants identify personal values related to possessions.
2. To help participants prioritize the value they put on their possessions.
3. To aid participants in making decisions that align with their values.

Program Description:

Preparation:

Gather needed blank paper and pencils.

Introduction:

Begin with discussion of personal values and how each person has values that guide his or her behavior and choices. For example, if someone values health, he or she makes time to exercise and eat well; if someone values people, he or she tends to be around people often; if someone values leisure, he or she makes time for it every day. Have each participant try to think of one of his or her personal values that can be shown through his or her behavior or actions. Explain the activity.

Activity Description:

Hand each participant a blank sheet of paper and a pencil. Explain that the participants are being placed in a hypothetical situation of their house being on fire. All humans and pets are safe. The participants have only five minutes to go through the house and collect the most important items and possessions they have in the house. The specialist should use guided imagery to help participants see themselves going through each room of their house, such as the bedroom, kitchen, living room, and garage.

As the imagery continues, participants are to jot down any possession they would want to bring safely out of the house. Size or weight of the item is not considered. They are to write down any possession that means a lot to them.

Each person lists the items that he or she would want out of his or her house. Remind them they only have five minutes to recover these possessions. Most people will have between 10 and 20 items.

When the lists are complete, instruct participants that they can only keep three items on the list. They are to make decisions and choose only three items.

First in pairs, and then with the whole group, ask participants to discuss what items they brought out of their houses. Ask participants to explain why certain items were chosen.

The closing discussion can focus on how people chose their items, and how they narrowed down the list. Remind them that their values are reflected by their choices. Ask them to identify what values prompted them to choose the items they did. Close with debriefing questions.

Debriefing Questions/Closure:
1. How did your items relate to your personal needs?
2. What memories do these items have for you?
3. Would you change anything about your lists after you hear other people's lists?
4. What was difficult for you as you made up your lists?
5. What values were identified by the possessions you wanted to keep?
6. What other actions do you take that help identify these same values?
7. How easy or difficult were the decisions of which items to take?

Leadership Considerations:
1. Give examples of items you would take and how to do guided imagery.

Variations:
1. May want to split the group into several smaller groups or dyads and have the participants practice interviewing techniques.
2. Have the dyad partner present the information and have the group give feedback in conversational skills.

Creator: Linda Maurer, CTRS, RTCR, Veterans Administration Medical Center, Chillicothe, Ohio.

Leisure Choices

Space Requirements: Classroom or activity room

Equipment/Resource Requirements: Accompanying form, pens or pencils

Group Size: Small group

Program Goals:
1. To have participants identify the factors that influence their leisure choices.
2. To have participants identify the advantages and disadvantages of leisure choices.
3. To have participants identify whether to continue, discontinue, or change leisure experiences or choices made regarding particular leisure experiences.

Program Description:

Introduction:

Begin by discussing leisure choices. A number of decisions are made as leisure experiences are selected and carried out. Choices may influence the nature and quality of our leisure experiences. Leisure experiences may be continued, discontinued, and/or changed as a result of weighing the decision variables. Review the purpose and goals of the activity with the participants.

Activity Description:

Hand each participant a copy of the Leisure Choices form and a pencil. Instruct the participants to list in the first column, their valued leisure experiences and any they would like to pursue yet, to date, have not.

In each of the columns, they are to answer the W question accordingly:

- Who—who is involved in this experience with you?
- When—time required for the experience?
- Where—location or place of the experience?
- Why—goal or outcome expected of the experience?

After responding to the W questions for all listed experiences, they are to determine their "future" leisure preferences and action plan by recording their experiences and courses of action.

- Advantage/Disadvantage—use the information presented in the previous columns to explain the pros and cons of your choice.
- Continue/Discontinue/Change—explain decisions that you might make to enhance the quality of the experience or your leisure as it relates to your listed experience(s).

Allow adequate time for participants to complete the work sheet. Share within pairs, then with group as a whole. Use the following debriefing questions to close the session.

Debriefing Questions/Closure:
1. What patterns influenced your leisure choices?
2. What advantages and disadvantages did you list?
3. Which choices appear appropriate or require changes and how will they impact future leisure preferences?
4. Why do you make specific leisure choices?
5. What will influence your decisions in the future?

Leadership Considerations:
1. Encourage participants to first respond to the *W* questions for each experience separately before examining responses to all listed experiences.
2. Require participants to list current active interests as well as current inactive interests.
3. Suggest participants project future needs based on anticipated life situations (e.g., two and five years in the future) by contemplating the "why" (e.g., goals and outcomes).
4. Use the Continue/Discontinue/Change column to present specifics for each previous *W* response.

Variations:
1. Complete as a partner or group activity so participants facilitate alternative decision making among themselves.
2. Complete for various life stages then compare. For example, past and present patterns and selection processes, projecting into the immediate future.

Creator: Marcia Jean Carter, Re.D., CLP, CTRS, Ashland University, Ashland, Ohio.

Leisure Choices

Leisure Experience List	Who	When	Where	Why	Advantages/ Disadvantages	Continue/ Discontinue/ Change
1.						
2.						
3.						
4.						
5.						
6.						
7.						
8.						
9.						

Planning a Luncheon

Space Requirements: Classroom or activity room, kitchen area, and grocery store

Equipment/Resource Requirements: Chalkboard or dry erase board, chalk, markers, grocery ads from local newspapers, paper, pens or pencils, calculator(s), cooking equipment, cooking and eating utensils, cookbooks, money for grocery shopping, transportation to grocery store

Group Size: Small group

Program Goals:
1. To increase participants' ability to plan a meal for a small group.
2. To increase participants' ability to comparison shop for groceries within a budget.
3. To increase participants' ability to cook a meal for a small group.

Program Description:

Preparation:
This activity requires that participants shop for groceries, and that a kitchen be available for participant use. The entire activity may take three to four days from start to finish. Obtain all supplies, secure money, grocery ads and transportation for the out-trip. Know how much the group may spend buying groceries.

Introduction:
The purpose of this activity is to help participants develop skills in planning, shopping for, and preparing a meal for a small group. Begin the first session of the activity by presenting the idea of planning a luncheon for the group, as a group. Discuss the possibilities of participants planning this activity by themselves after discharge from treatment. Focus on the decisions that must be made to be able to prepare a meal for others. Explain the procedures of the activity.

Activity Description:
Part One:
Ask the group members to decide on day and time to have the luncheon. Help the group identify how much time and money it will take to shop and prepare for the luncheon. Present the actual amount that the group can use to spend on the luncheon.

Have the group brainstorm ideas on what meals could be prepared for that designated amount. Write their ideas on the chalkboard. As a group, decide what will be on the menu. Have a cookbook or two available if needed.

After the menu has been determined, have the group make a list of all the food items that need to be purchased. When the list is complete, have participants estimate the cost of each item. Record this on the board next to each item. Add up the cost to see if it is within the range of the allowed budget. Delete items on the menu if over budget. Make a final list of items to be purchased on the shopping trip.

319

Part Two:
Distribute grocery ads to the group and have them look for the most economical prices on the needed food items listed. As a group, decide what store would be the most cost effective to shop at. Divide responsibilities among group or divide into pairs. Determine which people or pairs will be in charge of looking for a particular item at the store. Plan time for grocery shopping outing.

Part Three:
On day of shopping outing, distribute calculators to participants prior to entering the store. Use these to help tally the costs to ensure that participants do not go over budget. Remind participants of their responsibilities and decide on a time and place to meet back with the group to tally the total cost of items before checking out. Remind participants to be cost efficient.

When reconvening, tally up the total cost of all items gathered. If total is over the budget, as a group decide how to solve the problem. Designate a person to be in charge of the money handling and check out.

Part Four:
Gather cooking equipment and designate areas for the food preparation. Make a list of responsibilities on the chalkboard and ask participants to decide who takes what food preparation duties. Prepare food in designated area.

Have participants prepare area for luncheon and arrange room as needed for the activity. After food preparation is completed, have participants take food to luncheon area, and proceed with meal. Encourage interaction during the luncheon. Have participants clean luncheon and food preparation areas.

Debriefing Questions:
1. What skills did you learn about meal planning for a small group?
2. What skills did you learn while grocery shopping?
3. What skills did you learn while helping prepare the food for the luncheon?
4. Would you be able to plan, shop and prepare a meal for a small group in the future?
5. What skills do you need to work on?

Leadership Considerations:
1. This activity may be done in a variety of treatment areas, such as day treatment and inpatient.
2. Best when used with a group that has difficulty structuring social time, money management or planning skills.
3. This activity works best when co-led with an Occupational Therapist and can serve as an assessment session.

Variations:
1. This could be an activity that participants have to plan from start to finish.

Creator: Shelley A. Vaughan, CTRS, and Patricia Grimm, OTR/L, St. John's Hospital, Springfield, Illinois.

Leisure Resources Activities

Back to Back

Space Requirements: Classroom or activity room

Equipment/Resource Requirements: Accompanying form, blank paper, pencils

Group Size: Small group

Program Goals:
1. To improve participants' ability to communicate clearly with a partner.
2. To improve participants' awareness of leisure resources.

Program Description:
Preparation:
Make copies of Back to Back form, one drawing per each pair of participants.

Introduction:
The purpose of this activity is to help participants identify leisure resources, specifically leisure equipment, through an activity that requires clear communication with a partner. In this activity, partners are placed back to back, and while one partner describes the picture in his or her hand, the other partner draws what the person is describing. Explain the procedures of the activity to the participants.

Activity Description:
Ask participants to line up two rows of chairs, backs together, facing in opposite directions, in the middle of the room. Divide group into partners. One partner will be the describer and the other partner must remain silent and will be the drawer. Have the partners sit back to back in the chairs.

Hand one partner in each group one of the drawings. Hand the other partner blank paper and a pencil. (The drawer may need a firm surface to write on.) Make sure pairs sitting next to each other do not have the same drawing so directions from another pair cannot be overheard.

Have the describer begin describing the drawing as the other person draws it. The describer is to give clear, concise directions to help the drawer. Allow five to 10 minutes for the partners to complete this process. Do not have the partners show each other the drawings when finished.

Have partners change roles, the drawer will now become the describer and vice versa. Hand the new describer a different drawing and proceed as before. Allow five to 10 minutes to complete.

When completed, place chairs in a semicircle facing the front of the room. Have each pair come to the front of the room and show the group their drawings. The leader should facilitate a discussion about the drawings, the process, and leisure equipment. Debriefing questions are provided below.

Debriefing Questions:
1. How essential was clear communication to completing the drawings?
2. What did the describers say that helped the drawers draw more correctly?
3. What are other situations in daily life that need clear communication?
4. Were you familiar with all the leisure resources named today?
5. Which of these pieces of leisure equipment have you used before?
6. Which of these pieces of leisure equipment would you like to use in the future?
7. How will this activity help you in the future?

Leadership Considerations:
1. Each drawing can be as simple or complex as it needs to be, to meet the abilities of the participants.

Variations:
1. Change the drawings to meet the needs, abilities, and interests of the participants.

Back to Back

Drawing 1:

Drawing 2:

Drawing 3:

Personal Leisure Directory

Space Requirements: Classroom or activity room

Equipment/Resource Requirements: One hundred four-by-six-inch index cards per participant, pens or pencils, list of leisure activities and resources, telephone book and/or newspaper, four-by-six-inch picture binder, page tabs

Group Size: Individual or small group

Program Goals:
1. To increase participants' ability to identify resources available to improve personal leisure lifestyle.
2. To increase participants' ability to identify new resources to be used upon discharge.
3. To increase participants' knowledge and use of resource materials.

Program Description:
Preparation:
Make lists of leisure activities and resources. Gather materials as described above.

Introduction:
This is a tool that assists in increasing the knowledge and use of the activities and recreation possibilities close to participants. Participants should look through the list of activity possibilities provided and be encouraged to think of their own. Forty-five activities is quite a few, but encourage persistence. Review the purpose and goals of the activity with participants.

Activity Description:
Day 1, Part 1:
First, go through the list of activity ideas provided. Using those and ideas of your own, list on the first 15 cards provided, activities in which you would like to participate. Do not think about reasons not to choose activities when you are deciding. If you enjoy it, write it down . . . where there is a will, there is a way!

Day 1, Part 2:
You have a good start of things you would like to see or participate in. Now do something with them to make them useful. Fill out an information card about those 15 activities that you just chose. This includes the name of the activity, the address where the activity takes place, the telephone number there, and the cost of the activity. Some of this information may require a little research, so jump right in!

Day 2:
(Day 2 looks very similar to Day 1.) Choose another 15 activities from the list (or from your brain) and fill out information cards about them. You should be familiar with this process by now. Just as a helpful hint, the telephone book, the local newspaper, magazines, and friends can be very useful resources for this part of the project.

Day 3:
Today you need to fill out just 15 more items from the activity list. Just keep in mind what a great resource you will have when you are finished—you will probably use it more than you think! If you have thought of new activities and ideas for your project, do not be afraid to add them at any time. You can never have too many options for recreation!

Day 4:
Last day on the project! Today you are going to make your list something easy to use. Using any method you choose, categorize your activity cards. You may have as many or as few cards in a category as you wish. After you categorize, return the cards to the binder and mark the category with tabs that you name appropriately. All that is left is remembering to use your new tool! Have a great time on your new adventures!

After each session, help participants review the goals of the activity and the purpose of their own personal leisure directory. When projects are completed, ask participants to share their directories with other participants and explain what resources are included and why they are important.

Debriefing Questions/Closure:
1. How will you be able to use your personal leisure directory on a daily basis?
2. What activities did you include that are new to you?
3. How easy or difficult was it to find out information about new activities?
4. Could you find new leisure resources information on your own?
5. How does your directory differ from other participants'?
6. Why do you think we included so many different activities?
7. How can you use this tool following discharge?
8. What new information did you learn about the community and resources around you?

Leadership Considerations:
1. This activity may be completed independently by individuals who are not cognitively impaired. As the facilitator, an introduction may be necessary, and a check up every now and then, but the participant should be primarily responsible. The facilitation questions for closure also need to be conducted by the facilitator.
2. The activity cards may be prepared prior to the beginning of the activity, or may be completed by the participant.
3. It may be helpful to suggest ideas for categorization when all activity cards have been completed. "Things to Do," "Places to Go," "People to See," and "For Your Information" are suggestions for categorization.

Variations:
1. This activity can also be simplified by limiting the available resources to specifically home, family, personal, community, state, or national resources. This limits the activity possibilities, but it increases the amount of research needed for finding the activities.
2. The activity can also be modified through the addition of pictures with the activities instead of only activity information on the activity cards. It is suggested that the name and telephone number always be kept, but additional information can be changed or omitted.

Creator: Nikki Colba Harder, CTRS, Illinois State University, Normal, Illinois.

Leisure Circle

Space Requirements: Classroom or activity room

Equipment/Resource Requirements: Accompanying form, magazines, scissors, glue, pencils

Group Size: Individual or small group

Program Goals:
1. To increase participants' ability to identify preferred leisure activities.
2. To increase participants' knowledge of potential leisure resources.

Program Description:

Preparation:
Make copies of Leisure Circle form, one for each participant.

Introduction:
The purpose of this activity is to identify what the participants like to do so they can find resources that they can use. Review the purpose with the participants prior to beginning the activity.

Activity Description:
Hand each participant the Leisure Circle form. Ask participants to look through magazines and cut out pictures or words that describe activities that they enjoy. Have them paste or write these activities in the circle. Explain that by narrowing down activities into a list (the circle), the next step of finding possible resources will be easier.

After the circle is completed, have the participants choose two or three of the activities from their circles. Ask the participants to identify resources in their home, community, or state which can assist them in participating in the activity. They are to write these resources on the outside of the circle. The finished product should include a list or pictures of leisure activities in the middle and resources needed to implement them on the outside.

Have participants share their circles with others in the group. Facilitate a discussion about similarities and differences between participants' circles.

Close with a review of the activity goals and the following debriefing questions.

Debriefing Questions/Closure:
1. How did identifying your leisure interests make it easier to find possible resources?
2. Was it easy or difficult to identify positive leisure activities?
3. Do you feel that you need to broaden your knowledge of possible activities and resources?
4. How did your activities and resources differ from others in the group?
5. How often are you able to participate in these activities and use these resources?
6. What would help you increase your participation?
7. What did you learn about leisure resources that you can use in the future?

Leadership Considerations:

1. Be sure participants are choosing a variety of activities.
2. Explain that knowing your personal leisure interests makes it easier to find resources to accommodate your choices.

Variations:

1. The outside of the circle can be used to identify negative leisure habits.
2. The outside of the circle can be used to identify activities in which the participant would like to participate.

Creator: Becky Klein, Illinois State University, Normal, Illinois.

Leisure Circle

Leisure Resources A
1.
2.
3.
4.
5.

Leisure Resources B
1.
2.
3.
4.
5.

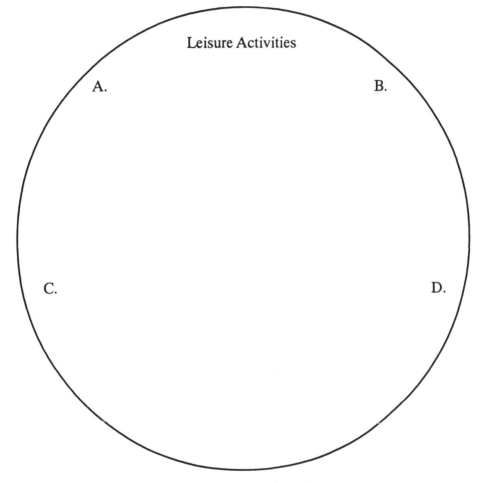

Leisure Activities

A.

B.

C.

D.

Leisure Resources C
1.
2.
3.
4.
5.

Leisure Resources D
1.
2.
3.
4.
5.

Leisure Phone Book

Space Requirements: Classroom or activity room

Equipment/Resource Requirements: Several copies of accompanying form per participant, several magazines containing leisure activities, a hole punch, and yarn or string or fasteners for notebook, tape or glue, several local phone books, pens, pencils or markers.

Group Size: Small group

Program Goals:
1. To increase participants' ability to identify preferred leisure activities and resources.
2. To increase participants' ability to communicate leisure preferences.

Program Description:

Preparation:
Make copies of the Leisure Phone Book form, several for each participant. Gather other listed materials.

Introduction:
Begin activity with discussion about leisure activities. Ask participants what activities they enjoy, where they participate in these activities, and how often they participate. Introduce the concept of leisure resources—things that are necessary in order to participate in leisure activities. For example, a partner or a tennis racket may be considered leisure resources to play the game of tennis. Discuss the goals and outcomes of the activity.

Activity Description:
Participants will be provided either magazines with pictures of leisure activities, or, if they cannot use scissors, with a large selection of pictures depicting leisure activities already cut from magazines. Participants will be asked to select those pictures of activities which they enjoy the most. Ask participants to assemble a number of copies of the Leisure Phone Book form to make pages of a "book."

Once participants have selected their desired pictures, they will paste or tape each picture to a page, leaving space at the bottom of the page to write where this activity may be performed locally, including facility name and phone number. Depending on the participants' disabilities, the specialist will help participants look up information about each activity in the local telephone book and write it in the space provided on the page.

The specialist will explain that the Leisure Phone Book can be used in several ways. For those with severe disabilities, this phone book may be a way of communicating what that person might want to do when asked.

For those who are higher functioning, this can serve as a beginning tool to learn the use of a telephone book, and allow them to be more independent in their leisure planning. Participants will be encouraged to look for more pictures in the future and keep adding pages as needed.

Close the activity by reviewing the goals of the activity. Debriefing questions are provided as examples to help reinforce the projected outcomes of the activity.

Debriefing Questions/Closure:
1. What are some of your favorite activities?
2. What are the advantages of having a Leisure Phone Book that is custom designed by you?
3. How will you be able to use your Leisure Phone Book?
4. What kinds of activities would you like to add in the future?
5. What activities did someone else have that you would like to try?

Leadership Considerations:
1. Have an adequate number of copies of the accompanying form per participant.
2. Have an adequate and diverse supply of magazines or pictures appropriate to the group of participants.

Variations:
1. Have pictures already drawn on the pages and have participants find the resource information.

Creator: Jeff Thompson, Illinois State University, Normal, Illinois.

Leisure Phone Book

Leisure Activity:

Facility Name: _____

Facility Address: _____

Facility Telephone Number: _____

Hours of Operation: _____

Cost: _____

Other Information: _____

_____

_____

_____

_____

Find a Resource

Space Requirements: Classroom or activity room

Equipment/Resource Requirements: List of possible community resources specific to the places the participants will visit.

Group Size: Small group

Program Goals:
1. To improve participants' ability to identify possible resources within the community.
2. To improve participants' ability to identify activities that can be done at each resource.

Program Description:

Preparation:
Prepare list of community resources (see Activity Description).

Introduction:
This is to be done as a community out-trip with participants with adequate cognitive functioning. The specialist will take participants on a walk or a bus ride around the community. The specialist should know the route being taken and the resources along the way.

Before the out-trip begins, explain what community leisure resources are to the participants. Ask each participant to name a favorite leisure resource in the community. Explain the purpose of the out-trip and review the goals of the activity.

Activity Description:
As the out-trip begins, give each participant a list of community resources. (These should be in no particular order.) Explain that all the resources will be found somewhere along the way.

When the resource is spotted, participants must identify the name of the resource and what activities can be done there. For example, an item on the list might be the park. Participant will say the name of the park and at least one activity that can be done there.

Continue throughout the community, asking specific questions to test participants' level of knowledge, for example:

- How far are we from your home?
- What kind of transportation would you use to get here?
- How much do you think that activity costs?
- Do you have to purchase tickets in advance?
- With whom could you come here?
- What else is close by?
- If you wanted to eat a meal, what restaurants are close to here?

When the out-trip is over, review the purpose and goals of the activity, and stress carry over by using the following debriefing questions.

Debriefing Questions/Closure:
1. How easy or difficult was it to find the resources?
2. How easy or difficult was it to identify leisure activities that can be done at those locations?
3. Do you need any accommodations at any of the facilities?
4. How can you find out if they can accommodate you?

Leadership Considerations:
1. If using public transportation, be sure that all participants' disabilities can be accommodated.

Variations:
1. Have a specific destination in mind.
2. Just go for a walk and have the participants find as many resources as they can along the way.
3. Let the participants make a list of where they want to go.

Creator: Becky Klein, Illinois State University, Normal, Illinois.

I Walk the Line

Space Requirements: Classroom or activity room

Equipment/Resource Requirements: Paper and pencils

Group Size: Small group

Program Goals:
1. To increase participants' awareness of local community resources.
2. To help participants identify leisure resources that may be used in their future.

Program Description:
Preparation:
Gather blank paper and pencils.

Introduction:
Discuss the purpose and goals of this activity. Discuss how, sometimes, we are least familiar with what is closest to us—sometimes we see something so often, we do not give it much thought. This often happens to us when we travel to work or school.

Activity Description:
Distribute paper and pencils to participants. Ask each participant to draw a map of his or her town or neighborhood—perhaps the route he or she travels to work or school.

Ask participants to draw a line representing the path they usually take within this area. Have the clients note on the paper the stores, buildings, parks, and open areas that are along this path. Participants should provide as much detail as possible.

Have the participant note any store or building that he or she might use for his or her leisure (e.g., a video store to rent movies, a park bench for relaxing, a fitness center to exercise, a mall for shopping, a restaurant for dining out). Have the participant circle this facility or area.

Review the purpose and goals of the activity. Allow participants to keep their drawings for use as future reference. Use the debriefing questions for closure.

Debriefing Questions/Closure:
1. How many things did you identify that could be used for leisure?
2. How many of these have you already used, and how many were new?
3. Select one and tell how you might use it, when, with whom, for what purpose?
4. How many of these can you and will you use in the future?

Leadership Considerations:
1. Allow enough time for participants to draw their neighborhoods and think about what is located there.
2. Do not focus on the artistry of the drawings.

Variations:
1. Have participants draw their homes or rooms at the facility, and identify leisure resources.
2. If participants are local, have them draw one specific area (for example, downtown) and have them identify, as a group, leisure resources they can use.

Leisure Resources Box

Space Requirements: Classroom or activity room

Equipment/Resource Requirements: Shoebox with lid (one for each participant), construction paper, magazines, markers, scissors, glue, several blank slips of paper

Group Size: Small group

Program Goals:
1. To increase participants' ability to follow directions.
2. To increase participants' ability to identify leisure resources found in the home and community.
3. To increase participants' awareness of how to make use of home and community resources.

Program Description:

Preparation:
Gather materials.

Introduction:
The tables in the room should be prearranged with the materials in the center of each table. The participants should be asked not to touch the materials on the table until directed to do so. The specialist should have a sample box to show to the group prior to the start of the activity.

Activity Description:
Each participant will be asked to choose a shoebox. The participants are then to use the construction paper to cover the outside of the box so that any writing cannot be seen. The inside of the box should remain open. The lid to the box should then be covered, using the same material, so that any writing cannot be seen. The lid should still fit over the top of the box.

The participants must then cut a hole in the center of the lid of the box. The hole should be approximately one-half-inch wide by four-inches long. (The specialist may show the sample box as an example.) Holes can also be cut prior to the activity to save some time.

Once the hole has been cut, the participants will be asked to spend the next 20 minutes looking through magazines to find images of home and community resources (e.g., telephone, television, stereo, movie theater, park, playground). Once these images are found, the participants may cut the photos out of the magazine. If an image is not found, the participants may write the resource on the outside of the box.

Once the images have been cut out, the participants may glue the images to the outside of the box. When the 20 minutes have passed, the participants need to take a blank slip of paper for each image or word pasted on the outside of the box (15 images = 15 blank slips).

For each of the resources pasted on the outside of the box, the participants must list three uses of that resource. When the slips of paper have been completed, they are placed inside of the box. (If time runs out, participants may complete their slips of paper at a later time.)

At the end of the session, the participants are asked to clean their work area, leaving behind the leftover magazines, scissors, glue, and construction paper. The participants are asked to bring their boxes to the next group session.

At the next group session participants are asked to choose three resources pasted on the outside of the box. Each participant will read the corresponding slips of paper to the group, for each of the three resources chosen. When all of the participants have had the opportunity to share, the group will have a discussion about the activity and Leisure Resources.

Debriefing Questions/Closure:
1. What are some of the resources you found to put on your box?
2. Did anyone in the group have similar ideas?
3. Name other resources not pictured on the boxes and uses for each.
4. Name any resources you were not aware of prior to this activity.
5. How often do you access the resources pictured?

Leadership Considerations:
1. Specialist should have a sample box available while describing the activity.
2. Specialist may want to precut the holes in the lids to avoid any potential injuries from working with the scissors.
3. Specialist should check with participants during the activity to ensure that the directions are being followed and to answer any question.
4. Plan on spending two group sessions to complete this activity.

Variations:
1. Leisure Benefits Box—photos of activities on outside and list benefits on slips of paper.
2. Positive Messages Box—photos of activities enjoyed on outside and positive messages from other group members on inside.
3. Chemical Dependency Box—box divided into two sides, one for barriers to leisure when using and one for benefits of leisure when sober.

Creator: Theresa M. Connolly, CTRS, Illinois State University, Normal, Illinois.

Leisure Resource Tick-Tack-Toe

Space Requirements: Classroom or activity room

Equipment/Resource Requirements: X cards, O cards, tick-tack-toe board, and phone book

Group Size: Small group

Program Goals:
1. To increase participants' awareness of leisure activities.
2. To increase participants' awareness of leisure resources available in their community.
3. To increase participants' ability to find leisure resources using a phone book.

Program Description:

Introduction:

Prior to the start of the activity, prepare X and O cards. Each card has a question about a specific leisure resource (e.g., Where is the local YWCA? What pieces of equipment are needed to play croquet? Where would you look up the telephone number of the fitness center?) Also prepare the tick-tack-toe boards, large enough to accommodate the X and O cards.

Start by discussing the rules of tick-tack-toe. One person goes at a time. One person is X and the other is O. Three of the same letter in a row are needed to win. The winner may have three in a row across, diagonal, or up and down. Review the purpose and goals of the activity with the participants.

Activity Description:

Explain the following rules:

1. The participants must answer the question on the back of their X or O card before they can put it down on the board.
2. If they are unable to answer it, the specialist may give hints.
3. The participant who does not get three in a row has to take the winning Xs or Os and find the address and phone number of the resource in the phone book matching the questions on the back of each X or O card.
4. In case of a "Cat's Game" (no one winning), both participants together choose three Xs or Os and find the phone number and address of the resource matching the clue on the back of the X or O.
5. No two Xs or Os can be placed in the same square.

Pair off participants. Hand each pair a tick-tack-toe board, and X and O cards. Each player chooses whether he or she is Xs or Os. The X player begins by reading the question on the back of the first X card. He or she answers the question by naming the leisure resource matching the description. If he or she cannot answer the question after hints are given by the specialist, a new X question is read. More clues are read until the participant matches the clue with the resource. The O player follows the same rules using the O cards.

Close with a discussion of leisure activities and resources. Refocus on the goals of the activity, and review the following questions.

Debriefing Questions/Closure:
1. How easy or difficult was it to answer the questions about resources?
2. How many new activities or resources did you learn about?
3. Were you reminded of any resources that you had forgotten about?
4. How many resources did you discover that you would like to learn more about?
5. How will you use this information in the community, in the future?

Leadership Considerations:
1. The specialist should have questions relating to resources available to the participants in the community and in their homes written on the backs of the X and O cards.
2. The difficulty of the questions should be based on the participants' cognitive ability.
3. The clues should be for age appropriate resources.
4. A master list of the clues and answers might be helpful to have around if the participants do not know the answer from the first question on the backs of the cards.

Variations:
1. The participants could have to name the answer to the opponent's question before going instead of answering their own question.
2. Small teams could be made instead of the activity being for only two people.
3. The phone books or pamphlets could be used during the tick-tack-toe game to help participants answer the questions.

Creator: Julie Keil, CTRS, Illinois State University, Normal, Illinois.

The Resource Exchange

Space Requirements: Classroom or activity room

Equipment/Resource Requirements: Paper and pens or pencils for each participant

Group Size: Small group

Program Goals:
1. To increase participants' awareness of leisure resources available in the community.
2. To increase participants' awareness of leisure resources available in their homes.
3. To promote interaction between participants.

Program Description:

Preparation:
Gather materials.

Introduction:
Begin with a discussion about the importance of knowing what leisure resources are available for one's use. Ask the participants how many of them feel as though they have a good awareness of what leisure resources are available to them. Introduce the purpose and goals of the activity to the participants.

Activity Description:
Hand each participant a piece of paper and a pen or pencil. Have the participants divide the paper into four sections. Label the four sections "1," "2," "3," and "4."

Instruct the participants to write down, in section 1, as many leisure resources they have available in their homes and within a two block radius of their homes. Allow three to five minutes.

Have the participants switch lists with a partner and discuss the similarities and differences. In section 2, have them write down some of these differences and similarities. Allow three to five minutes. Again, have participants discuss their answers with their partners.

In section 3, have the participants list as many community resources as they can. Allow three to five minutes. Again, have the participants switch lists and compare answers, writing down the similarities and differences in the fourth section of the paper.

Ask participants to carefully look at their lists of home and community resources and see the similarities and differences between their answers and their partners' answers. Allow three to five minutes.

Refocus on the goals of the activity, helping participants to increase their awareness of home and community resources. Close with the following debriefing questions.

Debriefing Questions/Closure:
1. What did you learn about leisure resources in your home?
2. What did you learn about leisure resources in your community?
3. How many of you have people listed as leisure resources?
4. How did your lists compare with your partner's lists?
5. What did you learn about leisure resources that you can use in the future?
6. How did this activity increase your awareness of leisure resources?

Leadership Considerations:
1. Participants may first need some help getting started with their lists. The specialist should be prepared with some examples like bike, television, pictures, paper, a friend, and a telephone.
2. The participants could discuss their answers from the home resources before switching to the community resources.

Variations:
1. Participants could switch partners a few times during the activity to have a broader variety of ideas.
2. Instead of listing leisure resources, the participants could list leisure barriers in their homes and in the community or just barriers in general and ways to overcome the barriers.
3. The participants could act out their resources in a leisure charades sort of manner and have the other participants guess what they are acting out instead of just listing or saying what the resources are.

Creator: Julie Keil, CTRS, Illinois State University, Normal, Illinois.

346

Leisure Resources Game

Space Requirements: Classroom or activity room

Equipment/Resource Requirements: Game board, one die, prepared game cards, game pieces (e.g., paper clips or coins), accompanying form

Group Size: Small group

Program Goals:
1. To increase participants' ability to identify personal leisure resources.
2. To increase participants' ability to identify leisure resources in the home.
3. To increase participants' ability to identify leisure resources in the community.
4. To increase participants' ability to identify leisure resources in the state.

Program Description:

Preparation:

Prepare game cards. The questions to place on game cards are located on the Leisure Resources form. The specialist should make a copy of the game board and a set of cards per every four players.

Introduction:

The specialist should explain the idea of leisure resources, and give some examples. Discuss personal resources, home leisure resources, community leisure resources, and state leisure resources. Ask participants to give some examples of each of the four kinds of resources. Continue until all participants are familiar with the concepts and terms. Review the goals of the activity.

Definitions:
- Leisure Resources—Items that allow opportunities for satisfying leisure experiences.
- Personal Resources—Abilities and interests that you possess.
- Home Resources—Items found in the home that allow opportunities for satisfying leisure.
- Community Resources—Resources in the community and surrounding area which provide potential leisure experiences.
- State Resources—Opportunities located within the state which are enjoyable for leisure.

Activity Description:

Explain the rules of the game. Each person rolls the die once and the one with the highest number goes first. Play will continue to that person's left. Make sure all players understand the concepts before beginning.

Have each person select a game piece and place it on the *start* square. The person who won the roll of the die begins and rolls the die again. He or she moves his or her game piece that number of spaces, and selects the top card that corresponds with the space on which he or she landed.

He or she picks up the card, reads it aloud to the other participants and either answers the question or completes the action required. When completed to the satisfaction of the other players and the specialist, play continues with the person to the left. He or she rolls the die, moves that number of spaces and responds to the card he or she picks up.

Play continues in this fashion, until time to quit, or someone crosses the finish line. The specialist should facilitate discussion throughout the game.

Close with a focus on the goals of the activity and the following debriefing questions.

Debriefing Questions/Closure:
1. What did you learn about personal leisure resources?
2. What did you learn about home leisure resources?
3. What did you learn about community leisure resources?
4. What did you learn about state leisure resources?
5. What interests did you have in common with other group members?
6. How will this knowledge help you in the future?
7. Why are leisure resources important to you?

Leadership Considerations:
1. Encourage players to think about new resources and not ones used every day.
2. Players should use resources appropriate to their ages and disabilities.
3. The specialist should help focus on discussion of topics, beyond just quick answers.

Variations:
1. Change content of cards according to what participants need to learn from the game.
2. Change the number of squares, adding more of one resource if desired.
3. Add appropriate pamphlets or magazines to help participants come up with new resources.

Creator: Norma J. Stumbo, Ph.D., CTRS, Illinois State University, Normal, Illinois.

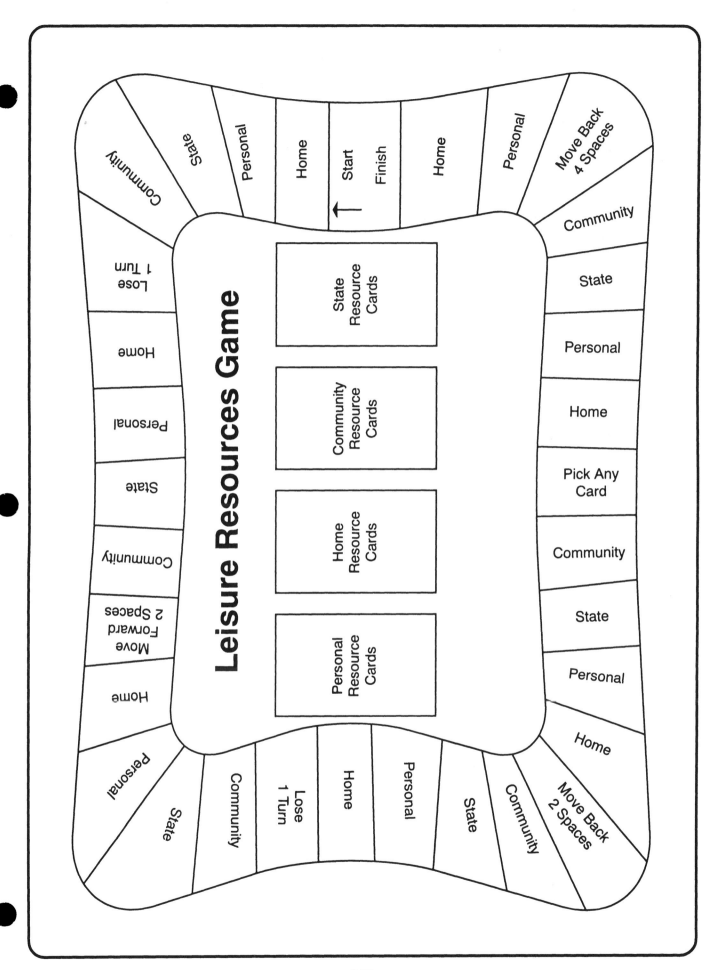

Leisure Resources Game

Leisure Resources Game

Ideas for personal resource cards:

Name one way to use your voice for leisure.

Name one leisure activity that you have gotten better at in the last year.

Name one way your level of risk taking affects your leisure.

Where do you go when you want to be alone?

How have your social skills helped you in leisure?

Name one of your assets as a child and explain how you used it in leisure.

Name one leisure activity that really requires you to think.

What personal resources do you have in common with family members?

Name one leisure activity that can be done by yourself.

Ask the person to your right to recite a short poem.

Ask the person to your left what he or she does when bored.

Name one physical asset that helps you in leisure.

How much money do you usually spend per week on leisure?

Name one leisure activity that you are really good at.

How have you used your five senses for leisure?

Ideas for home resource cards:

What is your favorite piece of electronic equipment?

Where is your favorite place for leisure within your home?

What is your oldest leisure resource in your home?

Name two ways a telephone book can be used as a leisure resource.

Name one way a newspaper can be a home resource.

Ask the person to your left his or her favorite home resource.

Ask the person to your right about his or her next planned home resource purchase.

Name one way a personal computer can be used as a leisure resource.

Name one home resource you borrow from a family member.

Ask the person across from you to name one home resource he or she uses for exercise.

Ask the person across from you to name one home resource he or she uses for relaxing.

Name one way a pet can be a leisure resource.

Name one leisure resource that you keep within easy reach.

Name one home resource that you always show people who visit your home.

What is your favorite place in your room or home? Why?

Leisure Resources Game

Ideas for community resource cards:

Where would you go to play tennis?

Where's your favorite place to eat? Why?

Where could you learn to play soccer?

Where could you go to a movie?

How much does it cost to buy an ice cream cone?

Where would you go if you had an hour to yourself?

Where would you go for a walk?

Where can you shop for clothes?

What's your favorite place to find a bargain?

Where could you go to watch a sporting event?

Where would you go to spend the afternoon?

Ask the person to your left his or her favorite night spot.

Ask the person to your right for directions to the YMCA/YWCA.

Where could you go if you did not want to spend any money?

Where is the nearest museum?

Ideas for state resource cards:

Name one state park that is close to here.

Name one place within the state listed on the National Register of Historic Places.

What is the state's most famous tourist attraction?

Where in the state have you visited most frequently?

Where would you go to study state history?

What's the most famous sports team in the state?

What leisure resource would you find at one of the state universities?

What could you do in the southern part of the state?

What could you do in the state capital?

What does a hunting or fishing license cost in this state?

Ask the person across from you to name his or her favorite spot in the state.

Ask the person to your left to name the place in the state he or she has been to most frequently.

Ask the person to your right to name the most beautiful place in the state.

Name two reasons someone would want to visit this state.

For what is this state most famous?

Leisure Resource Influences

Space Requirements: Classroom or activity room

Equipment/Resource Requirements: Accompanying form, pens or pencils

Group Size: Individual or small group

Program Goals:
1. To help participants examine the influence resources have on their leisure participation.
2. To help participants consider the relationships of leisure resources used in various leisure experiences to one another.
3. To explore how participants might adjust resource influences to accommodate their leisure behavior patterns.

Program Description:

Preparation:
Make copies of Leisure Resource Influences form, one for each participant.

Introduction:
What we choose to do as leisure is influenced by available and accessible resources. Participants make decisions and choices influenced by knowledge of resources needed with specific experiences. Leisure patterns are altered when adjustments are made to gain access and use available resources. Review the goals of the activity with participants.

Activity Description:
Hand each participant a copy of the Leisure Resource Influences form and a pencil. Have participants list experiences that typically occur during their leisure in a given time period (e.g., week, month) in the first column on the Leisure Resource Influence form.

They are to consider the weight or percent the listed factors have on their leisure in each of the other columns. The outcome or last column should total 100 percent.

Have them place, under each column heading, a numerical value (percentage) that best represents the influence of that particular factor on their specific leisure experience. Ask them to keep in mind for each activity listed, the final column should total 100 percent.

In the Other column, ask them to note any additional influences that impact participation but which are not found in the listed subheadings.

Ask participants to find a partner and share their information. Allow five minutes for discussion, then have the partners share their information with the larger group. Facilitate discussion, focusing on the purpose of the activity.

Close by reviewing the goals of the activity, and use the following discussion questions.

Debriefing Questions/Closure:
1. Is there a pattern in your resource usage that prevails regardless of the listed experience?
2. Which influences might be controlled by making decisions or taking action to "change"?
3. How do changes you make in, for example, time, or skills, impact other influencing variables?
4. Which influences are negative or limit your leisure and which seem to enhance your expression of leisure?
5. What did you learn about how resources influence your leisure?
6. How might you use this information in the future?

Leadership Considerations:
1. Encourage participants to respond to each listed experience separately prior to making comparisons among the influences.
2. Include in the introduction a discussion on leisure barriers and constraints so participants gain a sense of the variety of influencing factors.

Variations:
1. Adjust the column headings to accommodate the particular group characteristics (e.g., add Work for adults or Transportation for youth).
2. Complete the activity with and without the last column so participants examine the relationship among the influences for a particular experience.

Creator: Marcia Jean Carter, Re.D., CLP, CTRS, Ashland University, Ashland, Ohio.

Leisure Resource Influences

Influences (List % Under Each Heading)

Leisure Experience List	Family and/or Friends	Interest	Time	Health	Cost	Other	Total (100%)
1.							
2.							
3.							
4.							
5.							
6.							
7.							
8.							
9.							
10.							
11.							
12.							

Scavenger Hunt Community Outing

Space Requirements: Activity conducted in the community

Equipment/Resource Requirements: List of local community resources for reference, transportation for community outing, clues for the scavenger hunt

Group Size: Individual or small group

Program Goals:
1. To help participants identify local community leisure resources.
2. To increase participants' awareness of the activities that the community leisure resources have to offer.

Program Description:

Preparation:

Prior to the start of the activity, the specialist should decide what community resources are to be introduced to the participants while on the outing. The specialist should make a list of clues in reference to the selected resources, for example:

- Clue 1—A building with a wealth of knowledge. Answer: local library.
- Clue 2—A hit song of the Village People in the 1970s. Answer: YMCA.
- Clue 3—At this place you may see some horseplay. Answer: horse stables.
- Clue 4—There are plenty of greens at this place. Answer: golf course.

Introduction:

Begin group activity by discussing the variety of leisure community resources available locally. Ask each participant to identify the resources that they utilize. Introduce the goals of the activity.

Activity Description:

Select one participant to read the clues. Have the person read one clue at a time. The participants are encouraged to figure out the clue as a group.

When the participants have guessed it correctly, ask the group members if they already know where the resource is located and have them guide the specialist to the location. The specialist drives to that specific community leisure resource and gives details about it (e.g., price, hours, leisure activity that is available). Also encourage the participants to offer any information about the resource they may know.

This continues until all clues are read and located. Allow one and a half to two hours for this activity.

While returning to the facility, end with a discussion using the following debriefing questions.

Debriefing Questions/Closure:
1. What community leisure resources do you feel you would most benefit from?
2. Would you do this alone or with others? Is the cost affordable?
3. What new leisure resources did you learn about?
4. What did you learn about the location of these resources?
5. In what new leisure activities will you participate in the future?

Leadership Considerations:
1. Take this time to do leisure time discharge planning with the patients.
2. Give a typed list of the community resources introduced on the outing to each group member (including all the needed information, i.e., cost, hours).

Variations:
1. Pick a couple of sites to actually get out of the van and let the clients experience the resource first hand (e.g., take a walk at the local park, get out at the YMCA and ask for a tour and acquire some extra information).

Creator: Shelley A. Vaughan, CTRS, St. John's Hospital, Springfield, Illinois.

What's Out There?

Space Requirements: Classroom or activity room

Equipment/Resource Requirements: List of community leisure activities and where to participate in them (approximately 15 activities, more if time allows), note cards on each of which is written (and drawn where possible) one of the activities

Group Size: Small group

Program Goals:
1. To increase participants' awareness of leisure resources which are available in their community.
2. To increase participants' awareness of the leisure activities available at specific community resources.

Program Description:
Preparation:
Prior to the start of the activity, prepare activity note cards. Each note card should have a leisure activity written on it, along with a drawing or picture of the activity (e.g., skiing, bowling, archery, walking). Prepare about 15 cards. Also prepare a list of those 15 activities with a corresponding list of where in the community participants could go to participate in that activity (e.g., skiing—ski resort; bowling—bowling alley; archery—archery range; walking—local park). You may put specific community locations, like the name and address of the bowling alley, if you wish.

Introduction:
At the start of the activity, briefly review what constitutes a leisure activity (e.g., free time, fun, relaxing, freely chosen). Explain that this group will involve a discussion about leisure activities and leisure resources in their community. Review the goals of the activity with the participants.

Activity Description:
Announce that one leisure activity has been written (and drawn) on each of a series of note cards. One participant begins by randomly selecting a note card from the deck and announcing the leisure activity to the group.

That participant is then asked where in the community the activity could be done. Use the participant's response and the list that was prepared ahead of time to generate discussion with the group about the activity.

After each specific activity has been examined, generate further discussion about the following categories of activities:

- special attractions (zoo, library, museum),
- special events (concerts, carnivals, exposé),
- parks (identify them and all that can be done there, e.g., picnics, playground activities), and
- activities that can be done anytime (walking, playing catch, driving).

Close the activity by discussing the program goals and the following debriefing questions.

Debriefing Questions/Closure:
1. Why is it important to know what's available in the community?
2. How often do you think we should do community activities?
3. What considerations do we need to keep in mind when planning a community leisure activity?
4. Is it good to have a balance between community leisure activities and activities at home? Why?
5. Were there any activities or resources mentioned that were unfamiliar to you?
6. How will you use these resources in the future?

Leadership Considerations:
1. Be aware of the time allotted for your group, particularly if your community is large and available activities are numerous. If necessary, you may leave the extra leisure categories for another activity on another day.
2. Emphasize that community leisure opportunities can be both those in which we participate and those in which we are spectators.

Variations:
1. Include discussion regarding the proximity of these leisure resources, i.e., how close they are to the residences of the participants.
2. Include discussion about those activities that cost money and those that do not.
3. Participants may discuss their experiences with various resources and facilities.

Creator: Tim Leer, West Central Human Service Center, Bismarck, North Dakota.

Leisure Treasure Hunt

Space Requirements: Classroom or activity room

Equipment/Resource Requirements: Different colored construction paper or copy paper, premade clues, and accompanying form

Group Size: Small or large group

Program Goals:
1. To increase participants' awareness of leisure resources and activities available to them.
2. To increase participants' ability to participate as a team member.
3. To increase participants' ability to solve problems.

Program Description:
Preparation:
Prior to the start of the activity, prepare "clues" on the different colored paper, to the different leisure activities and resources at your facility. Each clue should be made on each color of the paper, but in a different order. Number the clues in the order they are to be found, for example:

- Basketballs, baseballs, we are not. This ball is played in the sand when it's hot. (sand volleyball court)
- Oak, ash and pine are some you may find. This one you are allowed to climb. (tree)
- Keys are what make me sing. Making music is my thing. (piano)
- Are you looking for a community activity? Here's what you should do. Go to this board and you might find a clue. (activity bulletin board)
- You know Babe Ruth would tell you the truth. Go to this "plate" and "home" runs are your fate! (baseball diamond)
- Minnesota Fats played this game with a cue, this will take you to the next clue. (pool table)

After the clues are made, the specialist should keep the first clues separate to give each team to begin the treasure hunt. Hide the rest of the clues according to each previous clue. For example, the first clue explains where the second clue should be hidden.

Introduction:
At the start of the activity, discuss with the group members the different leisure resources that are available to them. Also discuss why it is important to know these resources and how to find and use these resources. Ask for participants to volunteer examples of resources throughout the facility or in the community. Review the goals with the participants.

Activity Description:
Explain to the group the importance of teamwork with this game. Divide the group into small teams, or have the participants select teammates. The number of teams and the number of people on a team can be decided by the specialist.

Hand out the Leisure Treasure Hunt form, copied on the team colors, to each team. Read through this form with the group and ask for questions.

Set the physical boundaries of the treasure hunt with the group (e.g., within the activity room, within the gym area, on grounds not past the parking lot). Also set a time limit.

Give each team the first clue in its color, and ask the group to return when it collects all the clues. Close with a discussion focusing on the goals of the activity. Use the following debriefing questions.

Debriefing Questions/Closure:
1. How easy or difficult were the clues? Which was easiest? Which was most difficult?
2. How did your group work as a team?
3. What were activities or resources that were new to you?
4. How can you use this information in the future?

Leadership Considerations:
1. The specialist may want to laminate clues and Leisure Treasure Hunt rule sheet if the game will be used often.
2. The specialist can organize clues in individual envelopes as to where the clues should be hidden.
3. The specialist could make a clue describing himself or herself, so that participants would come back to the specialist for the next clue.
4. A staff member might need to be with each team.
5. The more clues are spread out in areas, the more time and active participation this will require.

Variations:
1. Instead of small group teams, it could be played with individuals as teams.
2. Instead of participants searching for clues, the specialist could read them to the group and the group members could guess.

Creator: Amy Payne-Johnson, CTRS, Orchard Place Child Guidance Center, Des Moines, Iowa.

Leisure Treasure Hunt

1. Do not remove other team's clues. Only collect your team's clues. You will know this by the color of your team.

2. Qualification to win is to return each one of your team's clues. If you have any missing, you will need to go back to find them.

3. You may look around, as you are searching, to see any upcoming clues. However, it would be to your disadvantage if you were to remove them out of order.

4. Keeping this is mind, it would be a good idea to check for the number, making sure you are keeping your clues in order.

5. Work together as a team! There are many roles that might be needed on the teams; for example: the Reader of the Clues, the Runner(s), the Collector (responsible for holding all the clues found), the Thinker(s)—hopefully this will be everyone. The more input from everyone on the team, the better your chances of finding the clues.

6. Most important rule: *Have Fun*!

Let's be careful out there!

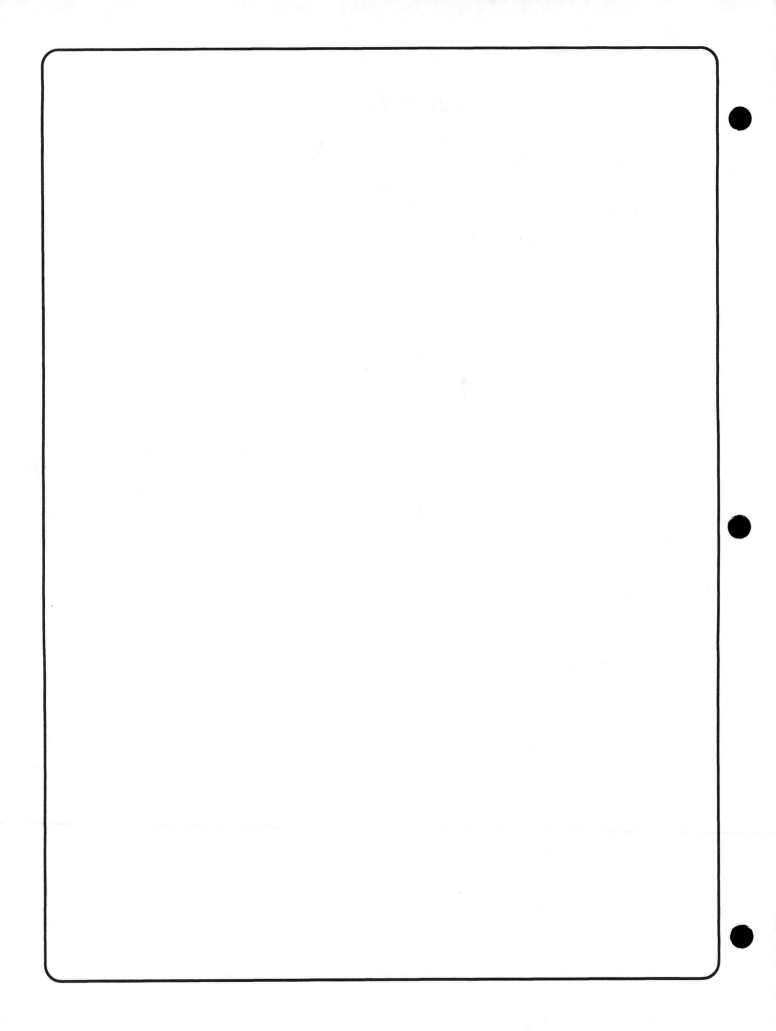

Leisure Resources Bingo

Space Requirements: Classroom or activity room

Equipment/Resource Requirements: Accompanying form and slips of paper prepared ahead of time by specialist, bright markers, a hat

Group Size: Small group

Program Goals:
1. To increase participants' ability to recognize leisure resources.
2. To increase participants' ability to match a picture of a leisure resource with its name.

Program Description:

Preparation:

Prior to the start of the activity, the specialist should prepare several game boards, using the Leisure Resources Bingo form as the pattern. For example, several pictures of leisure resources need to be located. These can be found in magazines, catalogs, and product supply catalogs. Make several copies of each picture and reduce or enlarge to fit the squares of the Leisure Resources Bingo form game boards. Place these pictures randomly on different game boards. (Each finished game board should have pictures in different orders so not everybody gets bingo at the same time.) Remember that the purpose of this activity is for participants to recognize leisure *resources,* not just leisure *activities.* The leader should create slips of paper with the names of the leisure resources written on them, to be placed in a hat that will be drawn from during the game.

Introduction:

At the start of the activity, facilitate a discussion on leisure resources and why they are necessary for participation. Ask the participants to name several leisure resources that they use on a weekly basis. Introduce the goals of this activity, and for those who do not know, go over the rules of bingo.

Activity Description:

Hand everyone a copy of the completed Leisure Resources Bingo form. The leader begins by drawing the name of a leisure resource out of the hat, and calling it out loud. If participants have that leisure resource on their cards, they use the bright markers to place an *X* over the square. The specialist should ask participants questions about that resource:

- For what activity would that resource be needed?
- How much do you think that resource costs?
- Where is that resource located?
- How many of those do you need to participate in the activity?
- If you cannot afford one, where could you rent one?
- How many people do you need with you to use this resource?

Play continues until someone has a bingo, with four in a row, vertically, horizontally, or diagonally. New game boards are distributed and a new round begins.

Debriefing Questions/Closure:
1. How would you define a leisure resource?
2. Name three leisure resources you have in your room or home.
3. How easy or difficult was it to match the picture with the spoken word?
4. What new things did you learn about leisure resources?
5. How can you use this information in the future?

Leadership Considerations:
1. Keep focused on the goals and content of this activity—to identify and match leisure resources.
2. Prepare the game boards and list ahead of time.
3. Laminating the game boards, and using dry erase markers, makes them reusable.

Variations:
1. As a separate activity, participants could prepare the game boards, and then in the next session use them to play Leisure Resource Bingo.

Creator: Melissa Capenigro, Illinois State University, Normal, Illinois.

Leisure Resources Bingo

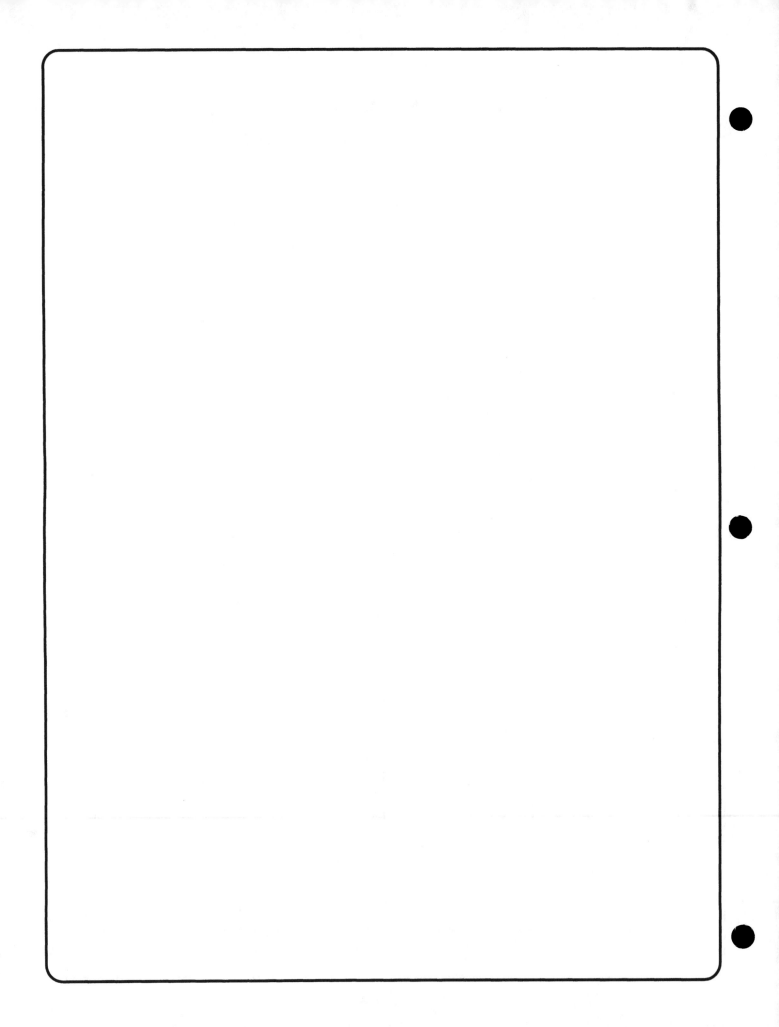

In the Bag

Space Requirements: Classroom or activity room

Equipment/Resource Requirements: Accompanying form, pencils, paper bags, chalkboard, chalk, timer, scissors

Group Size: Small group

Program Goals:
1. To assist participants in identifying equipment used for various leisure activities.
2. To improve participants' ability to work cooperatively with peers while participating in a group activity.

Program Description:

Preparation:
Copy the In the Bag form and cut into pieces. Place half the pieces in one bag and half in the other bag.

Introduction:
Ask participants to name a few activities that require equipment, such as tennis, hiking, gardening, reading, softball, and Frisbee. Ask them to name two or three pieces of recreation equipment that they own or have access to. Introduce the purpose and goals of this activity to the participants.

Activity Description:
Divide the group into two teams and have them go to opposite sides of the room. Hand each group one bag, asking each team member to take out one or two pieces of paper. Each person is to write one piece of equipment that is required to participate in the activity named on the slip of paper. For example, the name of the activity might be archery, and the person is to fill in a piece of equipment, like target, bow, or arrow. When finished, have the group members place all their pieces of paper back in the bag. Team members are not to discuss what they wrote on their slips.

The teams are to exchange paper bags. Select one person from each team to start. The person from Team A draws a slip of paper out of the bag and goes to the chalkboard to draw the piece of equipment named on the slip. The members from Team A are given 30 seconds to guess what activity the piece of equipment represents. Five points are awarded if Team A guesses correctly. While Team A is guessing, Team B is to remain quiet. If Team A does not guess the activity correctly, Team B gets a chance for one guess. If Team B guesses correctly, they get 10 points.

A person from Team B then draws a slip of paper out of Team B's bag and goes to the chalkboard to draw the piece of equipment named on the slip. The members of Team B are given 30 seconds to guess what activity uses the piece of equipment the person is drawing. Points are awarded as previously.

Play alternates teams and continues until all slips of paper are used or time runs out.

End with discussion focusing on the following debriefing questions.

Debriefing Questions/Closure:
1. How easy or difficult was it to name a piece of equipment to go with the leisure activity?
2. What difficulties did you have trying to guess the activity that was represented by the piece of equipment?
3. How often do you participate in leisure activities that require some type of equipment?
4. What types of recreation equipment would you like to get?
5. Where can you rent equipment if you do not want to own it?
6. How else might you access recreation equipment?

Leadership Considerations:
1. Use activities and equipment that are familiar to the participants.
2. Keep the focus on naming the equipment, not drawing.

Variations:
1. This can be changed to matching of activities and locations (for example, ocean and swimming).

Creator: Norma J. Stumbo, Ph.D., CTRS, Illinois State University, Normal, Illinois.

In the Bag

Horseback Riding	Tennis
_____	_____
Gardening	Reading
_____	_____
Crocheting	Traveling
_____	_____
Watching Television	In-Line Skating
_____	_____
Sewing	Playing Baseball
_____	_____
Crossword Puzzles	Sledding
_____	_____
Jogging	Dancing
_____	_____
Swimming	Canoeing
_____	_____
Listening to Music	Playing Cards
_____	_____

Community Reintegration Trips

Space Requirements: Classroom or activity room

Equipment/Resource Requirements: Accompanying forms, other resources depend on trips taken

Group Size: Small group

Program Goals:
1. To increase participants' knowledge of leisure resources in the community.
2. To increase participants' ability to utilize leisure resources in the community.

Program Description:

Preparation:

This is an eight-week program which encourages participants to become more independent in the community. The first four weeks take place in the immediate community surrounding the facility; the next four weeks are spent exploring another community. Prepare Community Reintegration Trips forms, and make arrangements per the proposed schedule.

Introduction:

A pretest and post-test are given at the beginning and end of the eight weeks to determine if the program was a learning experience and to identify weak areas in the participants' knowledge that need to be addressed prior to discharge.

Each session has its own introduction, based on the activity or event of the day (see Activity Description).

Activity Description:

Each session discusses the events, problems and recommendations of that particular trip. Also discuss expectations of the next trip, such as destination, cost, and time to arrive at group.

Schedule of Activities	Money Needed
Week One	
Interest survey taken	
Pretest given	
Discussion of Program	
Week Two	
Visitor's Center	Transportation $2
Park Department	Lunch $
YWCA Tour	
Week Three	
Venture Shopping	Transportation $2
(Comparative shopping)	Lunch $

Week Four
    Library Tour   Transportation $2
    Memmens Tour   Lunch $
    Public Aid Office
    Aurora Assignment

Week Five
    Fox Valley Mall   Transportation $2.50
      (Comparative shopping)   Lunch $

Week Six
    Recreation Trip   Transportation $2.50
      (e.g., bowling, mini-golf)   Bowling $2
                                           Mini-Golf $4.75
                                           Lunch $

Week Seven
    Nature Day   Transportation $3.50
                                           Lunch $

Week Eight
    Post-Test
    Program Evaluation

Debriefing Questions/Closure:
Each session has unique debriefing questions, depending on the activity or event of the day. All debriefing questions should refocus the participants on the goals of the program.

Leadership Considerations:
1. This exercise can be used and adapted for any town to which the participant is discharged.
2. Contact the community staff as early as possible to establish a schedule.
3. The first three trips the participants should assume leadership with staff there for supervision only.

Variations:
1. Go to facilities that meet the needs of the group participants.

Creator: Cathy Pacetta and Julie Beck, Elgin Mental Health Center, Elgin, Illinois.

Community Reintegration Trips

Pretest and Post-Test Example

1. How much does it cost to ride the bus from Elgin Mental Health Center (EMHC) to:

   Elgin bus terminal _____   Springhill Mall _____   Aurora _____   Venture _____

2. Is there a library in Elgin? _____   How would you find out? _____

3. It takes three buses (2 transfers) to arrive in Aurora from EMHC? True or False

4. Which bus departs and arrives at EMHC?
   a. 800   b. 801   c. 802   d. 803

5. Where do you go to see a cultural event in Elgin? _____

   Where do you go to see a cultural event in Aurora? _____

6. The Metra train runs from Elgin to Chicago? True or False

   The Metra train runs from Elgin to Aurora? True or False

7. How long is a bus transfer good for? _____

8. Blackberry Farm is a:
   a. berry picking farm   c. historical village
   b. amusement park   d. shopping center

9. Where are the swimming pools in Elgin? _____

   How do you find out? _____

10. You are new in town, where do you call to find out what is going on in town for entertainment?

    _____

    _____

Name: _____

Date: _____

Unit: _____

Score: _____

Community Reintegration Trips

Comparative Shopping

Item	Discount Store	Specialty Store	Department Store
Shoes	_____	_____	_____
Socks (1 pair)	_____	_____	_____
Socks (pkg.)	_____	_____	_____
Underwear	_____	_____	_____
Jeans	_____	_____	_____
T-Shirt	_____	_____	_____
Skirt	_____	_____	_____
Blouse	_____	_____	_____
Lotion	_____	_____	_____
Shampoo	_____	_____	_____
Sunglasses	_____	_____	_____
Gym Shoes	_____	_____	_____
Music Tape	_____	_____	_____
Towels (Bath)	_____	_____	_____
Towels (Kitchen)	_____	_____	_____
Purse/Wallet	_____	_____	_____
Jacket	_____	_____	_____
Shorts	_____	_____	_____
Perfume/Cologne	_____	_____	_____
Sweatshirt	_____	_____	_____

Community Reintegration Trips

Aurora Assignment—Exploring a Different Community

1. You are new in town, where do you call to find out what is going on in town?
   Place:

   Address:

   Telephone:

2. Is there a public library? If so list:
   Address:

   Telephone:

3. Is there a zoo in Aurora? If so list:
   Place:

   Address:

   Telephone:

4. Where can you see a movie?
   Place:

   Address:

   Telephone:

5. Find three shopping areas:
   1.

   2.

   3.

6. Are there any colleges in Aurora? If so list:
   Place:

   Address:

   Telephone:

7. Find two Mental Health Centers.
   Place: Place:

   Address: Address:

   Telephone: Telephone:

Aurora Assignment (Continued)

8. How much does it cost to ride the bus to Aurora? _____
   How much is a transfer? _____   Where is the terminal located? _____
   Address:
   Telephone:

9. Is there a Recreation Department? If so, list:
   Place:
   Address:
   Telephone:

10. Are there a YMCA and a YWCA in Aurora? If so, list:
    Place: Place:
    Address: Address:
    Telephone: Telephone:

11. Name a place where you can see a concert.
    Place:
    Address:
    Telephone:

12. What is Blackberry Farm? _____

13. Where is Fox Valley Mall located? _____

14. Does the Fox Valley area have an orchestra? _____

15. List any other recreational, educational or treatment-related facilities you can find.

    _____

    _____

    _____

    _____

    _____

    _____

Other Books From Venture Publishing

The A•B•Cs of Behavior Change: Skills for Working with Behavior Problems in Nursing Homes
    by Margaret D. Cohn, Michael A. Smyer and Ann L. Horgas
Activity Experiences and Programming Within Long-Term Care
    by Ted Tedrick and Elaine R. Green
The Activity Gourmet
    by Peggy Powers
Advanced Concepts for Geriatric Nursing Assistants
    by Carolyn A. McDonald
Adventure Education
    edited by John C. Miles and Simon Priest
Aerobics of the Mind: Keeping the Mind Active in Aging—A New Perspective on Programming for Older Adults
    by Marge Engelman
Assessment: The Cornerstone of Activity Programs
    by Ruth Perschbacher
Behavior Modification in Therapeutic Recreation: An Introductory Manual
    by John Datillo and William D. Murphy
Benefits of Leisure
    edited by B. L. Driver, Perry J. Brown and George L. Peterson
Benefits of Recreation Research Update
    by Judy M. Sefton and W. Kerry Mummery
Beyond Bingo: Innovative Programs for the New Senior
    by Sal Arrigo, Jr., Ann Lewis and Hank Mattimore
Both Gains and Gaps: Feminist Perspectives on Women's Leisure
    by Karla Henderson, M. Deborah Bialeschki, Susan M. Shaw and Valeria J. Freysinger
The Community Tourism Industry Imperative—The Necessity, The Opportunities, Its Potential
    by Uel Blank
Effective Management in Therapeutic Recreation Service
    by Gerald S. O'Morrow and Marcia Jean Carter
Evaluating Leisure Services: Making Enlightened Decisions
    by Karla A. Henderson with M. Deborah Bialeschki
The Evolution of Leisure: Historical and Philosophical Perspectives (Second Printing)
    by Thomas Goodale and Geoffrey Godbey
File o' Fun: A Recreation Planner for Games & Activities—Third Edition
    by Jane Harris Ericson and Diane Ruth Albright
The Game Finder—A Leader's Guide to Great Activities
    by Annette C. Moore
Getting People Involved in Life and Activities: Effective Motivating Techniques
    by Jeanne Adams
Great Special Events and Activities
    by Annie Morton, Angie Prosser and Sue Spangler
Inclusive Leisure Services: Responding to the Rights of People with Disabilities
    by John Dattilo
Internships in Recreation and Leisure Services: A Practical Guide for Students (Second Edition)
    by Edward E. Seagle, Jr., Ralph W. Smith and Lola M. Dalton

Interpretation of Cultural and Natural Resources
    by Douglas M. Knudson, Ted T. Cable and Larry Beck
Introduction to Leisure Services—7th Edition
    by H. Douglas Sessoms and Karla A. Henderson
Leadership and Administration of Outdoor Pursuits, Second Edition
    by Phyllis Ford and James Blanchard
Leadership in Leisure Services: Making a Difference
    by Debra J. Jordan
Leisure and Family Fun (LAFF)
    by Mary Atteberry-Rogers
Leisure and Leisure Services in the 21st Century
    by Geoffrey Godbey
Leisure Diagnostic Battery Computer Software
    by Gary Ellis and Peter A. Witt
The Leisure Diagnostic Battery: Users Manual and Sample Forms
    by Peter A. Witt and Gary Ellis
Leisure Education: A Manual of Activities and Resources
    by Norma J. Stumbo and Steven R. Thompson
Leisure Education II: More Activities and Resources
    by Norma J. Stumbo
Leisure Education Program Planning: A Systematic Approach
    by John Dattilo and William D. Murphy
Leisure in Your Life: An Exploration—Fourth Edition
    by Geoffrey Godbey
Leisure Services in Canada: An Introduction
    by Mark S. Searle and Russell E. Brayley
The Lifestory Re-Play Circle: A Manual of Activities and Techniques
    by Rosilyn Wilder
Marketing for Parks, Recreation, and Leisure
    by Ellen L. O'Sullivan
Models of Change in Municipal Parks and Recreation: A Book of Innovative Case Studies
    edited by Mark E. Havitz
Nature and the Human Spirit: Toward an Expanded Land Management Ethic
    edited by B. L. Driver, Daniel Dustin, Tony Baltic, Gary Elsner, and George Peterson
Outdoor Recreation Management: Theory and Application, Third Edition
    by Alan Jubenville and Ben Twight
Planning Parks for People
    by John Hultsman, Richard L. Cottrell and Wendy Zales Hultsman
Private and Commercial Recreation
    edited by Arlin Epperson
The Process of Recreation Programming Theory and Technique, Third Edition
    by Patricia Farrell and Herberta M. Lundegren
Protocols for Recreation Therapy Programs
    edited by Jill Kelland, along with the Recreation Therapy Staff at Alberta Hospital Edmonton
Quality Management: Applications for Therapeutic Recreation
    edited by Bob Riley
Recreation and Leisure: Issues in an Era of Change, Third Edition
    edited by Thomas Goodale and Peter A. Witt

Recreation Economic Decisions: Comparing Benefits and Costs (Second Edition)
    by John B. Loomis and Richard G. Walsh
Recreation Programming and Activities for Older Adults
    by Jerold E. Elliott and Judith A. Sorg-Elliott
Recreation Programs That Work for At-Risk Youth: The Challenge of Shaping the Future
    by Peter A. Witt and John L. Crompton
Reference Manual for Writing Rehabilitation Therapy Treatment Plans
    by Penny Hogberg and Mary Johnson
Research in Therapeutic Recreation: Concepts and Methods
    edited by Marjorie J. Malkin and Christine Z. Howe
A Social History of Leisure Since 1600
    by Gary Cross
A Social Psychology of Leisure
    by Roger C. Mannell and Douglas A. Kleiber
The Sociology of Leisure
    by John R. Kelly and Geoffrey Godbey
Therapeutic Activity Intervention with the Elderly: Foundations & Practices
    by Barbara A. Hawkins, Marti E. May and Nancy Brattain Rogers
Therapeutic Recreation: Cases and Exercises
    by Barbara C. Wilhite and M. Jean Keller
Therapeutic Recreation in the Nursing Home
    by Linda Buettner and Shelley L. Martin
Therapeutic Recreation Protocol for Treatment of Substance Addictions
    by Rozanne W. Faulkner
A Training Manual for Americans With Disabilities Act Compliance in Parks and Recreation Settings
    by Carol Stensrud

Venture Publishing, Inc.
1999 Cato Avenue
State College, PA 16801

Phone: (814) 234-4561; FAX: (814) 234-1651

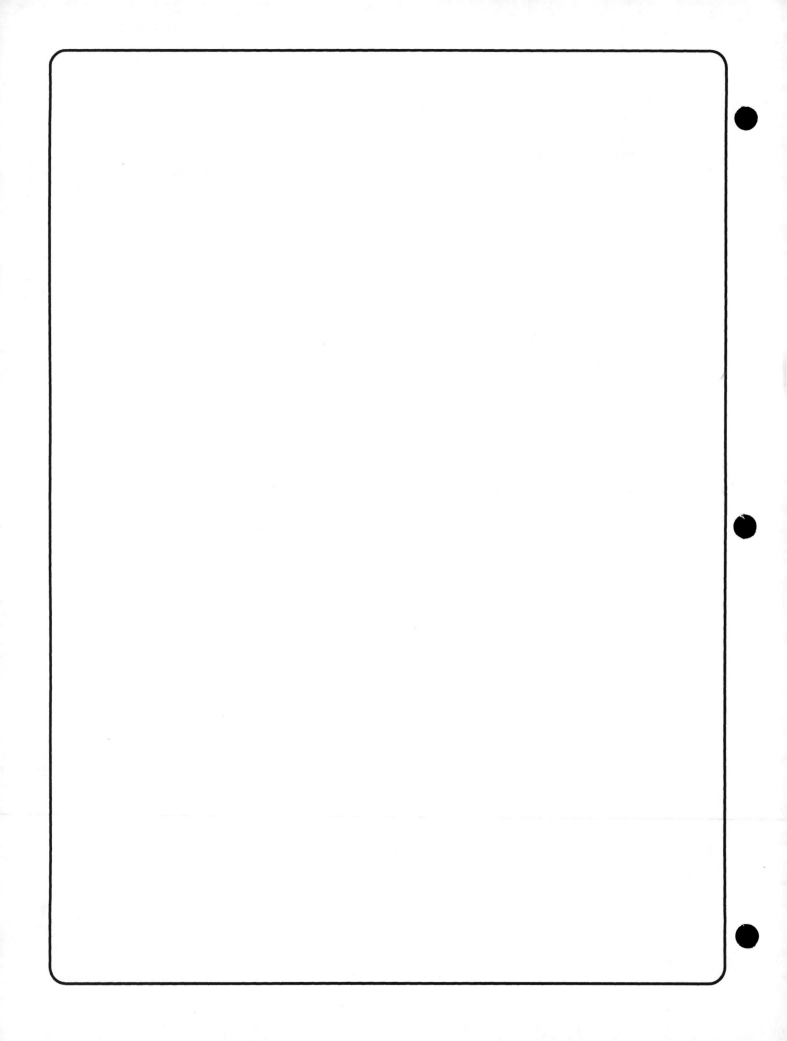